HOT CARS
cool drivers

Lew Boyd

edited by Jim Rigney

To Rick -
Hope this brings back GREAT memories!
Lew Boyd
22 Dec. '06

Coastal 181
PUBLISHER

Cover photo credits:

FRONT:

Top: Reino "The Flying Finn" Tulonen on fire at Westboro. *(Balser photo)*
Middle: "Dynamite" Ollie Silva at The Pines. *(Conway Collection)*
Bottom: Leo "The Lion" Cleary after another win at Norwood. *(Balser photo)*

BACK:

Top, left: A full field of Midgets ready to go at Westboro. *(Silvia Collection)*
Top, right: Stock cars head for the start at Norwood. *(H. White photo, Silvia Collection)*
Bottom: Legendary Kenny Small throws the green from trackside at The Pines. *(Conway Collection)*

ISBN: 0-9709854-5-2

For additional information contact:

Rigney Motorsports
Coastal 181
29 Water Street
Newburyport, Massachusetts 01950

Second printing March 2005

Printed in the United States of America

CONTENTS

WESTBORO

High Banks and Long Neck Knicks 1
Long Neck Knicks 14
They Called Him "The Doctor" 24
The Fence Factor 32
"Two Gun" Beeso 42
The Fallen Falconi 58

THE PINES

Oscar in The Pines 81
Casterline 96
Big Starter Small 112
The Mayor of Randolph 120
A Fan's Perspective 134
Same Start, Different Tracks 140

NORWOOD

Racing on the Auto Mile 151
A View from the Top 162
Trigger and the Thing 174
Jack Lundin's Explosive Career 204
The Preservationists 212

Index 219

This book is dedicated to the memory of Bill Welch,
Dean of New England Auto Racing, gentleman, and friend.
This one's for you, Welchie.

INTRODUCTION

One Saturday night in May of 1953 a neighbor came by to take us kids for a ride. On our rounds we happened by a newly opened speedway, and I caught a glimpse of a pack of gaudy stock cars bumping and grinding around the dusty oval. That single spark ignited a burning passion I have carried with me for over fifty years, including forty two behind the wheel of a race car.

In talking with hundreds of people while researching this book, I was amazed by how many others had a very similar experience. At the end of World War II conditions were perfect for the development of a dramatic, consuming sport for the people, performed by the people. Jalopy and midget race car tracks popped up all around the country, often utilizing county fairground facilities. At the height of the racing craze in the late forties and fifties, hundreds of thousands of people attended races each week in New England. It was captivating stuff.

People reminded me again and again of how the bleachers would sway with excitement as Ollie Silva in his "Big O" and Don MacLaren barreled side-by-side around The Pines Speedway with sparks and exhaust flames piercing the nighttime air. They spoke of the wonderful sounds—the throaty, unmuffled roar of Fats Caruso circling Norwood Arena in the pink and black "Circle Two" cut down with Del Shannon's *Runaway* in the background on the PA system. They even reminisced about the exotically pleasing smells of Castrol fumes wafting over the stands at Westboro, co-mingled with the smoke from frying onions and hamburgers and moistened by the musty scent of hundreds of recently opened beer bottles. By any measure, it was an extraordinary phenomenon.

Another definite thread through all my conversations, however, was one of sadness. Virtually everyone acknowledged that racing has grown enormously in visibility and professionalism. The ascent of NASCAR was certainly one of the major American commercial moonshots of the last fifty years. However, this success has come very much at the expense of local racing. Allan Brown reports in *The History of American Speedways* that while 56 oval tracks have been active in Massachusetts, only one, Seekonk Speedway, offers racing for full-sized cars today.

Frankly, it is not all that surprising that so many of the tracks eventually folded, and it is quite unlikely that places like Norwood, Westboro, and The Pines will ever open again. The pages of this book describe an activity that was far too dangerous to be tolerated today, especially given the litigiousness of our society. Noise and land values have become major issues, especially in populated areas. Environmental concerns have changed automotive technology such that the rugged, heavy chasses and muscle motors so popular for racing are no longer being widely made. And, finally, over the last five decades there has been a veritable explosion of competing alternatives for Everyman's entertainment dollar.

Because local racing was so rudimentary and was considered downright undesirable by upwardly mobile communities, speedways typically received minimum media attention. Very little was recorded about the racers, the fans, and the tracks, let alone the entrepreneurs who ran them. The bulk of the information in this book was, therefore, provided by individuals recalling what they saw. It is inevitable that there are inaccuracies. After forty or fifty years, incidents can be imperfectly remembered, even if still perfectly felt.

It is not the purpose of *Hot Cars, Cool Drivers* to be an actual history. However, in an attempt to make the book as factually correct as possible, we asked the following expert readers to review the text. We are especially grateful to Mark Alden, Dick Berggren, Bruce Cohen, Russ Conway, Ed Duncan, the Falconis, Ed Gendreau Jr., Dwight Lowes, Ron Marcorelle, Carl Merrill, Steve Newman, Wes Pettengill, Rick Riberio, RA Silvia, Kendall Smith, John Spence, Don Thomas, and Peter von Sneidern. Each was generous with his time and made helpful suggestions about some or all of the text.

Many other folks contributed stories, photos, clippings, and programs. Some are listed below, with appreciation. A very special thanks goes to Ed Duncan who served many hours doing research and cross-referencing.

This is the fifth motorsports book that Jim Rigney, MaryRose Moskell and I at Coastal 181 have now published. Jim's talents as an editor and compositer are unmatched, and his knowledge and experience in racing are amazing. Meanwhile, MaryRose has faced the formidable tasks of keeping us organized while she has concentrated so effectively on developing this brand new market for regional racing books, largely over the Internet. It has been a wonderful experience for us, and we already have further titles in the works.

Finally, we would like to thank Sandra Rigney for her interior design, which successfully depicts the functional style of the 40s and 50s, and Joyce Wells for yet another eye-catching cover design.

LEW BOYD
June 2004

Special thanks to the following contributors:

Andy Anderson
Bill Aramian
Archie Archambault
The Archambault Family
Johnny Arrigo
Dick Batchelder
Bob Bachiocchi
John Bain
Dave Balser
Bill Balser
A.J. Begin
Buzz Bezanson
Bob Bonin
Fred Borden
Bob Bouchard
Bones Bourcier
Joe Buccilli
Tommy Caruso
Joe Cast
Rene Charland
Leo Cleary
Pat Cleary
Bob Cloutier
Paul Conley
JC Crossley
Dave Dion
The Dolliver Family
Rick Eastman
Roy Elderidge
Hobart Esty
Ray Farnell
Peter Fiandaca
Ed Flemke Jr.
George Fowler
Tommy Gargango
Henry Graham
Dave Grantz
Peter Hamilton
Roger Hathaway
Marty Harty
Johnny Harty
Lee Hurd
Pete Hurn
Vic Kangas
Roger Lancey
Roland Lapierre Jr.
Red LaRoche
Joe LaRochelle
Glen Legere
Freddie Luchesi
Jack Lundin
Red MacDonald
Don MacLaren
Jack Malone
Jim Martel
Lenny Maughan
Bob Merrick
Buddy Merrick
Kenny Merrick
Dan Meservey
Gene Michaud
Mike Murphy
Neil Murray
Ron Narducci
Steve Newman
Sean Newman
Bo Noyes
Bob Pearson
Fred Peterson
Jack Peterson
Junior Prescott
Paul Richardson
Artie Rousseau
Bob Santos
Bob Santos Jr.
Mike and Sandy Sargent
George Savary
Ollie Silva
Frank Sivert
Barbara Skofield
Jim Slater
Bill Slater
John Smith
Phil Smith
Ken Smith
Ray Spognardi
Greg St. Hilaire
Paul Starta
Bugs Stevens
George Summers
Billy Tibbert
Bill Tibbert
Doris Toombs
Butch True
Reino and Anna Tulonen
Dick Volante
Bentley Warren
Trigger Watson
Dick Watson
Paul Wellington

Only trees and leaves lined the Boston-Worcesrter Turnpike when Westboro Speedway was built. *(Falconi Collection)*

WESTBORO SPEEDWAY

High Banks and Long Neck Knicks

ANNA TULONEN DIDN'T THINK TOO MUCH ABOUT IT. She was nursing her first child that summer in 1946 when her husband Reino and his buddy Ray Hill headed off on their motorcycles on a balmy Sunday afternoon. She knew they were going to check out the car races in New Hampshire. It seemed like everyone was checking out new things those days. The war had ended, the economy was beginning to pick up, and the country was in a springtime state of mind.

Ray and Reino motored North from Fitchburg across the state line into Keene and to the Cheshire Fairgrounds, a basic, no nonsense half-mile dirt track that ran parallel to a country highway. There promoter Jimmy Green was presenting racing under the sanction of the New England Big Car Association. Big cars, carryovers from auto racing's start in pre-war years, were serious, custom-built machines. The best of them would converge each May to compete on the lumpy brick surface of Indianapolis.

When they arrived at the Fairgrounds, Reino and Ray sought out another friend from Fitchburg, Harry Billington. Harry was fielding a car that day, one quite typical of the times. It was a single seater with a hand-built body sitting on a rail frame, high atop a tractor-like spring setup and wire wheels. Beneath the expansive hood was a Hisso, a thundering World War One airplane engine. Big cars were fast and surely not for the faint of heart.

Keene had many fatalities, as the cars often flipped, tossing their drivers skyward like rag dolls. The rickety splintering guardrail around the dirt surface claimed its own pound of flesh—so much so that in the middle of one night a group of disgruntled drivers secretly cut the whole thing down.

It was not, therefore, altogether surprising that afternoon when Billington's designated driver, Larry Page, got cold feet about the whole affair. But what was a surprise was when an official walked up and asked who would drive. Hill and Billington pointed instantly to Tulonen.

Anna recalls not being too upset by this turn of events when she heard what had happened. "I was too young to really understand things. By the time I realized how dangerous it was, Reino had the bug. That was it. There was nothing I could do."

Neither the bug nor the danger took too long to realize. Almost immediately the infatuated Tulonen was on the road with the Billington big car. The car was defi-

Reino Tulonen awaiting the start in the Billington Hisso. *(Tulonen Collection)*

nitely a handful—so hard to steer that Tulonen's fingers and palms would be bleeding after each feature, especially after he manhandled his way around the dirt bull rings, steering wheel locked right into the broadslide.

It was obvious to any seasoned railbird that young Reino, already nicknamed "the Flying Finn", had the goods, even if he was short on experience. His emerging skills, however, could not shield him from mishap as the team picked up momentum. One particularly scary incident at Franklin, MA Fairgrounds saw Reino crash mightily with the car burying itself beneath the guardrail. Reino's helmet was ripped off and he slumped unconscious with his hair singed by the exhaust header until he was rescued. He bears the scars today.

As the Fitchburg gang became increasingly engaged in racing, word began to circulate about a new racetrack on the Boston-Worcester Road called Westboro Stadium.

Tongues were wagging about Westboro with good reason. Located several miles to the east of Worcester, the facility featured imposing high banks, sculpted from the flat, then-isolated farmland. Grandstands with 8000 seats encircled the quarter-mile oval, paved with a fine bituminous concrete mix, while the asphalt itself surrounded a football field in the infield.

Westboro Stadium was the lofty vision of a group of enterprising ex-servicemen, Leo and Roland Turgeon of Westboro, Richard Trum from Natick, and Joe Hennebry and Norm McDonald, both of Framingham. Their goal was to develop a world-class speedway for midget cars, and they used all manner of entrepreneurial cleverness in its construction. They offered contractors partnering arrangements paid from future attendance, eerily similar to the way much of business is done today.

The gamble surely seemed a score early on. Excitement about midget racing was reaching a crescendo, and when Westboro opened on Tuesday night August 5, 1947 with the Bay State Midget Racing Association, it was a madhouse. Leo Turgeon reported, "We had 10,000 people and we could hardly handle the money fast enough."

The show was well received and it was apparent that the track's steep slope lent itself to multi-groove competition. The first two heats ever run were copped handily by Joe Sostilio and Joe "Fat Boy" Ross aboard the famous McNutt Offy. In the third heat a torrid duel developed between Frankie Simonetti, Johnny Black, and Hermie Delisle, with Delisle scooping the checker. In the second semi, Simonetti and Delisle went at it again, joined aggressively by Bob Blair and Bud Tatro. Simonetti won what long time midget writer and official "Mac" McLeod termed "the finest race I have ever had the pleasure to see."

A 25-lap feature was run off essentially without incident in a time of 6:21:27. The victor was Natick's Joe Sostilio by a wide margin.

Wildly enthusiastic crowds continued to be huge for the nine remaining shows of the season, but the winds of discontent were already stirring. Sostilio, aboard his own well-tooled Leader Card Special, was so dominant that he was only beaten twice in features, each time by legendary Bill Schindler in the Caruso Offy.

"Rosey Joe" Sostilio was the winner of Westboro's inaugural main event. *(Silvia Collection)*

(left) Sostilio works his Offenhauser engine in the basement of his home in Natick. *(Bob Miour photo)*

(right) The awesomely talented Bill Schindler was the only Westboro winner the first year other than Sostilio. The one-legged legend is shown here with one-armed legend, Wes Saegesser. *(Caruso Collection)*

Sostilio, colorfully labeled "Rosey Joe", was by the mid-forties a veteran campaigner. He had begun in the treacherous big cars on the dirt at Readville in 1923 and by age 17 was a winner. He came hot out of the box after the war, finishing second to New England Hall-of-Famer Bob Blair in BSMRA points. By 1947, teamed with Johnny Bernardi, he was at the top of his game and he swept the point race by a full 1000 points. In the fifties he would venture out of New England, appropriating the 1951 AAA Eastern Sprint Car title. Sostilio is credited with an amazing 300 open cockpit wins and was quite properly inducted by John Notte into the Hall of Fame in 2003.

Over the course of the summer the local guys in their outboard and Ford V8-60 powered racers could see they were no match for the big boys with state-of-the-art Kurtis Kraft chasses and Offenhauser engines. And the big boys like Sostilio were in town. The nightly midget shows run in New England attracted competitors from far and wide. Many rented cabins near Westboro, as a centrally located base for their weekly circuit.

The tensions were to reach a boiling point over the winter. Even though Westboro purses in 1947 had averaged over $3,000 (very big for those days and far above the $1,100 guarantee), prize money and technical rules were at the heart of the dispute. No resolution had been reached by spring, and after an April 19 opening day, the Bay State Midget Racing Association, represented by Johnny Whitehouse, Bill Welch, Bill Randall and hundreds of others, struck Westboro (and other tracks), marching in widely publicized picket lines along Route 9. The ugly situation was covered by all major New England newspapers. Many race dates were cancelled, and—desperate not to lose their investments—the track owners reached out to the nationally based American Automobile Association and brought in even bigger names —with even faster cars. The racers included Ronnie Householder from Detroit, Jim Florian, and Johnny Parsons.

(left) "Boston Blackie" LaMachia in a Ford V-8-60 *(Caruso Collection)*. *(right)* BSMRA officals picket Westboro in the Spring of 1948. *(Silvia Collection)*

Over time some of the problems were resolved and by July regular racing was presented on Tuesday nights. The great Johnny Thomson was the big winner, joining single-race victors Sostilio, Bernardi, Bill Randall, Jim Florian, Chet Gibbons, and Charlie Ethier. Sadly, however, the bloom was off the rose of the midgets. The winter of '48-'49 brought further discontent, and Westboro's management opted to bring in new types of competition for the 1949 season. For purists like Leo Turgeon, it was a death knell. "The midgets were nice clean racing, he lamented, "not just cars slamming into each other." The midget craze abruptly over, Turgeon sold his interest in the track.

Johnnie Parsons was one of the national names brought in to compete at Westboro around the time of the strike. He went on to win the Indianapolis 500 in 1950. *(Duncan Collection)*

There must have been rekindled excitement in the big car community when they were invited to Westboro for a trial show in 1949. Usually performing on longer dirt tracks such as Keene and Topsfield, big car riders looked forward to the novelty of running at the tight and spiffy asphalt quarter-miler. A number of clubs were competing for dates in the big car circuit, and it was New England Speedways, Inc. that sanctioned the event.

That Saturday was a barnburner, recalled in vivid detail by veteran Shrewsbury, Massachusetts racer Frankie Sivert. Driving Paul Lyon's Riley that night, he was second in the first heat and had high hopes for the feature. Pole sitter, Hartford's Eddie Edwards aboard the Paquin Hal, paced the throbbing field down for the green. Suddenly, at the last second just as starter Wally Faulkner unfurled the green, Edwards raised his hand, as if to request another lap. It was too late. Everyone was already on the hammer, and Sivert remembers the pandemonium. In Bob Bonin's race report, "Art Rousseau who was directly behind Edwards crashed into his tail and hurtled high over his car, turning end-for-end in the air, and landing upside down in front of Jimmy Little who crashed into Rousseau's overturned car, causing it to roll over twice into the infield where it landed upside down with the driver pinned beneath." Rousseau was hospitalized with an injured wrist, torn shoulder ligaments, and a concussion, while Little was taken away unconscious with severe facial lacerations and a concussion.

It was not over yet. When the carnage was cleared and the ambulances had returned, the fans must have flipped out. There was Art Rousseau back in the lineup. While he was escaping the clutches of the doctors and nurses, his crew had been pounding out the damaged Pete

The bionic Art Rousseau in the Pete Galka Riley, immediately before the feature. Note his bandaged wrist—he has just returned from the hospital. The now hoodless car's tail and cowl have been banged out, and he's ready to go. *(Berggren Collection)*

Galka four-port Riley racecar. Amazingly, Rousseau would go on to win, causing Bonin to write, "This was indeed the most spectacular speedway achievement I have ever witnessed—for a driver to set such a blistering pace for 20 laps while suffering untold pain from injuries sustained only shortly before in a crash which would cause the average man to retire from racing for life." Second across the line was Frankie Sivert—and, in third, that Flying Finn, Reino Tulonen. Edwards, King, Knox, Bob White, and Jerry Russo trailed.

It is quite likely that Anna Tulonen—like other drivers' wives—had some words with Reino that night going back to Fitchburg about the dangers of his passion. However, there was another topic of discussion as well. Big cars really weren't the big time at Westboro Stadium in 1949. It was something brand new. It was stock cars.

Art Rousseau tries on a stock car for size. The flimsy cage and the seat mounts speak to just how little thought was given to issues of safety. *(Berggren photo)*

I can remember as yesterday sitting in the office at Westboro in the early sixties during a rainout talking to one of the track promoters, Bill Welch. Welchie, a Hall-of-Famer and as fine a man as they come, had really dug into midget racing when he returned from the war. He became a virtuoso engine builder, first with V-8-60s and then the Offies. He had even taken a fling at driving until he crashed while testing Oscar Ridlon's Offy at Hudson, NH. There he flew off the track and flipped through the trees, causing the curved Kurtis Kraft windshield to penetrate his forehead, permanently diminishing his vision. Welchie told me of the times in the late forties and particularly of a very early stock car race in Lonsdale, RI in 1948. He said just watching the show made him predict the end of the midgets. "The jalopies were cheap, unlike our expensive midgets. Anyone could afford them.

John Tortona (#55) and Jug Menard mix it up in the zany world of stock cars. *(Alden Collection)*

Tommy Dupont
(Tibbert Collection)

And the fans went crazy about the action." NEAR founder and race historian Al Fini wrote of that "wild and ragged show of thrills and spills with Red Cummings the winner," so popular that it propelled Lonsdale attendance to an average of 15,000, with an astounding 200,000 for the season. Welchie adjusted immediately, partnering with Dave Morton, a top-notch carburetor and ignition guy, in a shop in Somerville. Calling themselves Morton Welch Engineering, they began building flathead Ford motors for stock cars. "Wild Man" Georgie Lewis, Ray Janelle, Billy Tibbert, Rufe Anderson, Ralph Moody and a host of others were also part of that huge first migration over to the hard tops.

Most significantly, though, by 1949 almost all of the Massachusetts tracks suspended the midgets as their headliner and booked the stock cars along with big car and thrill shows. Westboro's diminished ownership team, now functionally led by Joe Hennebry, switched to Friday nights and joined the New England Stock Car Racing Association. Run by former midgeteers Maurice "Bud" Tatro and speed-parts businessman, Ed Stone, the caffeinated NESCRA weekly tours consisted of Tuesdays in Hudson, NH, Wednesdays at Cherry Park in Avon, CT, Thursdays at West Peabody and West Springfield, MA, Fridays at Westboro, Saturdays at Norwood Arena, and Sundays at Lonsdale.

A new breed of traveling and competent stock car invaders such as North Carolina's Speedy Thompson and Frank "Rebel" Mundy began to spice up the mix, and they were joined, of course, by hundreds of Average Joes who suddenly found racing accessible and affordable.

The end result was some pretty intense racing. Red Cummings, Tommy Dupont, Ralph Moody and Junior Pooler were among the winners, but Bill Tibbert showed special stuff, copping three of Westboro's first four shows. A frightening but not untypical incident

Red Cummings in the Dynamite Special and Bill Tibbert in the Wentworth Jennings racer were huge names in Massachusetts. *(Silvia Collection)*

took place on June 24. Parading down for the start of the fourth heat, former open wheeler Ray Janelle and newcomer Jack Griffin touched. Janelle slammed through the guardrail like tooth picks, annihilating Lee Hiltz's starter's box. Lumber flew everywhere, striking Hiltz on the head and throwing him to the surface of the track as his stand was being flattened. Hiltz was rushed to Worcester Hospital, but guests from the speedway had short stays. In outrageous Rousseau tradition, he was back to wave off the feature that night.

By the end of the season, the whole Northeastern racing community had stock cars on the brain. Reino Tulonen was among them. The Finn was watching closely when his old buddy Ray Hill built a car and was finishing up front. That September Ray took a flyer and towed out to the New York State Fairgrounds in Syracuse for the state championship on the one-mile dirt. Incredibly, Hill returned victorious over Frank Mundy, Bob Cameron, and drivers from across the country in the accident- and injury-laden event, witnessed by an overflow Labor Day swarm of fans. What really caught Reino's attention was the $2,250 purse that Ray and his mechanic, "Hunk" La Cuier, brought back with them. Anna probably took note, too.

Ralph Gurney was red hot in 1950. *(Silvia Collection)*

In 1950 the scene was still in flux, as the new flavor of competition tried to take a set. Crowds were still large and teams with the necessary energy and resource could compete almost nightly. The New England Auto Racing Association joined promoter Hennebry at Westboro for the season. It featured a Class B "jalopy" division to complement the hard tops that were already becoming speedier and now known as "modifieds". Trophy earners included Ralph Gurney who snagged five straight in June, Tibbert, Stan Woods, and two Reds,

Bolduc and Foote. New names, too, padded the roster, names such as Freddie Luchesi, Hop Harrington, Carroll Sleeper, Gene White, and Gavin Couper that would become so very familiar over the course of the decade.

It was certainly spirited entertainment, but really primitive. Announcer Lee Emmerick talked the crowds through some remarkable situations. On Friday, August 11, Dick Gaumond and Jack Horan locked wheels in turn one on the start and Horan was slammed violently by journeyman driver, Jug Menard. Horan's car exploded in a towering ball of flame. The race report speaks to the rudimentary conditions of the time by praising the attendants for saving Horan by "pulling him from the car, rolling him on the round, thus putting out his burning clothing."

Perhaps because of changing ownership, Westboro's progress was shy of what was taking place at some other Massachusetts tracks, especially the Saturday night facilities Norwood Arena and Riverside Park. In fact, Westboro was already shaping its long identity as a second sister to Norwood, offering many of the same cars on Friday nights, but with reduced purse money, pomp, and circumstance.

Nonetheless, the stockers were here to stay, and Reino Tulonen had jumped in with bells and whistles. One of his first rides was in a #32 car—becoming #132 and then #732—owned by Custom Auto Body in Fitchburg. Bruno and Reino (another one) Maki owned Custom and they hired skilled mechanics from open wheel days to get them going. They were among the first to find speed with the flyweight 1932 Fords, also preferred on the dirt in New York by such mudslingers as Pete Corey. The combination clicked right off the trailer. The Finn was flyin'.

So, too, was Ray Hill, but his season ended a bit rockier than Reino's. He won widely, but was sidelined with injuries following a

Custom Auto Body's '37 Ford slant back sure started out pretty. *(Falconi Collection)*

(left) Ray Hill wadded this one up very badly and got hurt. (right) Reino Tulonen and Ray after Reino won Ray's benefit race. Following the ceremonies, Anna says they had quite a discussion about who should get the trophy. *(Tulonen Collection)*

savage mishap. A benefit race—the Ray Hill Handicap—was run at Manchester, NH's Motordrome on October 25, and the boys from Fitchburg would shake hands on the victory podium.

They were fast the next spring as well. Reino launched '51 with a win at the Medford Bowl opener and kept right on going. A tasty plum was a $1,000-to-win championship on the dirt at Oxford Plains, ME. He also copped convincingly a four-way combined contest of the Atlantic, American, Yankee, and Merrimack Racing Associations in the Maki 732.

Other hot shoes getting it done on Route 9 included Red Castor, Ralph Moody, and Charlie Ethier who won the first midget competition run in three years. Hully Bunn, Trigger Watson, Funzie Caruso, Mario "Fats" Caruso, Bob Hersey, Chink Howard, Bill Andrews, Bob McGee, Larry Plant, and Gordon Martin of the credentialed Martin Brothers also joined the roster. The most interesting show of the year came on August 28. The hot new modifieds were pushed aside for a "New Car" show, sanctioned by an organization from Daytona Beach called NASCAR. Featuring 1949-1951 show stock models, the competition was advertised to match national auto gypsies such as Bill Rexford, Frank Mundy, the Flock Brothers, and Wally Campbell against the best of the locals, including Fat Boy Ross and Sammy Packard.

Most especially because of its bulging announced purse of $3,100, the race snagged the attention of the Custom Auto boys. They acquired a Henry J for Tulonen and took it a sixth place finish at Westboro behind Connecticut wheelmen Charlie Gattalia, Pappy Hough, and Paul Petit, Cleveland's Don Bailey, and Ed Gauvin from Boston. Spurred on by their good finish, the Custom boys and the Finn went to Thompson in October where he was fifth and on to

(top left) Reino and his Custom Auto Associates pose with the Henry J. before their adventures at Thompson, Westboro, The Pines, and Darlington. *(Tulonen Collection)*

(top right) Pappy Hough was a colorful midget owner and proponent for years before his involvement with NASCAR's short track endeavors. He's shown here with his Ford at Westboro. *(H. White photo)*

Darlington SC with the Henry J. It wasn't as tough a tow as one might think. The car was registered and Reino drove it down. His teammate, Natick's virtuoso chauffeur Bill Tibbert, did the same. They finished 40th and 49th respectively.

NASCAR's foray into Massachusetts did not last, and the Southerners were not to return regularly until they brought their coveted sanction to Norwood in 1960.

Westboro, meanwhile, was to enter a kind of motorsports Dark Ages that saw a gradual diminution of car counts and an overall deterioration of physical plant over the next ten years.

As the modifieds—mostly all flathead Ford V-8s—grew in technical sophistication, a supporting Sportsman class grew up beneath them with the same rules save some engine limitations. New modified

By the time Custom brought out this coupe for Reino, fenders and running boards were gone, and there was a lot of mixing and matching of parts. (Tulonen Collection)

A great field of midgets returned for a show on June 23, 1951. Charlie Ethier got the win. *(Silvia Collection)*

stars began to shine, Ralph Flannery, Red Allard, Freddie Schulz, Ronald LaPierre, Red Bolduc, Porky Kinsman, Red Sequin, Dan Stanton, Red Hill, and Wellesley's Doc McKenzie among them, while Sportsman competitors such as Lee Hurd, Buster Nelson, and Fats Caruso were quick. A third division was also created in line with Norwood. The new Jalopy division required drivers to run over infield ramps on every third lap. A 1952 division novice was a burly young man from nearby Upton named George Summers. He attacked the four-foot ramps installed at Westboro with vigor, but by his own admission he got off to a pretty modest start, trashing no small number of cars. Oh, how that was to change.

Another newcomer in those days was an unlikely fellow by the name of Marty Harty. Harty, along with his brother Johnny, owned a scrap yard in Barre, MA and became intrigued with racing in 1949. They decided to have a car built and they farmed the construction out to various mechanics, welders, and engine builders. Thunderously disappointed by the results, the exacting Marty began digging in himself. An uncommonly bright man, he studied everything he could lay his hands on and totally immersed himself in the emerging field of stock car engineering. He took his first car to West Peabody with Bobby Tolman in the seat in 1950 with limited success. Then he and Johnny heard about a motorcycle racer from Gardner named Leo Richard and they inquired about his services. This combo clicked and they won five of their first six shows, while the next year they were on top of the points at West Peabody, Hudson, and Mohawk Stadium, a facility near Lunenburg that operated but two years.

In 1952 the Hartys arrived at Westboro, barely missing a win on their first night. Ralph Flannery, driving the Sully Panetta entry out of Lincoln, nipped them on the last lap. Marty was taken with the skills of some of the Westboro wheel twisters. "I began to recognize good drivers," he recalls. "They drive, but every great driver drifts. You should have seen Reino Tulonen back then. He practically owned Westboro in 1952. He drifted. It goes beyond driving—beyond the

Long Neck Knicks

Good times and bad, there was one cash register at Westboro Speedway that was always ringing. It was at the beer stand, so accessible to the front stretch bleachers and to the pit area.

Opened early and closed late, the rough-hewn structure was so much a part of the Westboro experience back in the fifties that several car owners would not run on Fridays, lest their drivers be too fuzzy to pursue Norwood's Saturday purse. It was still going on many years later when one of the promoters told me on a Monday morning that close to four beers had been sold the previous weekend for every adult ticket holder.

An especially popular custom was for a feature winner to swagger over, buy everyone a round, and proceed to carry on about how fast he was. What became of greater concern over the years was how fast people might be going down Route 9 after the races. Mercifully, no significant problems were reported.

Father Knickerbocker was clearly very pleased with Westboro's consumption, so much so that he showed up himself on May 13, 1963 to present Joe Csiki with a trophy that would hold more than one. That's Maury Dumas on the right, a great benefactor to Massachusetts auto racing. *(Balser photo)*

In more recent years, the brands switched around a bit. But on September 2, 1978 podium finishers Freddie Schultz, Roland LaPierre, Jr., and Johnny Falcon were in an obvious Budweiser state of mind. *(Balser photo)*

Bobby Sprague (#6) and Jimmy McGuire (#37) dance in their cut downs beneath Father Knickerbocker. *(Silvia Collection)*

Marty Harty poses with his #329 square top. Note the vertical extensions to the exhaust system by the rear quarter panels. Marty smiles about them, "The guy who owned Lonsdale told me it was the sweetest sounding car he had ever heard." *(Harty Collection)*

edge. I used to see Fats Caruso come through the turns at Westboro with his front end straight. I didn't know till later what I was seeing. I had to learn to adjust my cars for them. When Reino first asked me to change my front ends around for him, I was a little offended. Then I realized."

The person who made the deepest impression on Harty was a young driver fresh to Westboro and Norwood from a brilliant early career at the Medford Bowl. He was driving pickup rides at the time, but Marty's selection was right on the money. Soft-spoken Freddie Borden would mature into the winningest driver in Westboro's history.

Always seeking to spice up the show in these years, promoters scheduled occasional events for women drivers. A Powder Puff was

NEMA, the Northeastern Midget Association, was organized in 1953 as an essentially lower-cost "Ford" club. Bert Brooks was top man for their Westboro swing on June 27, while Bill Eldridge was their first champion. The irrepressible Reino was racing midgets in these years, as well. This particular outboard midget, "The Whisperer," sits at his home today, ready to go. *(Tulonen Collection)*

George Summers' first car didn't last all that long. Running over the ramps was a jarring experience to say the least. *(Summers Collection)*

the last event of the show on September 18, 1953. Hop Harrington had just snatched a 24-car main away from Joe McNulty, Red Cummings, and Fat Boy Ross. Somehow this Powder Puff, the third one run, would make things much more real. A grandmother named Ann Howe lost it off the fourth turn and flipped down the front stretch. She was reportedly "badly shaken,"

In tune with the new sound of Elvis Presley over the radio waves, Westboro car builders were more adventuresome over the winter of 1953 and 1954. The modified cars, now starting to be known as "hot rods" or "cut downs," were getting lower and lower, lighter and lighter. Guys like Marty Harty were taking space frame technology utilized by the Germans and Lotus engineers to produce flyweight creations. Westboro racing would go largely without problem that summer while Bolduc, Tulonen, Borden, Harrington, Wally Silva, Big Joe Rosenfield, and Leo Cleary all visited the checkerboard. The stories of the year were, in fact, largely out of town.

Ralph "Hop" Harrington was winning in the cut-downs in 1954. Legendary Indy car Engineer, Jim McGee once said of him, "After seeing the likes of Hop Harrington and Ralph Moody drive, I knew I should never try. I knew I should concentrate on the cars." *(Silvia Collection)*

George Summers, the ramp driver from Upton, had really taken a liking to racing. The popular young man, son of American League umpire Billy Summers, befriended Jack Griffin, a well-known cut down driver. The relationship matured, and Griffin became the mentor, helping Summers with mechanical issues and with driving insight. On Saturday August 26, Griffin and Summers were together, installing a new cam in Summers' car, before setting off in opposite directions for the evening wars. Summers headed to Norwood, Griffin to New London, CT.

Later that night, George was to call Griffin's house, beside himself with excitement about telling Jack that he had just won his first feature. The response was solemn: Jack had been killed that very night. He climbed a wheel and flipped violently in the first turn of the Speedbowl.

(left) Jack Griffin was all smiles at New London. In the feature things would go terribly wrong. *(Summers Collection)*

(right) After Griffin was killed, his family gave all the racing equipment to George Summers. Here is Griffin's car as it arrived at Summers' garage. *(Summers Collection)*

The implications of this Connecticut accident were profound, especially in the aftermath of an unsightly incident the year before at Thompson. Reino's friend, Ray Hill, had been on a tear, racing and winning everywhere. His driving was extraordinarily brave, witness his shocking run a few years earlier at Syracuse. Reino and Anna figure that to some degree Ray just didn't care. He had a 4F from Uncle Sam for juvenile diabetes and he had been unable to participate in the war. Over time he did not appear to be in the best of health. He was warned that the car he took to John Hoenig's blisteringly fast 5/8th mile Thompson Speedway might not be suitable for such high speed. It was not. In a grinding crash on September 27, Ray Hill was ejected through the covered roof of the former cloth-top coupe before a horrified crowd, and he succumbed a few days later to his massive injuries.

These two events contributed significantly to the course of racing in that Connecticut tracks banned the cut downs and returned for good to full coupe configuration the next year.

A flicker of light shone on the Route 9 raceway in 1955, but it turned out to be short-lived.

Races that year were sanctioned by Harvey Tattersall's New Haven-based United Stock Car Racing Club. Tattersall was one of the last to attempt a serious "roll up" of stock car activity in the Northeast. He had weekly racing at Riverside Park in Agawam, West Haven, CT, Lonsdale, RI, and Old Bridge Stadium in Old Bridge, NJ, as well as the Friday night venue in Westboro. Tattersall tried to sew the tracks with threads such as hosting special 100-lappers for late model cars.

Only marginally successful, the circuit's champion turned out to be NEAR Hall-of-Famer, Jokko Maggiacomo. "Fabulous Freddie" Luchesi, one of Rhode Island's all-time best, won Westboro's United point chase definitively. Red Barbeau, Roland LaPierre, Bobby Edwards, and Junior Pooler were among those in pursuit.

A real benefit to Westboro from United was the strengthening of a non-Ford division. By the mid-fifties, Ford Flatheads had come to dominate stock car competition. For the last seven or so seasons, motor builders were learning a lot, and a mini-support industry grew up around them. Innovators sought advantage by using "trick" stuff such as higher compression heads that Ford was installing on Canadian buses. An old time racing family from Rhode Island, Sam and Caesar Litterio, were designing and grinding racing camshafts for flatheads, and their technology was masterful. Much of this new kit was available from Ed Stone, a fixture in New England racing circles, and his pioneering emporium, New England Speed Equipment.

For these Ford-powered "hot rods," more and more rocket-like, the expense of construction was getting out of hand. Even some successful owners such as the Panettas threw in the towel. Bill Tibbert reflects on it today: "Just like what happened with the Offies and Kurtis Krafts, it seemed to grow to money. Things always start simple and easier, then get complicated and expensive. Then the pattern starts again."

The non-Fords were a kind of new start. Based on Chevy, Hudson or other straight (as opposed to V-8) block configurations, the non-Ford rules allowed essentially the same cars but much cheaper power. The cars were going great guns at New York speed plants such as Freeport Stadium on Long Island and Rhinebeck Speedway a little

In 1955 Freddie Luchesi was the fastest at Westboro. *(Silvia Collection)*

That's Ed Stone in the center by the door of his Brighton emporium. Bill Welch is at the far left while Joe Ross flashes his usual smile second from the right. *(Caruso Collection.)*

Larry Antonellis, master driver from Quincy. *(Balser photo)*

further up the Hudson. Soon they were tearing around Norwood, the Pines, and West Peabody, as well as Tattersall's sanctions, Riverside and Westboro. One of Westboro's earliest non-Ford standouts was a crane operator from Quincy named Larry Antonellis. Both competent and enduring, Antonellis racked up many, many checkers at Lonsdale, Westboro, Norwood, and elsewhere. Along the way, he also became a very successful businessman.

A spectacular non-Ford (or "Bomber") misadventure occurred at Westboro in August of the next year. George Summers was leading the 20-lap feature with two to go. Vastly improved, Summers was in the office of a #29 coupe owned by Bo Noyes who would become a popular fixture on Route 9 for years. Suddenly, dueling with Dick Durand, Wally Dudley, and Worcester's well-known Tommy Bourget near the starter's box, Summers rubbed a wheel and spiraled into a series of flips, landing in a broken, smoldering heap in the first turn. He was extricated and rushed to Worcester Memorial Hospital with painful shoulder and leg injuries.

If the mishap was memorable for Summers, it surely was as well for North Grafton's Margaret Kneeland who watched with terror from the stands that night. Peg and George were scheduled to be married the next Saturday. George managed to keep the date, but required considerable assistance to reach the altar. He was in an immobilizing body cast for weeks . . ..

After Tattersall and United retreated at the end of 1955, a familiar promotional team arrived at the high banks. There was actually little substance to it, and hardly anyone would have predicted that in one form or another it would remain in place for twelve years, and, after a very slow start, clearly become responsible for saving and then stabilizing the race track.

The lead dude was a cheerful, dapper fellow from Lincoln, RI named Jimmy Costello. Costello, who counted car dealerships and Rhode Island state politics among his weekday activities, partnered with long-time associate Wally Faulkner, and formed the Atlantic Auto Racing Association. They were to guide Westboro, by this time a bit disheveled and run down, steadily and unspectacularly for the rest of the fifties. The first attempt to build some leverage came when the duo also took on West Peabody Speedway and pushed a dual-track circuit. It was an interesting experiment, co-mingling for the first time in a few years the state's more Southern cars with those competing in the Merrimack Valley area.

Undaunted by eventual disappointment in Peabody, the pair continued to reach out, and by the early sixties they were in control of the Westboro, Brookline, NH, and Thompson, CT Speedways.

Faulkner and Costello nurtured the growing resumes of cut down stars such as Red Sequin, Hank Stevens, Red Barbeau, Red Hill, and Fred Luchesi in these years, pitting them against newer throttle jockeys like Somerville's Jovial Joe Cast, Smokey Joe Delginio, Russ Hazard, and Lloyd Putnam. One of the most colorful was Dick "Jet" Jackson who built signature #27jr hot rods.

The Finn was still flying high these days, still towing wild cut downs out of Fitchburg each weekend. The final race of '57 must have been reminiscent for him, though. Faulkner and Costello brought back the New England Big Car Association for what turned out to be the division's final appearance ever at Westboro. Ed Brown, steering

Freddie was the first of the great Astle Brothers to venture up to Westboro. This night in May of '54 he probably wished he hadn't come. *(Silvia Collection)*

Most always in racing the best drivers end up eventually in the best cars. In 1957 it was Ernie Gahan in the #97 and Freddie Luchesi—great Westboro champion—in the familiar Leaning #2. *(Silvia*

The Finn's hot rods were always cutting edge. Looking at the number(s), one would think the sign painter was covering his bets on the side of this one. *(Tulonen Collection)*

his brother's Thunderbird Special out of Scituate, just beat Earl Halaquist in the Ted Blair Chrysler across the line. Hank Duggan, Jerry Russo, Al Pillion, and Smokey Boutwell also suited up to drive open-wheelers owned by guys like Jim Moffat, Forrest Dame, Frank Sivert, and Reino's old owner, Harry Billington.

Marty Harty's predictions about Fred Borden were materializing. In 1956 Borden showed up in a tiny red and black cut down, #10, out of nearby Southboro. Owned by John Falconi, the car had been driven earlier by Bill Tibbert, and then his friend Joe Ross and subsequently by Andy Anderson and Gordon Martin.

Falconi had originally become interested in racing when his buddy Win Rich from Wellesley fielded a coupe for Tibbert. When Rich called it a day, the equipment went to Southboro and Tibbert built a new car with the pieces. Finished on a Saturday, it even looked hot and was fitted with a state-of-the-art 60-over flathead from Morton Welch Engineering to boot. Dave Morton and Bill Welch became an integral part of Falconi's effort.

Looking at their watches that afternoon, Falconi and Tibbert realized they could reach New London in time for the show and in time for a test run. Arriving in Connecticut, they found that Tibbert was on the "black list," having competed in shows not sanctioned by United, New London's sanction at the time. Such lists would be tested at Norwood in the sixties, as their legal validity was certainly challenged by right-to-work laws. Tattersall did allow the car to run that day, however. Ray Delisle, a much-heralded Nutmeg State driver, qualified it, and Tibbert was allowed to shoe it in the main, provided

Jimmy Costello and his daughter Debbie congratulate Borden on a win in 1956. *(Falconi Collection)*

that he did not win. Tibbert loved the car instantly. It responded to his every wish. But he contained himself, climbing no higher than third place. Then, charging down for the checker, race leaders Dick Beauregard and Don Collins, two of New London's greatest, lost control, tangled, and took each other out. Despite intention to the contrary, Tibbert coasted across the stripe victorious. "Johnny Falconi sure was happy," Tibbert recalls. "Tattersall was not."

Falconi, Welch, and Morton's selection of Borden not long afterwards was good from the git go. The laid-back welder never seemed spectacular out on the race track, but somehow in the end he was always there. Marty Harty recalls that, "Freddie just knew how to pass each person—differently. He was very fast, a drifter, but he did not look it. His mind must have been a computer."

On multiple occasions Freddie would deliver the #10 to victory circle not only at Westboro but Norwood as well. And by this time Norwood had far surpassed the increasingly shabby Westboro in terms of competition, prize money, and prestige. The dichotomy between the two tracks became so great that the #10 team, like several others, built two cars, an understated model for Route 9 that could get beaten up on Friday nights and a second one that would be strong and fresh for the big Saturday bucks on Route 1.

By the end of 1959, however, the little red and black hot rod sat beside Route 30 in Southboro, decommissioned and stripped. The deep-throated overhead valve engines were creeping into the field. It was obvious to everyone that once chassis builders could make use of all that new music, the flathead engines would be playing second fid-

They Called Him "The Doctor"

Also known as "The Jumping Jack," Faulkner shows his flag form as Pete Vigeant goes by. *(Balser photo)*

It seemed that Wally Faulkner had been around forever. Way back in Chesire County Fairgrounds big car days, he was both the starter and the concessionaire. Always in motion, he was an effective and agile starter, while at his food stand you could buy some juice that had quite the bite to it.

He hooked up in the early fifties with Jimmy Costello and the Atlantic Auto Racing Association. It was a tough time for the sport and the two often could not afford a full complement of staff at all the shows they promoted hither and yon. In these years he became known as "The Doctor," as he would grab a first aid kit and administer to any wounded himself.

The Railway Express worker himself, however, would need his own medical attention and lots of it for a long time in 1953 when he was run down and over by several cars while flagging at Manchester Motordrome, leaving him in critical condition.

As time went by, the sport matured and the Doctor went along with it—somewhat. Especially after the linkage between AARA and Motor Wheel Enterprises, Westboro was offering up a relatively professional and well-run program. Occasionally, though, he

"The Doctor" (right) receives an Oilzum appreciation trophy from Jim Moffat. *(Balser photo)*

would revert right back to the old days and the old ways.

About seven o'clock one rainy evening, Wally was closing up the concession when to his surprise in drove a bunch of cars, trucks, and trailers. It was the folks who were going to put on the animal show that night as an added attraction to the races. Their lead guy was soon in the office, sparring with The Doctor. He was of the mind that, despite the rain-out, he had still brought all his animals, people, and equipment, and he should be paid. In full.

The Doctor, less than thrilled with this arrangement, shot back, "When I pay for an animal show, I get an animal show." He forced the troupe to unload in the pouring rain and to perform in front of a completely empty grandstand.

The big boys, Barbeau, Cleary, Luchesi and Tulonen, do something unplanned. *(Silvia Collection)*

dle. Bill Welch and Dave Morton did not wish to make the change and they quit. So did Falconi. But, as it would turn out, they did not let Borden ride-hop for too many seasons.

Towards the end of the fifties another division was evolving at Westboro and its little sister track located just over the line from Townsend in Brookline, NH. It featured full-bodied—though usually fender and hoodless—straight axle cars, mostly Fords, of pre-1949 vintage. Bernie "Tinker" Progin, Milt Blood, Lee Ward, Homer Eggleston, Marty Boise, Bob Baker, and Jim Travers were a few of the players in this short-lived but enthusiastically received division.

Chassis men like the Harty Brothers were busy keeping these cars going. Harty, now a road warrior equipped with all necessary tools to build/rebuild a race car, worked with Bob Cook, a winner out of Orange, with Jim Travers, a Brookline Speedway ace, and with Roger Lancey. One of his more curious creations in the next few years was

There's a lot of going on outside Bob Pulsifer's windshield in the #87 as he picks his direction off the second turn on June 23, 1960. That's Bob Bacchiochi backwards. *(Balser photo)*

Roger Lancey in the Harty-built Model A at Thunder Road. The car was owned by some folks in Troy, NH with a gas station, and it seems they wanted everyone to know what they were charging per gallon. *(Harty Collection)*

among the few Model A-based cars to win big in New England. Built for a New Hampshire group, the spiffy sedan was taken to Thunder Road in Barre, VT and Lancey won with it immediately. Thunder Road, a brand new track carved out of a quarry by a young racing entrepreneur named Ken Squier, became a hot-bed of flathead racing for years, and it is one of the nation's most admired short tracks even today. It was definitely to Westboro and Brookline's disadvantage that no serious cross-promotions would ever take place with Squier's Green Mountain endeavor.

By the beginning of the 1960 season, Westboro Stadium, now known as Westboro Speedway, was barely getting by. Still lacking inherent strength of its own, it was blown around like a wind sock, and the biggest gusts were coming from the direction of Norwood.

Bill Balser's spectacular shot captures Larry Antonellis freestyle in the Woodward Spring Shop #4. The scene is more frightening that it first appears. Note that wheel headed at a high rate of speed towards the fence. Uncontained wheels were a major problem with stock cars in the early years. There was at least one attributable death and several serious injuries at Westboro alone. *(Balser photo)*

(left) An ever-calm Fred Borden works to break a victory smile on September 2, 1960. That's car owner Andy Smith with the flag. The #99 was one of the first overhead cutdowns and it had a very unsophisticated A-frame front end. *(Balser photo)*

(right) That's Bo Noyes congratulating his driver George Summers while Jimmy Costello looks on. This combination was always a factor. Bo worked for the engine building firm, Bob Hitchcock in Framingham. He really knew how to make those six cylinders fire. *(Summers Collection)*

1959 had been an edgy time for the cut down guys. The overhead engines were bringing even more expense for the teams. There was talk that that the purses needed to go up, even at Norwood, once considered relatively generous. Everyone seemed to be in agreement, save the management at Norwood, that is.

Tension built towards the end of the season and surely came to loud climax when Norwood made the shocking announcement that it would bring in the NASCAR Sportsman-Modified cars in 1960. Although the stated intention was to offer up both cut down and NASCAR racing at the track, it was a mess. Some owners just strengthened their resolve to continue the hot rod configuration; others threw in the towel and began constructing NASCAR full coupes, hoping the national sanction would bring better prize money; some quit racing all together. Eventually in 1960 the cut down group, then called the Independent Race Car Owners Association, boycotted Norwood and went on the road. Their shows were not always strong as the fields were mixed and inconsistent. An attempt was made for a few weeks by Independent to compete directly with Norwood by hosting Saturday night events at Westboro. By the end of the year Norwood's NASCAR show was building momentum, while the cut downs were floundering.

Faulkner and Costello would suck it in and do the best they could. They advertised open competition racing on Fridays, paying $200 to win to draw whatever competitors they could. They even attempted—with just marginal success—to recapture some enthusiasm for a previous Canadian connection, principally with Toronto's Pinecrest Speedway. A July 4 Canadian-American Stock Car Championship was scheduled, but scant few of the publicized "top Canadian stars with their own unlimited modified cars" were in the lineup.

In 1961, the situation seemed even bleaker. Westboro had become thoroughly a secondary track, relying on other speedways for its field. And it was in a real quandary now, as it could not afford the outlay to link with NASCAR.

And then came the second weekend in August. That Friday night Worcester's Red Sequin was the anointed jockey in Ed Bowley's infamous "Flying 5" cut down out of Tewksbury. One of the hottest race cars on the East coast, the glistening red and white machine won the heat handily, and Sequin looked to have them covered in the feature. Suddenly, leading at halfway, he dropped out with mechanical problems.

The next night Bowley's boys hauled out the new Interstates to New York, north of Syracuse, to joust with the finest cut downs in the country on the 5/8 mile asphalt of Oswego Speedway. A bounty had been placed on Nolan Swift, a crafty veteran who was winning everything in sight. The Sequin-Bowley combo was spun by the press as a likely contender to take Swifty's cake.

It was only a momentary setback in the Flying 5 pit when Sequin dropped out of his heat again—yet another little technical problem. By consi time, he was ready. They won it resoundingly, setting a new track record of 100.3 mph.

One can only imagine the excitement as the field thundered past Oswego's imposing grandstands with Sequin and Swift starting deep in the pack. The battle, sadly, was never to unfold. Sequin, broken loose by water from a blown hose, sideswiped legendary upstater "Irish" Jack Murphy and drilled the unforgiving steel wall. Sequin, a father of three, sustained head injuries and died that night.

Red Sequin had become a key player at Westboro, and news of his demise was a well-reported shocker. It was the symbolic nadir of the downward spiral at the once proud oval. Faulkner and Costello saw

(left) This was the Finn's final and most famous cut down. He built it in a tiny shed next to his house, so tiny he had to cut the wall down to get it out. The car was based on 1932 Ford rails with a bow spring up front and short springs down back. The roll bars were crafted from 1939 Chevy drive shafts. Reino's obsessional concentration on weight is demonstrated by welding nerf bars to the rear locating arms. A small block Chevy—multiple carburetors atop—was off-set. The car won right out of the box and was always hot. *(Tulonen Collection)*

(right) Things got a little too hot at Westboro on May 7, 1960. The Finn is leaning to his left to avoid the flames from up front. He's actually leaning right over his gas tank, which was also off-set, sitting there beside him. *(Balser photo)*

Red Sequin has a big grin for Bill Balser following his heat win. He died the next night. *(Falconi Collection)*

that to continue they would need to go back to the drawing board. Do something different. Do something new.

They sure did.

✣ ✣ ✣ ✣ ✣

Faulkner and Costello were old-time, track-to-track, traveling promoters, and they knew it. They understood that to pull something together of more permanent substance they would have to add to their resource. They chose wisely, with John Falconi, Bill Welch, and Dave Morton in the form of Motor Wheel Enterprises becoming their partner. The three surely knew racing inside and out and they were popular and well-respected, something not ordinary for promoters of the era.

Morton at the start was the least engaged in the effort, but come springtime he was omni-present in the pit area, reinforcing the rules. Wired with an early hearing aid, Morton, always quick with a smile, was fondly referred to as "Channel 2" by the racers. He remains a welcome presence at New England races still today.

While Falconi and Welch immersed themselves energetically in the turnaround, they brought different, though complementary, skills to the party. Falconi's would be felt over time.

Having started out in Southboro around the war as a pharmacist who also offered five gallon pails of kerosene out the back door, Johnny and his bride, the former Nancy Harwood, became leading citizens in their community. The petroleum side of their business flourished, and by the mid-sixties Falconi Brothers Fuel Oils afforded its founder a little time off in the summers. Falconi came to love the speedway grounds. He began treating them as his own, tending to broken,

Dave Morton was always in the thick of things. That's "Channel Two" with the cigar, coordinating the righting of Ed Potvin's car. *(Balser photo)*

unpainted seat boards in the stands, regrading access ways, bringing back a clean, lawn-like look to the infield, and, oh yes, maintaining that demanding wooden fence. A thousand times he would meander up Route 30 in the red pickup provided by Warwick Ford and over time he systematically purchased shares in the facility. By the seventies he was the largest single shareholder outside of the controlling interest held by Joe Mahoney, representing the Molaghan family.

There was an appealing no-nonsense wisdom about John Falconi, most often packaged in abbreviated—and much copied—vocabulary of his own. He so frequently referred to salesmen visiting Falconi Brothers as "Murphy" that he became known to many as "Murph" himself. (And "Murph" always seemed to be hiding under his desk when a "Murphy" arrived at the door).

I had perhaps the prototypical interaction with Murph in 1964. Coming off the fourth turn in a B-division car owned by Skip and Pat Sanborn, I lost control and spun down the front stretch. I ended up next to the starter's box facing traffic when hard-ball and feature winning driver Dick Chesboro, with no place to go, hit me head on full tilt. Smoke, steam, broken parts everywhere. Murph, observing all from his spot right next to starter Dave Faulkner, walked by me, calmly commenting, "too fast, too quick, Lew" on his way by.

Bill Welch, on the other hand, made many of his contributions from his desk at home in Winchester. Although Welchie's interest in actually fielding cars faded with the flatheads, he was always immersed in racing. He was at every race, greeting everyone, usually with his companion Shirley Jackman, a delightfully irreverent woman who, along with Anne Empey, was one of New England's leading racer scorers. Welchie was a bookkeeper by trade, and he had that thorough and systematic manner of thinking. There was instantly a new feel to Westboro, a sense of organization and care, sorely lacking before, in schedules, press releases, rules and the like.

In the sixties, professional wrestling had a spike in popularity. Sometimes fights were brought in to Westboro. Other times the promoters thought there was enough confrontation between the racers themselves. Here Argentina Rocca chums with John Falconi and Joe Mahoney. *(Balser photo)*

The Fence Factor

This desolate shot of Dick Volante's cutdown being worked on in the third turn shows Westboro's racy backstretch and the minimal nature of the wall even in the late fifties. The railroad ties protruding above the boards were especially dangerous. *(Volante Collection)*

The fence at Westboro was always a factor, much more so than at other Massachusetts speedways. It was not the smooth, sturdy concrete retainer Anthony Venditti poured so carefully around Seekonk, nor was it a product of the backfilled, more reinforced designs used at Norwood and Riverside Park. And while it did appear more substantial than the sand banks surrounding the Pines, it was arguably no safer and it sure was a lot more work.

The work orders came immediately. On the seventeenth lap of just the second feature race run, on August 12, 1947, Art Sprague threw a wheel from his midget entering the third turn. His midget clobbered the fence, flipped several times, and landed upside down on top of it, trapping Sprague. As he was being hospitalized for what was termed "chest injuries", several sections of the fence had to replaced before the restart.

After being beefed up in the very early fifties to stop any of the heavier wayward stock cars, the fence went through a period of long deterioration that was only accelerated with each pounding. By the time in 1962 that two new divisions, both featuring full-sized cars, were brought in, countless new holes had to be dug for the supporting railroad ties and the weighty, spiked connecting planks.

The Godfather, still early on in his lease and full of Westboro optimism, completely redid the front stretch wall. That was only small consolation for Murph Falconi and his right-hand man, Frank Pratt. A gentle, soft-talking bear of a man, Pratt patched the fence hastily a hundred times on race nights and backed it up laboriously during the week.

I penetrated the wall completely during a surprise trip to the pits in May of 1965 after tangling with Tommy Garganigo. My car owner, Rick Falconi, was not happy. *(Balser photo)*

The fly-weight midgets were not immune from the fearsome clutches of the wall. Here, Ed Duncan, a researcher for this book and long time racing personality, runs to check on Brian Handy and Robbie Hart. *(Silvia Collection)*

The heavy cars could really do a job. Witness the aftermath of some tree clearing by the great George Murray. *(Silvia Collection)*

Anthony Venditti took a major stab at the wall. *(Falconi Collection)*

Seasoned Westboro regulars had their tales about how they might have nicked it and how they were sucked in by the breaking boards. They used to kid about the outsiders from The Pines and Hudson who would approach the high banks with skittishness, not being accustomed to such an outside rail. It was the Westboro racers themselves, though, who should have been scared. The fence did do its job 1,000 times by keeping cars out of the bleachers, but not without the cost of occasional driver injury and, on rare occasions, death.

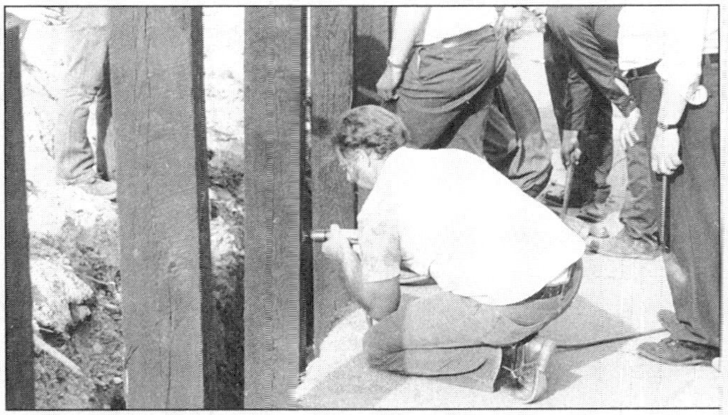

Bringing back the faster modifieds, Dick Williams was wise to give the wall further attention. That's Dick with the drill. *(Balser photo)*

Welchie, Shirley Jackman and Dave Faulkner. *(Balser photo)*

Nearby White's Corner Restaurant must have done banner business the winter of '61-'62, because the new group met there frequently, putting in a Herculean planning effort. They completely re-crafted Westboro's rule book for the first time making it a destination track. They switched to Saturday nights and their rules were written for Westboro cars only and for anyone who wanted to go on to Brookline on Sundays. Their decisions were fascinating.

The Class A rules were completely retrospective. As if to pull back in racing's renegades who had been put off by the recent march towards light-weight, overhead-powered cars, the division called for full coupes with Flathead or six-cylinder power, one carburetor, and small tires. The B Division was 180 degrees out: it was open to any American car 1949-1953 with virtually no modification allowed. Designed to be very cheap and to have lots of cars, the rules represented one of the first times that late model cars were featured in a weekly division in Massachusetts.

Flathead Fords and overhead Oldsmobiles mix it up in July of 1962. It was a contact sport for sure. It's hard to believe that these were all new cars that spring. *(Balser photo)*

Joey Kay, trademark camel showing the way on his hood, was good with his Olds and good with a Ford the next year. He faded from racing, to return briefly for a fling with the NASCAR modifieds. When he went to Stafford, he found that he needed much better stuff than he did at Westboro. A snow tire was all he needed on the left rear of his B car at the time of this win. *(Balser photo)*

Welchie and his media man, Herb Cole, pumped out releases all winter. The word was out. Like many others, I towed into Westboro with a car for the first time that summer. There was a definite feel of excitement in the air; there were folks in the stands; the pits bustled with the most curious combination of veterans and rookies.

The B Division became a fan-approved success from the very first lap. The inclusive, low-cost concept drew copious cars of every flavor —huge and heavy muscled overhead V-8 powered Oldsmobiles, little Chevy sixes, Plymouth flat sixes, and seemingly a million '49-'53 Fords. Entrants so jammed the pit area that for a time features carried thirty-three starters lined up in eleven rows of three. Not allowed any trick springs, lowering devices, or locked rear ends, the cars were topsy-turvy and rollovers were commonplace. And before safety hubs

Bentley Warren was a frequent visitor in the B-car division towing down from his haunts in Cape Ann. Even with this rather modest-looking equipment it seemed he could do nothing but win. *(Balser photo)*

(top left) Marty Boise and his Chevy six; (top right) Eddie Martin and Buddy Roggie; (bottom left) Buzz Leavins in the Donati Hudson; (bottom right) Fran Miller and Ed Broulette crash while Al Jacques seeks smoother waters down low. *(Balser photos)*

were even allowed—let alone encouraged, front wheels sometimes seemed to be flying towards the heavens in every turn.

It took a couple of seasons for everyone to get a handle on the coil spring front ends. It was typical for front ends to literally bounce up and down on the high banks. Uninformed participants tried everything to keep the front ends up before shock and stabilizer dynamics were understood. In an ill-fated attempt to keep the front of our first car up, we drilled a hole in the right front shock, inserted a fitting, and filled the shock with grease. It worked great for half a lap, but then, quite predictably, the huge pressure caused the shock body to slip, spraying grease all over the right front. I hit the wall. Hard.

Those bomber drivers who came to the fray with some experience understandably had their way in the early days. Marty Boise was back in a six cylinder Chevrolet and was an early champion, defeating many much beefier motors. After a season with a six cylinder, Eddie Martin returned with a V-8 in his new #XX and he, too, was champion. Waltham's Paul Leger returned to racing, as did Lee Ward and others.

Meanwhile a whole crop of new spring drivers brought welcome color. Like all good support divisions, it in turn became a breeding ground for those who wished to advance. Pete Fiandaca, Sammy Stern, Billy Bertrand, Jimmy Haywood, and Jimmy McCallum were

(left) Tommy Garganigo in one of the hot pink B-cars out of Lovey's in Shrewsbury, a garage with a long and storied racing resume.
(Balser photo)

(right) The MAN, one of Westboro's greatest, Pete Salvatore. That's Bob Bouchard with him, someone else who sure knew how to win.
(Balser photo)

especially quick as they motored up the learning curve. Some of the new names were seriously colorful personalities away from the track as well. Westboro, in fact, had its own international division. There was Tony "Zeke" Schanzle, occasional driver of a #187 Chevrolet out of Weston. Schanzle was about to be the first person ever to cross the central plains in Australia solo on a motorcycle. And then there was Bill Dunlop who apprenticed these years at Westboro before taking on Oxford Plains in Maine with a '56 Ford. The consummate adventurer, Dunlop set sail from Portland, Maine in 1983 in a nine foot boat called Wind's Will. His goal—global circumnavigation. Though he was last seen off the Cook Islands in 1985, his daughter, Pam, keeps vigil even today, awaiting his return.

Another favorite in this era was fun-loving Bob Sleeper, pilot of an electric blue #24 Chevrolet. Known as "Tucker" for his employment at Framingham Motor Inn, Sleeper was younger brother of Carroll "Iron Hat" Sleeper, the great fifties era Massachusetts competitor. The playful Tucker would perish not long afterwards when his snowmobile plunged through the ice on Lake Winnepesaukee.

The novel Class A experiment worked well too, for the first few years anyway. That first year and for a few of the next seasons the car count was jump-started in April because Seekonk cars were legal and that track often did not open until May. Joe Rosenfield, Tony Cortez, and a group of others towed up to Westboro and, in fact, one of them, Deke "The Little Man with the Big Cigar" Astle won the first show in 1962.

More locally-based Homer Eggleston, Dick Earle, Bob Pulsifer, Tom Koopman, and Fran Chausse all brought race cars. The fire in the stands those days, however, was lit by a red-hot competitor from Worcester, Pete "The All American Boy" Salvatore. Driving a flashy #2 owned by Bob Bouchard, Ron and Ken's dad, stand-on-the-gas Salvatore had become the man to beat at Brookline and Westboro where in 1961 he was track champion. As it turned out, his biggest competition for the next couple of years would come from that now time-honored name on Route 9, Fred Borden.

(left) A youthful Bob Karvonen went right to the A division when he showed up in 1962. *(Balser photo)*

(right) In 1964, Tulonen fit into Borden's seat, no problem. Johnny Falconi is supporting the hood. *(Balser photo)*

John Falconi and Bill Welch must have been pretty pleased to see their beloved flatheads come back, though at first they were likely worried about how many there would be. For whatever reason, they decided to campaign another car as well as promoting, and Freddie was quick to arrive in Southboro with his welding truck to glue it up.

Though Welchie offered up a couple of his perky but indestructible motors for it, Falconi himself had little involvement with the car. Concentrating on the track instead, he handed over the wrenches to his five boys, Ricky, Johnny, David, Peter and Jimmy. It was especially Ricky—about to embark on a college career at Franklin Pierce in Rindge, NH—who took up the challenge and soon showed serious mechanical wizardry.

As would be expected, Borden was quick right away in the red Falconi Brothers coupe. His duels with the gutsy Salvatore in the Red and White Movers Deuce were the stuff of legend.

Over the next couple of seasons, Westboro's fortunes grew nicely. As pit attendance swelled, the grandstands filled correspondingly. These would have been great years for the promotional combo except that they were probably losing an equal amount at the desolate Sunday evening shows they carried on at Brookline until it fizzled completely in 1966.

There was a real intensity about Westboro's racing, even if the cars were less powerful than those at other New England tracks. And there were constant reminders of that intensity. One gathered up Fitchburg's Frank Michaelson, a neighbor of Pete Fiandaca. Michaelson was a standout of earlier novice wars in a towering Vicky sedan. He was a factor from the start in the new A-frame B cars until he flipped badly at Brookline. Coming partially out of the car while it rolled, he sustained severe injury requiring a metal plate in his skull. Everyone was shocked to see him arrive at Westboro with another B-car after his long recuperation. Everyone was speechless when the

The door has flown open and that's poor Frank Michaelson on the way out. Again. *(Balser photo)*

exact same event transpired at Westboro, this time inflicting decidedly career-ending wounds.

Opening day of 1964 brought a surprise, as much to the Falconis as the folks in the bleachers. At the eleventh hour, Borden, weary of the exhausting two-night weekends and also a bit perturbed about accusations of being a favored "track car," suddenly elected to take the year off. Ricky Falconi and his brothers reached out to Fats Caruso. "The Shrewsbury Flash" agreed and won gallantly. In a couple of weeks, however, Caruso was off to his appointed ride at Norwood for the season, and Ricky asked his father for advice. Murph's response was immediate: "Call the Finn."

The cutdowns were pretty much sunsetting in New England except for their weekly contests at Pines and Hudson Speedways. Reino was ready for work, and it took him about a half a lap to adapt to the full coupe #10. For almost all of the 25-lapper the next Saturday night it was Tulonen upstairs and Salvatore on the inside in as outrageous a demonstration of testosterone as was ever witnessed at Westboro. Tulonen would win—barely—in a shower of sparks, after which the young Falconi crew had to deflate the right rear wheel to

Even as late as the mid-sixties, safety precautions were fairly minimal, especially in the Bs. With the side torn from my car in this flip, the single roll bar (without cage) is shown clearly. We didn't even have shoulder harnesses back then, so I guess I was pretty lucky. I had also rolled over the night before. *(Balser photo)*

When Bruce Tessier's car (left) came to rest, a track attendant called for assistance. Billy Bertrand, #111, a consistently fine driver from Southbridge, tried to help. As it is obvious here, Bruce was no longer in the car. He had used an old snow tire chain to secure the seat bolts. It proved inadequate when he rolled over and flew out the window. *(Balser photo)*

remove the wooden splinters. The hammer-down Finn had used the fence as a containment device, bouncing off it as he exited each turn. Rick Falconi speaks today of having Westboro's greatest drivers in his car. "Both of them were amazing, just doing things in an automobile you could not believe. Reino was aggressive while Freddie was a little more smooth—almost stealth. Reino was just plain on the gas. All the time." Reino proceeded to add the 1964 point crown to the Falconi laurels while Eddie Martin took measure of the B-car contingent.

Fred Borden and Rick Falconi had cake at the banquet in November 1965. *(Balser photo)*

In 1965, even after nearly twenty years of intense racing, the call of the wild still rang in the Finn's ears. In his normal Spartan way he put together a NASCAR modified. He drove with typical Tulonen verve, on the edge, resulting in a memorable flip at Norwood and a sky ride out of the ballpark at Thompson that brought him a concussion. Even the Finn's driving skills and mechanical aptitude could not match the big money being poured into racing at the time. Finally in the seventies, says Anna, "right after he bought a truck to carry all his stuff around, he decided to quit. He just could not keep going."

1965 was a strong year in attendance but also the most tragic in Westboro's history. A grisly midget crash along the top of the guardrail snatched the life of Ed Clothier on June 19. The former motorcycle racer from Schenectady was very popular and had been a New York State boxing champion.

Then, on August 28, Grafton's Bruce Tessier, a good friend of mine and other B-car racers, perished in an equally upsetting fourth turn mishap. Having just joked with Bruce about who would win, I was running with him at the time and I saw the whole thing unfold. It seemed surreal, especially later that night when Wally Faulkner called Bruce's family to inform them and to explain simply that a $10,000 insurance check would soon be on its way. It was a different time—and it still seems surreal today.

(top left) Lucky Thompson had to shut down his C+W band on race nights. (top right) Windy Deboise and his brother Teddy were popular shoes. (bottom left) Ken Kutney ran well and then left for Norwood. (bottom right) Quincy fire fighter, Carl Valenti, was always fast. *(Balser photos)*

Happily 1966 was a safer season, and the track did well. The buzz of the year was the success of newer drivers who were sharpening their skills. On May 19, young and handsome Jimmy Pyne from neighboring Hopkinton cleaned house—and that with barely two years' experience. Similarly, a 28-year old salesman named Jerry Page dusted them off in a spark-shedding blanket battle that was thought to be one of Westboro's all time great main events. As the weeks passed, however, the A division was beginning to show some signs of weakness. When on the last night Tinker Progin was first in a Clayton Thompson car built by Marty Harty, no one would have guessed that he had just won the last flathead race ever to be run in Massachusetts.

White's Corner had another good winter, as the AARA/Motor Wheel partners gathered to understand why their field was going away. Their conclusion: with Flathead engines not being manufactured since 1953 and becoming scarce and with all other tracks having gone overhead,

"Two Gun" Beeso

Red Beeso in one of his string of red #99 bombers. *(Balser photo)*

Most people were inclined to believe Red Beeso when he said he robbed banks for a living and so the nickname stuck.

Beeso appeared on the scene with the AARA division changes in 1962. He did not have far to tow, as he lived on a dilapidated farm just up Route 9 in Shrewsbury. Hubcaps adorned the walls of the outbuildings, some inhabited by retired hobos. He was soon a winner with his signature red #99 '49 Fords. The cars were crude and low buck, but lightning fast. And Red himself was a similar contradiction. Anyone who dismissed him for his unkempt appearance missed completely the clever, witty mind within.

In 1965 Beeso finished up second in the B standings, requiring him to move up to the A class. Deciding not to, he asked me to drive his "Batmobile." We were soon to develop our own set of rituals, the most memorable of which would occur right before the feature. Red would help me strap in, give me some last minute instructions, then turn around and throw up.

We ended up crashing often, but we won our share, too, and it was those wins that had me burping. Tech man Dave Morton had it in his brain that the

The "Beeso Batmobile" I drove during ARC days. Watching on, from left to right, are Billy Rowe, Cary Stratton, Ed LaRue, Red Beeso and Ralph Conant. *(Boyd Collection)*

Batmobile had a big carburetor, and the antics that Beeso went through to hide it from him during teardown were hysterical. That sort of complication behind us, we would often adjourn to the Fox Lounge where Red would entertain all comers spinning outrageous yarns and eating beer glasses with his few remaining teeth.

As the sixties sunsetted, Beeso took a fling at the A cars, but he had a total lack of funds. By the seventies he was married and settling down to a Worcester three decker with an attached repair shop. He briefly campaigned a winning Grand American after which he stayed connected to the sport by building motors for Jeff Fuller. Sadly, Red—one of Westboro's all time remarkable personalities—was seriously burned in a fire down South and eventually died.

The hastily built "Nashoba Valley Rocket", Freddie Borden's final ride. *(Balser photo)*

Westboro was stranded. They opened the rules to accommodate the more powerful engines.

However, just as was the case with America's problems in Southeast Asia at the time, Westboro's situation was quite complicated. The promoters found themselves changing the rules several times over the summer in a futile attempt to get things right. The car count —and the unforgiving crowd—went into free fall. On June 19 just ten cars took the green with Porky Kinsman, Jimmy Ryan, Larry Antonellis, Johnny Arrigo and Rocky Onorato deferring once again to Fred Borden.

Borden had no easy time of it in 1967. Uncharacteristically he suffered through a number of serious mishaps, the worse of which saw him, throttle stuck, scatter the timber of the first turn wall like kindling. Rick Falconi and the boys burned the midnight oil keeping iron under Freddie. The final version was a uniquely racy Corvair-bodied creation, modeled after Lebanon Valley dirt cars. Peter Falconi speaks with profound emotion still about overhearing Borden speaking with Welchie in the infield late that summer. Freddie's wife, June, did not like the new speeds and he was saying that he himself had not enjoyed the accidents. As he softly delivered the champion's speech at the banquet that winter, Fred Borden announced the end of his sensational career. And, as things would roll out, he was not the only one who was all done. So, too, was the curious promotional team that had brought refreshing effort and continuity to the raceway. For the first time in some twenty years, Jimmy Costello would now stay home in Rhode Island on the weekends. "Doctor" Faulkner married, moved to Thompson, CT, and finished out his career at the Hoenig's oval right there in town. Welchie opted to leverage the considerable talents he had developed on the microphone and went on the road announcing,

Shirley still at his side. Shareholders Joe Mahoney and "Murph" Falconi remained standing and it was fully understandable that they responded with relief to a phone call that fall. The "Godfather," Anthony Venditti, founder, builder, operator of Seekonk Speedway, was once again seeking to expand. He had toyed with West Peabody and Thompson with his ARC sanction. Now his goal was to lease Westboro and light it up on Friday nights, supporting his "Concrete Palace" on Saturdays near Providence.

The legendary Anthony Venditti whom racers called "The Godfather." *(Boyd Collection)*

Once again the mimeograph machines clunked away over the cold season creating spin. Many predicted the clever Venditti would show them—there would be grandstands to the sky.

That spring, his unfamiliar gaggle of boxy-looking Studebaker Larks, Chevy IIs, Chevelles, and Mustangs landed on Route 9. Big Joe Rosenfield, patriarch of the great racing family from Bridgewater, took the opener in a defiant performance. Bob Sprague, wheeling a wild Shelby Mustang tuned by the great Tiny Levesque, won on night two. But the third night was especially inspiring to Westboro regulars, as Waltham's Johnny Arrigo, raised every eyebrow in the place out-dueling Sprague and old favorite Pete Salvatore in a stirring confrontation over the last fifteen laps. The All American Boy now drove a 1965 Chevelle owned by Frank Panarelli. Affiliated with Shrewsbury's Lovey's Garage, a haven for race cars for many years, the bronze #9 was tooled by Pete Beneditto, Red Carlson, and Al "Funzie" Caruso.

Much of the chit chat in the following meets, however, concerned a nineteen year old who had just joined ARC from a year or so at Pines and Hudson. Mentored by Salvatore and funded amply by his Dad from the start, his name was Ron Bouchard, a name that would find itself in the very first induction to the New England Hall of Fame.

For whatever reasons, ARC simply did not seem to take outside of Seekonk, and Venditti abruptly announced his intention not to renew for 1969. Falconi and Mahoney were left scrambling, wondering where in the world they would find cars now when, most fortunately, that phone rang again. This time it was Harvey Tattersall, Jr., the very same one who had rented Westboro way back in 1955.

Tattersall signs *(Gazette)*

Joseph F. Mahoney (right), general manager of the Westboro Speedway, discusses Harvey V. Tattersall (left) and his father, Harvey Tattersal, Jr., who will direc stock car racing programs this year.

Tattersall to Direct Show

Westboro Speedway Plan To Step Up Auto Racing

Harvey Jr. negotiated to place his Tuesday night United show at Riverside Park into Westboro on Saturday nights, regulated by Harvey III, a newly anointed corporate attorney. Everyone, most notably the track shareholders, was pleased to see the facility reopen, but some grumbling understandably followed the issuance of the rulebook. Yet again, the new rules were supposed to reduce the cost of racing. John Janisaitis' press releases spun the spin: "Our races will put a premium on the drivers. Now drivers can enter cars that cost them no more than $2,000. They will take stock sedans, beef them up, and blue print

(top left) Bobby Sprague in his great-looking, great-sounding Mustang. (top right) Joe Rosenfield aboard Jim Rogers' ARC car. (bottom left) Johnny Arrigo was justifiably happy the third night. (bottom right) Jon Astle, aka "Johnny Angel," youngest of the brothers Astle. *(Sprague-Falconi Collection; others, Silvia Collection)*

the engines to perfect tolerances for the track." All that was fine for the guys out West who already had kit in place, but for Westboro regulars it meant a third major rule change in less than three years. They would have to weld up completely new cars. The economy was uncertain at the time, about to head into the recession of the early seventies.

As a reported 2500 filed through the turnstiles on the chilly evening of April 28, some familiarity at least was evident. John Falconi had the place looking spiffy and his son Peter's PA-friendly voice alternated with Al Fraser on the mike. In the pit area, policing the rules, was familiar motor magician, Bo Noyes. And there with a new role wearing starter's whites was long time Westboro favorite, Joe Cast.

To cover their bets and to keep the back gate full, the Harveys cleverly kept the B-class rules quite open. The bomber pilots such as Dick Hureau, Neil Simpson, Gary Holbrook, Ace Johnson, Cal Coolidge, and Jim Tedesco were part of robust lineups from the very beginning. John McCarthy's traveling NEMA midgets came through town frequently, with Len Thrall, Al Pillion, Johnny Kay, Ronnie Evans, and Dave Humphrey defying their age with gutsy velocity.

Sixteen "Grand Americans" sped past Joe Cast's feature green opening night and the finish spoke volumes. United racer Al Becker went home $300 richer, followed by unaffiliated newcomer—but surely no newcomer to racing—Russ Nutting of Limerick, Maine. Third and fourth were two of the great locals, Red Beeso and Billy Bertrand.

This wide geographic mix continued as the division grew. Agawam Grand American teams featuring George Rettew, Ralph Graham, Wayne Fountain, Gil Lamereux, and Dave Mastriani confronted more and more Westboro entries in new equipment, among them speedsters Jimmy Ryan, Ron Vars, Hard Luck Joe Havaliotti, Steve Bombara and Lenny Baker with his 312 Ford. Pleasing to fans was the arrival of completely unexpected entries such as Nutting—and Archie Sherman, Duncan Olson, Al Brooks, and Ronnie Pond, towing up from the vicinity of Seekonk.

Though the Grand Americans were physically the largest cars ever to compete at the aging midget stadium and although their motors were technically restrained, racing juiced up over time. There was emotion for sure one night when Red Pickering took energetic exception to a call by Joe Cast. Pickering slammed on the brakes next to the starter's box, jumped out, and pummeled Cast with his helmet. Anyone who knew Joe Cast turned to see this one. From his start in the early fifties, Cast was a colorful force, commonly making his presence known with loud and confident boisterousness. After the combatants had been separated, Pickering proceeded to sit right there on the track, unwilling to move an inch. A tow truck was dispatched to remove his race car, and Pickering himself was towed away by the Westboro police. The crowd went absolutely wild. Some of the older rail birds smiled and agreed that, had this happened in the old Faulkner and Costello days, it might all have been staged, with Pickering and Cast both going home a few bucks the richer.

(bottom left) Leister's "Pops" Duffries had bombers in the sixties, but his most skilled driver was his own son, Gary. They campaigned this huge appearing 340 ci powered Dodge, the only Mopar in the field. In later years Gary experimented with a Dodge Challenger-based NASCAR modified. *(Alden Collection)*

(bottom right) Bill Baldidga drove this Southboro-based Grand American for Bob Fox who subsequently went into the hotel business in Daytona. *(Silvia Collection)*

Jimmy Galluzzo ran B-cars in the sixties, but it was with United that his light really began to shine. The trophy giver is Harvey Jr. *(Silvia Collection)*

When a semi-successful first season wound down, the champion's wreath went to one of United's regulars, Agawam's John Rosati. A loyal Ford man, Rosati was in the early laps of a long, distinguished career behind the wheel. Following 1969, the wreath was to be passed to a Westboro local and it would stay to the East for the next five years. The 1970 championship in particular was won by a diverse group of talented characters.

John Rosati, first United Grand Am Champion, was up front on June 14, 1970. A scant few years later he was in much faster company. He is shown working the outside of Bugs Stevens in the Judkins #2X and Geoff Bodine. *(Silvia Collection)*

Back in 1959 an enterprising fifteen year old from Lunenburg named Vic Kangas ventured upon a battle-worn 1947 Ford stock car and he bought it on a whim for the princely sum of $15. Hardly knowing what to do with it, he called his Uncle, Walter Heikkila, and off to Brookline they went. Vic cannot say for sure which of the two was more surprised by their second place finish that day, but it was for sure that a switch was triggered deep in Vic's soul.

By the mid-sixties he was racing his creations widely, schooled in the nuances of construction and maintenance by mentor Marty Harty. His regular driver, Fitchburg's Tinker Progin, won so consistently that knowledgeable people in the racing community, always on the prowl for young talent, began taking notice. With Marty along either physically or by telephone, Kangas went on the road building cars. Among them were the first Seekonk car for dashing Ronnie Bouchard and a stout 1937 Chevy coupe that carried Hall-of-Famer Ernie Gahan to the 1966 NASCAR National Modified Championship. After Gahan had run the bionic car a seeming million laps, it was campaigned yet again by veteran Tommy Bourget.

By 1968 Bob Bouchard understood very well son Ronnie's remarkable potential, and he brought Vic in as crew chief to work with Dave Rossback. A brilliant move it was, resulting in an astounding run of four consecutive championships at the Concrete Palace. Ronnie was, says Vic, "the most natural driver I ever worked with. He had been around racing all of his life and he knew just what he needed and how to ask for it." Ronnie, however, was not Bob's only card. His brother, Kenny, was also soaking it all up.

Still way too young to drive himself, Kenny reached out to another of Fitchburg's fearless named Al Becker. They purchased a car in New York, dragged it back to Bob's garage. They reworked it under

At Calvin Coolidge's insistence, Ace Johnson (#66) makes a lane change. *(Alden Collection)*

Hopkinton's Jimmy Pyne left racing after a short but highly promising career. *(Falconi Collection)*

the watchful eye of Kangas, who was there massaging Ronnie's chariots. The trajectory of this neighborly threesome would be meteoric. While Becker snuck away with the Grand American championship that very year, Ronnie would go on to win big time in the modifieds, Vic often at his side. Both would end up with distinguished careers on NASCAR's superspeedways.

The 1970 and '71 point titles went to familiar B-car graduate, Jim McCallum. If not all of McCallum's early rides were pretty aboard his #108 '53 Ford, from the very start he was very fast. Over time the unflashy, unassuming McCallum developed into one of the best pro stock drivers of all time, still winning in a major way at the turn of the century.

Good racing citizen, Ronnie Pond, a teacher from North Attleboro with the handle "Hawk" colorfully and liberally splashed down the side of his Grand Am, romped home champ in 1973. He was joined

Billy Antonellis, Jim Libbey and Steve Orcutt ease up a groove, wide of spinning Henry Rondeau. Jim Libbey graduated from Red Beeso's pit crew to become one of New England's finest pro stock racers. His brother, Bryard, also a winning late model driver, now does world-class high-end automotive restoration. *(Silvia Collection)*

The bombers stack them up in May 1973. Wayne Gendron (#50), Elliot Bigelow (#7), Ed Weston (#100), and Joe Martin Jr. (#91) *(Alden Collection)*

at the podium when Framingham's Billy Antonellis stepped up as Novice champ, having driven his #88 1955 Chevy to ten feature wins. Antonellis' car recreated the look of the great XX cars of Ed Martin and Johnny Arrigo, recognizing the time Antonellis had spent on those crews. Proving the wreath no fluke, Antonellis with car owner Warren Lang was champ once again for 1974, this time very impressively in the much faster Grand Am community. To help finance the effort, Antonellis had sold their '55 Chevy. It was a good buy for Louie Russo who steered the car to the Novice championship for the second year in a row.

Sadly, not long afterwards, Louie Russo died of a massive heart attack. Antonellis and Lang also died prematurely, strangely reminiscent of what happened to another Westboro team from earlier times.

Dave Humphrey and John McCarthy look very pleased with their #47 NEMA car in September 1972. *(Silvia Collection)*

It's a study in style as flamboyant Gary Colturi and aging Porky Kinsman sink into the turn. Both knew how to win, but Gary's seasons would be few. He died on a motorcycle. *(Silvia Collection)*

He was jolly, roly poly—a presence in the pit area and at the beer stand. Porky Kinsman drove cut downs for noteworthy owner Andy Cote, flathead coupes, and with his buddy, hard-working Ray Lyko, the Snap-on tool dealer, he took on United's Grand Ams, too. It was not a cake walk, however, until in a magical turn of events in 1969. Kinsman swept all three of the season-ending 75-, 100-, and 125-lap championship races. It was a truly masterful bit of driving, the symbolic culmination of Porky's countless summer nights behind the wheel. Fate was not kind, however, and one winter evening Porky is said to have fallen and suffered head injuries, lying in the cold until discovered at first light. A year of rehab did little, and the round man from Natick quietly passed away. Meanwhile, as the story goes, Lyko one day decided he had had too much of the fray. He sold everything he had and moved to a lakeside cabin in Maine. On the very first night, he popped open a beer, sat on his porch to contemplate the sunset, and died.

Over the course of its six-year sanction United presented about 120 regular shows at Westboro in addition to a couple of more each season featuring the barking modified hot dogs, the fastest racers in the Bay State at the time. These 100-lap modified events, lively and well-attended, had the effect of returning many people to the high banks who had chosen to race beefier cars than the Grand Ams. Some old friendships were renewed—and some old rivalries as well.

Riverside Park's own modified stars dominated in the beginning, as the rules were skewed in their favor. Hall-of-Famer Buddy Krebs

(left) Ronnie Wycoff, veteran racer from the Connecticut Valley, drills Jimmy McCallum (#25). (right) It was definitely open competition this evening in 1972 as up and coming Kenny Bouchard mixes up with the great veteran Eddie Hoyle. *(Balser photos)*

collected the initial gold in the storied 10 PINS coupe from the Nutmeg State, while, quite surprisingly, an unpublicized Ernie Caruso won both the summer and fall events in 1970. Again in 1971 the big dollars went back to Connecticut, once to the benefit of Jim Cash and once to smoothie Steve Evonsion.

Finally in the early 1972 race a more regular Westboro name was up front—and in a big way. It was none other than good old George Summers. A devoted and proficient owner named Ken Curley kept the wheels under Summers at the time. That summer they had a Seekonk-based Camaro tuned by Calvin "Colonel" Blaisdel. For several seasons Summers had engaged in a friendly—almost mentoring—rivalry with up-and-coming Ronnie Bouchard. The relationship was also fueled from the back end as speed secrets and cases of beer were shared back and forth by Vic Kangas and his old drag racing friend, the Colonel.

East Hartford's Bobby Bard won the August open in the beautiful #124 coupe, though folks took note of a seventeen-year old Kenny Bouchard buzzing energetically around the oval in second place for the entire century grind. As the rules loosened for modifieds in the series, the back gate bulged. Freetown's Hall-of-Famer Lenny Boehler had his old blue in the winner's circle with Freddie DeSarro in 1973. Billy Greco, one of United's most famous, won one, as did Westport's Deke Astle. The versatile Astle, is one of the cleverest, self-resourced drivers in Massachusetts history. This night he outsmarted a field of 50 cars with his box-like Seekonk late model style car. He shot under Eddie Flemke, Sr. in the Judkins #2x Pinto on the 90th lap for the $1,000 win. Few drivers ever played such a trick on the respected Flemke.

"The Deacon", Deke Astle shows signs of some hard laps as he is interviewed by Paul Tremaine. And so he should. His victory was a magnificent performance. *(Silvia Collection)*

Freddie DeSarro fights a push in Lenny Boehler's #3. Leo Cleary is handling much better. *(Balser photo)*

Most would look back on Wednesday, August 7, 1974 as the best of all these open competitions, however. George Summers was having one unbelievable year in the #21 Vega owned by Connie LaJoie and Dave Conley. Wrenches Paul Susi and Jimmy Waterman were brilliant, and George put their product across the line first in 66% of Seekonk's races. This particular night, though, it did not look so good. Summers fell out of the heat with a heating problem, not the best thing when the pit area is jammed with 57 modifieds and only 24 qualify. The problem fixed, the big guy had to show his stuff. With truly inspired drives, he won both the A and B Consis, securing a 21st starting spot in the Paul Revere feature. By the halfway mark every fan in the place was standing cheering him on, already in a battle for the lead. Once held, he never relinquished it.

Summers' popular victory was symbolic of the positive feeling generated by all the old acquaintances coming back for this series. One can only imagine the business done at Joe Plamondon's beer stand. Hours after it closed, a crowd still surrounded Summers who had by now retired to the trunk of his friend Murph Falconi's Cadillac, staying very close to a cooler with still more beers. In the wee hours of that night, just as Murph was closing up, some wag stormed into the office warning him that something strange was happening to his car. Poor Murph, everyone's favorite, ran out, looked, and knew not where to run next. His Cadillac, no one seated inside, was going around the parking lot in circles. Murph could not hear George laughing joyously inside, lying on the floor, one hand on the wheel, one hand on the accelerator.

Summers took no prisoners this Wednesday night. He drove the wheels off Connie Lajoie's #21, and the hood and fenders as well. *(Alden Collection)*

He came to town as if riding on the tail of a comet and, according to his self-aggrandizing spin, he would propel the change-weary, thirty-year-old stadium with him to the sky. Truth be know, however, it was the beginning of the end.

Dick Robidoux was yuppie rather than racer. He owned a couple of car dealerships and his methodology was leveraging money—other people's money, just as would be done so widely and naughtly in the nineties. And, when his eye fell on Westboro, he approached Joe Mahoney who had represented the Molaghan family's interest for years and he got himself a deal.

As spring approached and Robidoux struck an agreement with Anthony Venditti to run the show, Murph likely watched with curious pleasure—if not wonderment—the copious sums of money being poured into the project. The new paint was one thing. But the look on Murph's face must have spoken volumes when the afternoon of opening night two guys appeared replete with card tables, adding machines, and green visors. When Murph asked who in God's name they were, the not unconfident Robidoux responded that they were there to count the money.

Robidoux and Venditti had in mind trying once again the failed ARC experiment of 1968. They switched Westboro back to Friday nights again and ushered in Venditti's modifieds and cadets, and, of course, the streeters.

George Summers won on June 20, 1975. Connie LaJoie, second from the left, thinks that's a good thing. *(Balser photo)*

By this time the ARC A Division looked more and more like NASCAR modifieds. In order to ensure full fields, the rules were opened up just a tad more. Cars with greater engine set backs were allowed in, and Seekonk-type cars were offered a bonus of $100 to win to help bridge the gap.

1975 did have its nights of steamy competition. The driver who was to excel the most was Ron Bouchard. He ended up firmly atop the season point chase with 610 contrasted to the 496 accumulated by both Fred Astle and George Summers in a tie for second. Fourth was Tiverton, RI's George Murray who had a great year. In the Seekonk championship, he beat out Fred Astle while George Savary was third. Hank Goff nipped Lou Russo for the Westboro Cadet title and Frank Carpenter was top in the streets.

Pat Richardson, a gym teacher at Southboro schools, was one of Westboro's few women drivers. *(Balser photo)*

To the experienced observer—and by this time there were many who had witnessed the constant change at the speedway, it was clear right away that this initiative was challenged. Robidoux's money counters were no more necessary by mid season than they were on opening day. Perhaps the specter of reality dampened Robidoux's enthusiasm or perhaps it was the very serious cancer developed by his wife, but for whatever reason he lost forward momentum almost immediately. Soon he wasn't even seen at the track in person. Venditti, meanwhile, was no slouch and was known for quick—sometimes harsh—decisions. Not long into the summer he announced his intention not to return, and the track closed earlier that fall than it had in years.

Thank goodness for that old beer stand. Joe Plamondon had become the concessionaire during the Tattersall years, after predecessor Herbie Bloom was dismissed. Plamondon was racing motivated because he

(left) Left to right, Pete Falconi, Dick Monahan (NEMA President), Earl Grant, and Larry Stevens at the nightly drivers' meeting. *(Falconi Collection)*

(right) Tom McCann upstairs and George Savary tucking in underneath. *(Silvia Collection)*

knew there was money in beer and hot dogs but you had to have the races. He met with the Falconis and joined Murph and the boys as co-promoter. He leased the Speedway from Robidoux and switched back to Saturday nights for 1976. Instantly the new management team, known to be racer-friendly, brought back lost positive karma. Their staff was one of familiarity and popularity: Bill Welch, managing consultant; Pete Falconi, racing director; Rick Falconi, chief steward; Larry Stevens and Joe LaRochelle, handicappers; Earl Grant and Ed LaRue, starters; Bo Noyes and Henry Rufo in tech; and Frank Hayes, Shirley Jackman, Ann Empey, Curt Garfield, and Lenny Poe handling the pits and the tower.

The modified assemblage was a curious mix-and-match of cars and drivers including Bobby Clark, Tommy Bourget, Jean Michaud, Gary Holbrooke, Don Dionne, Wayne Darling, and Billy Clarke. The belle of the ball, however, was a glistening black #7 modified. Owned by Bellingham businessman, Billy Hood, the car was a rocket right off the trailer. Hood, consulting with Ken Curley, chose his rocket rider

Long-time Westboro favorite Dick Jackson always built world-class cars. Here he is in 1976 with one of the last of the coupes. *(Silvia Collection)*

The Fallen Falconi

Johnny and Jimmy Falconi. *(Falconi Collection)*

All the old guard remembers the Falconi kids, forever it seems. There they were down at the coal yard in Southboro, lugging coal from the rail cars, barely old enough to hold a shovel, faces black as the night from dust. Weekends they'd be at the track, parking cars, painting seat boards, mowing the grass. And, of course, watching Freddie Borden in Murph's legendary #10 cars.

Four of the five developed a passionate involvement in racing. Ricky, Johnny, and Jimmy demonstrated definite mechanical aptitudes while Peter was drawn to the promotional side of the sport. None seemed interested in driving until 1972, when Johnny pulled a derelict B-car out of the woods behind Sammy Stern's house and dragged it to the office. Doing little more than cleaning out the leaves and changing the oil, he went racing at Westboro mid-June. By fall he had finished fourth in points.

"I saw immediately that he was a natural," says Jimmy, "and we made a good team. I was eight years younger. In the old days, he'd always look out for me. We never had a cross word. Now I could help him by keeping good stuff under him."

By 1976 it was up to the late model division and for Johnny many, many feature wins, first in a unit designed by Warren Lang of #XX fame and then by the talented Steve May. Success at Westboro and beyond led to the modi-

Johnny cruises at Daytona in the Dash car. *(Falconi Collection)*

fieds, starting in 1978 with a "Mayco" truck arm machine that ran second in points to Freddie Schulz that very first year on the high banks

Then it was down the road in the NASCAR mods, sponsored by Lou Horton—and even to NASCAR's super-speedways, very successfully in a Dash car formerly owned by Robbie Moroso.

Through the journey Johnny maintained his aura of calm. Soft-spoken with a perpetual half-smile, Johnny had little to say, did the right thing, and was ordinarily unflappable at the track. It was also his way at Falconi Brothers, which the brothers began taking to the next level.

By the nineties Johnny's John—John III—was ready to take a fling. This, as it turns out, was the way to push Johnny's button. As Jimmy puts it, "I can still remember John's first win at Lee. Johnny was all excited, flapping his arms all around. He was so proud."

That's because the apple falls close to the tree. Over the last two decades the thoroughly laid back, philosophical Murph had gotten to arm-flappin' big time if he thought anyone had crossed Johnny in the modifieds. On one such night at Westboro he went after his own former driver, Fats Caruso. Another time he went eye-to-eye with Hall-of-Famer Eddie Flemke for a miscue involving Johnny at Thompson.

In October of 2000 an unwelcome rumor leaked through the racing community. Johnny Falconi was very sick. It was true. Despite a few months of apparent improvement, cancer spread from his throat throughout his body, and in January of 2003 the quiet family man died.

"We had trouble racing last year", says Jimmy, whose eyes well up even now, referring to the robust late model operation they have for young John at Thompson. "I hated to even go over to the garage. But John's getting ready for this year, and I am, too. We'll keep going. We've got to."

(left) Eddie Weston won his first feature on May 14, 1976. His partner Mark Alden is on the left. Weston still drives for Alden today. They run beautifully constructed cars on the STAR circuit. *(Balser photo)*

(right) A very popular Westboro area competitor was Si Allen, 1976 late model track champion. *(Balser photo)*

well, and George Summers, who had started at Westboro 24 years before, immediately swept four of the first five events. The only person to beat him was "The Lion," Hanover's Leo Cleary. At the end of the fifth night, Plamondon announced to the fans a $100 bounty to anyone who could beat Summers in a feature he finished. The colorful Hood matched the ante, promising a second C-note would be paid to the Jimmy Fund.

Although Summers finished up with seven wins—more than anyone else, he came up short of winning the title. However, that, too, went to someone well known to Westboro management. Way back in the early fifties, Murph Falconi occasionally housed his cars at a garage and salvage yard in Medway owned by former racer Johnny Black. Murph frequently relayed with a smile how his crew would look up from their work and see an admiring 13 year old neighborhood boy, his faced pressed hard to the window so as to observe every little thing. Just a handful of years later, the kid would start racing in a chassis given him by Don MacTavish. He was an instant success at Norwood and he pops up in Westboro results, too, in the late fifties. But, when Bob Santos came to Westboro in 1976 in Joe Brady's time-honored "Brady Bunch" modified, he was thoroughly educated. His consis-

George Summers was a wanted man in 1976. Car owner Billy Hood, left, added to the ransom. *(Alden Collection)*

Woburn's Mike Murphy, a big winner at Hudson and The Pines, was also a top Westboro runner. Here he is with his sons, Paul, Doug, and Stevie. *(Balser Photo)*

tency won him the point title without the boost of a single feature win. Summers was second and red-hot John Rosati, wheeling primarily the Kevin Coan and Tuck Hoffman #73 was third. Si Allen prevailed on June 4 and July 12 and was the late model point champ over Johnny Falconi, Wally Hartman, and Byard Libby. Mike Zajdel was street stock champ.

The next three seasons brought desperately needed continuity, with the Falconis fulfilling all the key responsibilities. As other Saturday tracks were offering relatively lavish prize money and pulling away some names such as Santos, Stevens, Bouchard, and Bodine, Peter Falconi, now a dedicated general manager, sensed an opportunity to cater to "small block and small buck" teams. Through 1979 new names entered the gates, among them clever and self-reliant Red Kimball, veteran Bobby Glass, Larry Tosi, Steve Yankee, and racing entrepreneur Dick Dubois. A surprise visitor to the modified ranks at the helm of a coupe once owned by Will Cagle was Dover's Butch Walsh. Walsh had been a midget standout for many years, accumulating considerable titles with NEMA. He also followed his passion on a national scale, competing even at Ascot, the former palace of open wheel racing near Los Angeles. Not one to shy away from much of anything, Walsh was racing flat track motorcycles as recently as the turn of the century.

Geoff Bodine moved from upstate New York to Bellingham to drive for Dick Armstrong and to work on the NU Style Team cars. Armstrong spent awesome amounts of money and Bodine was awesomely fast. *(Silvia Collection)*

(left) Bill Welch (with mike) and Joe Plamondon load up Jeff Fuller with trophies following a win in the "Eli Whitney 50" in September of 1976. *(Silvia Collection)*

(right) Bobby Fuller was beyond fast with his late model rocketship. *(Balser photo)*

Three brothers, Jeff, Bobby, and Ricky Fuller, also blew into town in the late seventies and not one of them wasted much time with incidentals such as learning how to drive. They were all naturally good, so very reminiscent of the Astles, Deke, Fred, and Jon.

Jeff would come first, followed by Bobby and Rick. Jeff had a lightning fast, almost edgy, style that immediately caught the eyes of Tom and Mary Dunn, a car-owning duo that was not wrong very often. Jeff swept the 1979 modified championship in their racy, gray station wagon-bodied #T-5. Bobby was next and almost immediately was on a tear in a #17 late model that was as fast as any in Westboro's history and one built with an aggressive interpretation of the rule book. He, too, went modified right away—in 1980—only to retire to concentrate on operating a motor home business. Ricky, who earned 1980's street stock championship, followed his brothers' modified migration and remains active today as one of the foremost talents on

Good guy Lenny Jellesma in the #45 is followed very closely by Bobby Fuller, while Dan Dulude in the #14 tries it out downstairs.

the NASCAR Featherlite Tour. Jeff today is a nationally known Busch competitor.

To spike their promotions, the Falconis and enduring associate Bill Welch booked traveling shows as frequently as possible. The NEMA programs were always a thrill on the oval designed so specifically for their form of competition. Johnny and Joey Coy, Dave Humphrey, Johnny and Billy Mann, and Bobby White, 1975 NEMA champ, were notable. However, one of the saddest days in Westboro's long history, September 9, 1978, involved a NEMA incident. Steve Gillespie somehow got upside down and went over the first turn fence. He suffered a broken neck and permanent paralysis from the neck down.

In advance of the 1980 season, the Westboro promoters were once again feeling that old Westboro uneasiness. This time there were two reasons for sleeplessness. First, although it seemed sustainable at first, the "small block, small buck" theorem had not attracted very many Westboro-specific cars at all. Second, Dick Robidoux's fortunes had soured dramatically and lease negotiations were going to have to be with the bank. And, very much as one would expect, the bank as a landlord insisted on huge insurance policies. All legal issues had to be completely topped and tailed, something not necessarily adhered to in earlier days of stock car promotion.

A fresh and most welcome face often featured in Speedway Scene that winter was Dick Williams. Always smiling, Williams was a guy who worked from the last star until the first. He launched Coastal Racing Association from Westerly, RI and he signed up New London, Thompson, and Monadnock for his sanction. It sure seemed like a

(left) None of them looks happy, but they made a lot of people laugh. Dick "Hanscom Harry" Solt, Curt O'Keefe, John Spence, Bruce Cohen, and "Nasty" Neil Murray observe the steam and smoke. *(Berggren photo)*

(right) In terms of raw speed among all the local teams, Joe Howard's was probably best. His #1X was blisteringly fast and he drove it well. *(Balser photo)*

(left) Joe Brady and his bunch sure had their hands full. That's Bugs Stevens in the #41 and Bob "Frito Bandito" Santos in the #41M. *(Silvia Collection)*

(right) Dickie Williams also enticed Maynard Troyer to Westboro. Here he is rubber side up in the smoke and steam. *(Silvia Collection)*

good link for Westboro, and a deal was struck. So, opening day 1980 had a whole different feel. Again.

Just as the Falconis had tried to downplay the big names and big money over the past few summers, Williams went right back after the them with a vengeance. His press releases said it all: "With close to $16,000 in posted guaranteed money now up for grabs for the season opener at Westboro Speedway, what Leo Cleary says about 'winning with Williams' is more than just words." Everyone wanted it to work. Williams' positive persona attracted even more top staffers with Bill Slater, Dick Brooks, Henry Rufo, Carl Merrill, Karen Slater, and Jim Rigney all pitching in.

If all had been as it was in the Westboro Busch 100 that spring, life would have been all good. An incredible field of modifieds towed in from hither and yon and played host to a swelling crowd. Long Island's Greg Sachs, who today is in the sunset of an impressive Winston Cup career, speaks this way of that day: "My life has been filled with fond memories of racing. But one at the top would have to

One of the greatest foursomes in stock car history, (right to left) Bugs Stevens, Jerry Cook, and Richie Evans congratulate Greg Sachs on his Westboro win. *(Falconi Collection)*

be the first race I won off Long Island, at Westboro, Massachusetts, with owner Lee Allard. The race produced a podium finish photo that I cherish. It includes Richie Evans, Bugsy Stevens, and Jerry Cook, representing sixteen years of national champions." Fellow Long Islander, the late Charlie Jarzombek, was fifth.

And so it was that in 1980 and 1981 the big bucks would go to the big boys, just as expected. Ronnie Bouchard won 7 shows in 1980 alone, and it was Stevens, Bouchard, and Cleary on the podium at the banquet. However, there were a few stellar and inspired runs by less well-funded entries, too. Roland LaPierre, Jr. and Gomer Taylor both had impressive victories, while totally unheralded Somerville

(top left) Dickie Williams didn't mind at all when Roland LaPierre, Jr. socked it to the big buck cars. *(Falconi Collection)*

(top right) Lakeville graduate Gomer Taylor, under-financed and hat askew, could out-of-the-blue be very fast. He won a big one in 1981. *(Balser photo)*

(left) Peter Schwarz wins in a car wrenched by Dick Pratt. *(Balser photo)*

Ed DeVoe (#13) sails high above Dickie Eliot (#6) in this remarkable midget action. *(Balser photo)*

driver/owner Peter Schwarz was always in the hunt and was fifth in points in 1980.

By the end of year two, despite everyone's good intention, Coastal Racing Association would wash out to sea. It was a bitter pill for the now sickly speedway. However, there was at least one small flicker of hope, one that had been burning quietly in the background for the last couple of years.

When Bill Welch, Peter, and Murph Falconi were seated at Seekonk's 1978 awards banquet, they found themselves next to a trusted friend, Dan Meservey. Meservey had emerged over the seventies as the very effective kingpin of a strong new movement in racing, mini stocks. The conversation must have been engaging. The Falconis always had their antennae tuned for possible Westboro competitors of any description. Meanwhile, Anthony Venditti had just announced that, after running the minis at Seekonk weekly in 1978, he was going to set them adrift.

Dan Meservey is much more in the image of his Cape Cod home than he is of an old time stock car track. Tall, blonde-haired, and fit even today, Meservey still has some surfer to his look, and it was actually on the beach that he developed his fixation with racing.

In the late sixties Meservey and a band of buddies moved away from drag racing and were intrigued with some new dune buggy concepts, most of which were built up over VW running gear. Before long they had built a bunch of them. On Sunday afternoons it was off to a specially marked track way out in the dunes.

These informal scrambles grew so notorious that the gang feared (with good justification) that they would be shut down by environmentalists. They picked up the whole deal and moved to a local sand

Dan Meservey
(Balser photo)

pit. Shortly thereafter they carved out a 1/5 mile dirt track and anointed it Chatham Speedway. The land was owned by a friend and the lease was one dollar per year, a fee never paid.

How unlikely it seems that Chatham Speedway could ever have been constructed in the midst of some of the fastest populating, most valuable residential real estate in the Northeast. But there was such excitement about the dune buggy races that a special permit was granted, and by the early seventies several thousand spectators lined the banks around the tiny oval each Sunday, passing the hat around to cover club expenses.

Dan himself proved immediately proficient behind the wheel and, not one to suffer island fever in any way, he felt the urge to test his met-

Pete Schluter chases Dan Meservey and Charlie Doane (outside) at Chatham Speedway. *(Meservey Collection)*

tle on the road. In 1970 he entered Florida's Everglade "300", a six hour buggy enduro, and he brought the trophy back North.

Chatham continued on in its unusual way and was even paved before its final season in 1977. But the complexion of things had changed at a fundamental level when Meservey came back from his trip South. He had contracted a thorough case of wanderlust. In Dan's own words, "I became kind of a Pied Piper, dragging people off the Cape." Fellow buggiests Pete Schluter, Marcel L'Etoile, and Charlie Doane were quick to follow and they persuaded a few places such as Vermont's Bear Ridge and New Hampshire's Rattle Snake and Riverside to give them a date. It must have been a sight as they sallied forth for their initial adventures. Not accustomed to travel, they would take three cars on the back of a fish truck or pack any flatbed they could find.

Soon the merry wanderers began to be noticed by the racing papers. A big break came when Lou Modestino, the honored racing writer from Stoughton, arranged a meeting for them with the guys who had competed in the VW Division at Norwood. The Arena just closed, they had no place to go. The chemistry was excellent from minute one, and, by session end, the New England Mini Modified Association was hatched.

NEMMA responded to any assignment, hitting venues such as Claremont and Lee, NH and the tricky clay at Lebanon Valley and returning most often to the Cape for Sunday shows. An interesting interlude came, though, when NEMMA cars descended upon the

Stoughton-based Lou Modestino has been writing for 40 years. *(Balser photo)*

infamous Golden Spur Speedway in Lakeville. To say that the track was underfinanced, underconstructed, and undermanaged would be no overstatement. It was fast and fun. It was also perfectly situated for the old Norwood gang, for the Cape crowd, and for those who might shoot down the Mass Pike from Lebanon Valley. So, Meservey himself took another flyer and leased Lakeville for the 1975 season.

Dan and crew had done a lot of work by opening day. We towed in from a modified race at Fonda, NY the night before and found the infield dug out, the grounds cleaned up as best possible, and the track surface subtly banked and covered copiously with clay. The clay turned out to be just as problematical as it always is for daytime racing. No matter how much water was washed over it, the springtime sun would dry it out in minutes, aided in a big way by the wide, grooved racing tires of the day. Most of us, however, found the clouds of dust far more to our liking than the filthy oiled dirt—and Lakeville rocks—that we had raced on previously. Doubtless the Environmental Protection Agency felt the same way.

Lakeville town officials did not share the open minds of those in Chatham and they turned the screw down on the race track any way they could. Golden Spur closed for good at the end of the year, much to Dan's disappointment. Though he admits he would have loved to keep it going—even to buy it, his heart remained in Nomex. "My passion was not to run a race track, but to race one."

What Lakeville did accomplish in spades was to cement NEMMA's positioning as a serious division alternative. Mini specials at Westboro in the next few years generated especially large car counts due to the ease of access from New York. There were great contests when upstate's big mini names such as Bob Hackle took on NEMMA's best. Then, in 1978 Anthony Venditti had some concern about his show so he took on the minis. He paid good money, often attracted forty cars, and even promoted a National Mini Stock Championship. Meservey won the $1,000, but for whatever reason NEMMA lost Seekonk.

Welchie, Murph, and Peter were aware of all this at the Seekonk banquet that night in 1978, and they also knew through NEMMA dealings that Meservey was solid and reliable. By the end of the evening they offered him a silent partnership in their Westboro promotional team. He accepted.

Due to his NEMMA responsibilities and the grind of his own racing, Meservey was not always at Westboro when the club was not there. But, as an invested partner, you can bet he was on site for the meeting in the fall of 1981 with Welchie and the Falconis to decide what to do now that Dickie Williams had gone away.

In retrospect, the outcome of the meeting seems obvious. In the Spring of 1982, the mini mods, just a decade ago chasing each other around a desolate beach, became for the first time in New England the headline attraction at a purse-paying speedway.

❖ ❖ ❖ ❖ ❖

By 1982 the definition of a mini described quite a sophisticated race car. Custom-welded chasses at 85-100 inches were in the VW Bug, Rabbit, or Pinto size range, covered with bodies channeled down to 50-70% of their original size. Motors from VWs, Pintos, Toyotas, Datsuns, etc. were allowed major modification, but a strict formula of car weight times engine power potential was observed. The goal was to have inexpensive, fast, and relatively equally matched cars.

It worked fairly well. Fields were satisfactory in size from day one, and, as had become the norm at Westboro, there was variety in the background of the competitors. Former Westboro drivers like Sam Stern, Joe Lemay, Lee Ward, and Dick Dubois suited up, as did other former stock car shoes as Frank Kuhlman, Dave Lind, and Billy Schulz. As a group, they confronted a whole slew of new wheel twisters who came to the sport through the minis. These included W.J.

Lee Ward, a veteran from back in West Peabody days. *(Balser photo)*

Billy Tibbert (#47), Bill's son, won his first mini feature at Westboro. He would go on to be a Seekonk track champion. He is shown duking it out with John Grant (#73) and Richie Murray (#88) for the win. *(Tibbert Collection)*

Sam Stern was on top of his game with Dave Searle's power. *(Balser photo)*

Dick Houlihan was consistently fast in the minis. *(Meservey Collection)*

Grez, Rick Hussex, Tom Glazier, Duncan McDougall, Darryl Smith, and Mike McGinn.

Dave Lind, Dick Houlihan, Dan Mersevey, and Sam Stern were among the bigger winners in the four seasons that followed. Their accomplishments do deserve mention, especially as few fans knew just how fast this new breed of little cars was going. One night management hosted a match race between an SK modified and a mini to pump up a forthcoming SK special event. Ricky Fuller was selected to participate in his stout #99 SK, while Meservey represented NEMMA in his #11a. Meservey claims he worried for a week about what to do, even seeking counsel from his father. In his heart, he says, he knew he could beat Fuller and he wanted to for NEMMA's sake. But then, the goal of the race was to make hype. How would it look if a mini whipped one of those supposedly lightning-fast V-8 modifieds?

The SK mod-mini mod match race. Are Ricky Fuller and Dan Meservey both full throttle? *(Meservey Collection)*

(top left) Paul Gariepy hams it up with Dick Brooks and Bill Ambrosio to his left. That's Frank Procopio and Dan Meservey to his right. *(Meservey Collection)*

(top right) Joe LeMay (#0) and Glen Cabral (#26), whose son Randy has been an instant success in NEMA. *(Meservey Collection)*

Meservey says today, with his ever available grin, that he never told Fuller that he kept out of the carburetor just enough for Ricky to win.

From time to time, of course, the speed that the minis were running had to have its consequence. Marcel L'Etoile took many broken parts home when he flipped on the front stretch and rearranged the starter's box in the fashion of Ray Janelle thirty years before. Dave Lind will recall coming off turn two, catching the small concrete curb beneath the fence, and cart-wheeling down the backstretch. And anyone who saw it will still be grateful that Lou Horton walked away from his mini the night he got caught up in a tangle and broke a fuel line. Gasoline ran down the banking and ignited into a blazing inferno. Horton, a Southboro businessman big in both commerce and physical stature, was pulled out just in time.

Pictured left to right, back row: Joe LeMay, Bill Schulz, Rick Falconi (for Lou Horton), Doug Meservey, and Julian Gorman. Front row: Dan and Danny Meservey. *(Meservey Collection)*

It seems that the younger generation stays away from Cape Cod on the weekends too. Here's Danny Meservey Jr. in a Silver Crown car at Nazareth, PA. Both Danny and brother Doug are experienced drivers. *(Meservey Collection)*

✥ ✥ ✥ ✥ ✥

To fill the show bill late models and streets also competed at Westboro these final years. Eddie Weston, Len Jellesma, Dave Blanchard, GeGe Gravel, and Bobby Thompson were up front. The real story, though, involved two Westboro drivers—one from the late models—who were well on their way to becoming the track's most famous graduates.

Groton's GeGe Gravel was Westboro's last track champion. *(Balser Photo)*

Bob Santos Jr. was a winner in the eighties. His kids, Bobby III and Erica, are red hot in the Seymour open wheel cars today. *(Santos Collection)*

(top left) Westboro and Monadnock star Fran Colson. *(Alden Collection)*

(top right) The talented, unheralded, Dave Blanchard. *(Balser photo)*

(bottom) Ron Bouchard had great cars from day one. This '57 Chevy was a rocket at Seekonk. *(Tibbert Collection)*

When you think of Westboro, you must think of Fitchburg, home to so many of the Speedway's signature names. And, when you think of Fitchburg, you're right at Ron Bouchard and Peter Fiandaca. The two, near the same age, grew up near one another, started racing very early, won races almost immediately, and continued for many years. At the same time, however, it would be impossible for two young men to have chosen the same occupation while taking more different pathways to success.

Very much Bob Bouchard's son, Ronnie insisted on the best of equipment from day one. Right from his earliest forays to Brookline, Hudson/Pines, Westboro, and Seekonk, he had access to topnotch cars, tuned by the guys who had ushered Peter Salvatore to so many wins. It was quite likely that his early success gave Ronnie the confidence to reach out to even more well-resourced owners as he climbed

the ladder. He drove for Bob Judkins, his mentor Marvin Rifchin, Bob Johnson, and Lenny Boehler, breaking into the top ten in NASCAR national modified points four times from 1972 to 1980.

By 1981 Bouchard was able to leverage all the positive momentum, and he found himself in the seat of a Winston Cup ride. Handsome, athletic, and media-conscious, he had all the necessary packaging. He had the big-track ability as well. That very year he steered Jack Beebe's Race Hill Farms Buick into victory circle at the Die Hard 500 at Talladega and was chosen Winston Cup Rookie of the Year just as brother Kenny was seven years later. Though Ronnie would never move out of Massachusetts, from 1981 to 1987 he made 160 Winston Cup starts, nailing down 60 top ten finishes. He also strutted his stuff in the Busch Series, copping back-to-back Darlington checkers in 1984. Today, celebrated as a NEAR Hall-of-Famer, Bouchard is a well-known Massachusetts personality, especially familiar to the public for his continuous television advertising for the ultra-successful Ron Bouchard Auto Stores.

The well-scrubbed Ron Bouchard. *(Silvia Collection)*

To appreciate just how different he was, consider what Pete Fiandaca says about his first car down at Westboro in 1967: "I can honestly say that I was the worst car on the track. I was in the way." Though he had a supportive family situation, he was functionally on his own. In Peter's words, "What really saved me were two things. First, frankly, I did not know what I did not have. My Dad never went to the races. He'd come out to the garage and say 'nice car.' I thought it was. Second, I didn't have much else growing up. I wasn't good at sports or in school. This is something that came easily to me over time. Racing is about getting through the turns. I can do that. Somehow it came naturally to me."

In 1968 Peter won his first race, an ARC cadet feature at Westboro, after Vic Kangas had stopped by and flattened his rear springs with a roller. That day Fiandaca knew he wanted to be a professional racer. It is interesting to consider whom he chose to watch. Rather than latching onto someone just up the learning curve, he chose the Finn, the aging owner/driver on the other side of town. "I went to the Thompson 500 in 1969 and snuck into the pits to watch Reino. He qualified fine and was running with the top fifteen when he dropped out. He said he had no money to buy fuel. That night I told my parents that I needed a checking account. That way I could buy what I needed before the feature and pay for it afterwards. Since then I have written 7559 checks and 5000 of them have been cuffed, written before I raced and earned the balance."

By 1970 Fiandaca, building and maintaining his own kit and paying for it with winnings, was essentially racing full time. In 1974 he was racing a minimum of four times a week, often at New Egypt, NJ, Riverside Park, Monadnock, Hudson, and Westboro. Even with his adaptation of the "grundge" look and the sometimes shabby appear-

Paul Richardson and Pete Fiandaca *(Berggren Collection)*

ances of his "135s," he attracted an admiring fan following and was fondly labeled "the Traveling Man." He also won the loyalty of a cadre of long-time support players. There was certainly Steve Bird, son of Hudson and Pines official, Amos Bird, and a future winning BUSCH crew chief. Steve wrenched Peter's cars for years in the most difficult circumstances. There was the day they left Hudson, NH in the afternoon after winning the feature. Birdie was seen working on the car on the hauler as it raced down to Thompson, CT where they won that night. And there was the main event crash near midnight on Westboro's backstretch in 1978. Literally every wheel was ripped off the #135 Gremlin. Peter and Birdie were at Hudson at noon the next day, ready to rock and roll to another win.

Marvin Rifchin, the honored founder of M&H Tire, took the young Fiandaca under his wing and his patience about being paid for tires was deep, though in the end, rewarded. It was the same way with Tex's Engines in Woburn.

At the end of 1979, Fiandaca was still winning modified races everywhere against monstrously better-equipped teams. But the next spring he shocked the racing world by dropping a division and showing up with a late model. Everyone knew he would make shambles of the Division and everyone was right. Everyone also thought he would eventually drift away from racing. Everyone was wrong.

Amazingly Peter was able to continue to support himself by wearing Nomex—mostly full time—right up to the present, competing in the lesser classes. His kickoff in 1980 had a real good feel; he was track champ at Westboro, Thompson, Stafford, and Connecticut State Champion. He won 30 of 62 mains that year, wheeling a rag tag unit he called "The Skid Row Express." He did—and does still today—a huge amount of racing.

A reflective kind of person, Fiandaca is very much aware of how understated his pathway has been compared to that of his more glamorous neighbor, Ron Bouchard. All said and done, though, Peter does seem to understand, as do so many others, that his old-time way of winning hundreds of features has its own very special merit. It could be said that he built his life on the sides rather than on the top. "You know," he says, "I called Ronnie when I had close to 87 trophies—that's what he had. I kept saving them until I reached 200 and then I started giving them all to kids."

Prior to the start of the 1985 season, two events would shake what remained of Westboro Stadium to the core. Shortly after Christmas, Bill Welch, the beloved gentleman who had every racing person's welfare in mind, died following a gallant struggle with lung cancer. It was a major loss to motorsports in Massachusetts, and to no one's surprise Welchie was inducted into the Hall of Fame at NEAR's very first program.

Bill Welch was known as "the Dean of New England Auto Racing" *(Balser photo)*

Second, the much-feared specter of auction finally surfaced. The bank backing the speedway could find no alternative to recouping their funds save by forced, open sale. The winning bidder was a developer from Southboro, Dick McCarthy. Fortunately, he was known to Murph Falconi and they agreed the track could operate for as long as possible before the construction crews for the shopping center arrived. It would be for just one more year.

Almost before anyone realized, it was Sunday evening, September 29, 1985. The final race was over. Brian Wood, newest performer out of a great racing family from Pelham, NH, had bested a 24-car Super Street field in a 50-lapper over Mark Curtis and Greg Warzycha. Dave Bell, Smokey Fenton (aka Rick Falconi), and Don DeFusco topped the Rookies. Even the beer stand had closed. As the early autumn sun was about to set, Murph took even a little longer than usual in shutting everything down.

Done at last, he drove over to the pit gate. He glanced over the banking onto the track and at the stands. A score of images of summer nights must have crossed his mind. There was Sostilio and crowds of 10,000; Luchesi, the cutdowns, Argentina Rocca, Reino and Freddie; there were the AARA flatheads, Tessier and Clothier, the Grand Ams, and the modifieds. And, yes, there was Dick Robidoux. In the end the law shut him down for financial impropriety and he was sent to prison for a few winters.

As the sun disappeared over Worcester, Murph slowly closed the pit gate and locked it. Westboro Stadium went silent forever.

John Falconi, the quiet, steady force behind Westboro for nearly 30 years. *(Falconi Collection)*

The site where the Pines was built was a natural amphitheater next to the Merrimac river in Groveland, MA. It lent itself to recreation and entertainment for all. *(Ken Smith Collection)*

Oscar in The Pines

IF WHAT THEY SAY IS TRUE, IT MUST HAVE BEEN QUITE THE SCENE. There can be no doubting that Carl Tiberio, brother to Al, Butch, and Mike from Methuen, was one rough customer, both on and off the track. In his early days with a bomber and later with a cutdown, Tiberio was hard on the throttle, soft on the brake. In the pit area he was quick with both his temper and his fist.

One night in the sixties, after winning the "A" Feature at The Pines Speedway, Tiberio swaggered up to the pay-off window, very much The Man, puffing beneath his trademark T-shirt and sailor's cap. Fully expecting $500 for the win, Tiberio slammed down that fist when Oscar Ridlon, The Pines' promoter, stopped counting at $250. "Where's the rest of the money, you crook?", Tiberio demanded. Ridlon's response came slowly. "So, Carl, you think you're tough. I'll show you who's tough." Ridlon calmly reached up and unscrewed the single light bulb dangling above his table. He soaked two fingers from his right hand in his mouth and then jammed them into the socket.

Tiberio left with $250.

I believe the story. Not more than a couple of years later Bruce Cohen and I went to Hudson Speedway, a quarter-mile sister track to The Pines in New Hampshire, for the Easter Sunday opener. We were intending to test out our dirt modified by running a few laps on the asphalt. Amos Bird, the pit steward, made us race in the supermodified division, and we were like a whale in a sea of gold fish. Somehow, though, a bunch of cars dropped out, and we splashed home in fifth. Totally green and naive, Bruce and I were thrilled at the thought of a few extra bucks to start the racing season, until we got to the payoff window, that is. A weathered, cranky-looking guy wearing a rumpled old suit and a white shirt with no tie grunted, "Who the hell are you?" without even looking up. We responded that we had just taken fifth in the super main. He counted out five five-dollar bills and handed them to us and promptly snatched four back. "Twenty bucks to join the club, kid."

So, Bruce and I had just towed all the way to New Hampshire, run up front in the feature, and we were getting $5.00. What happened, we wondered. We should have known better. We had just run into Oscar Ridlon.

An extraordinary race car driver in the pre- and immediate post-war years, Ridlon became owner of The Pines in 1950 and retained it until it was closed down

Carl Tiberio and his brothers, Butch, Mike, and Al, were no shrinking violets underneath the pines. *(Berggren photo)*

in 1973. Unlike Westboro, which saw such constant change in promoters and sanctions, The Pines was developed largely under the strong, personifying rule of one unusual man. In short, Oscar Ridlon *was* The Pines Speedway.

Oscar G. Ridlon was anything but ordinary from day one. Born in Roxbury in 1906, he was smitten as a kid by the primitive lure of early auto racing. An enterprising sort—and certainly not short on self-confidence, Ridlon worked himself into big car rides by his early twenties. In 1932 he won his first race. It was on the lethal one-mile dirt ribbon in Readville.

It is difficult to imagine how unruly this early competition really was. The cars and competitors were primitive forbearers to the dramatic racing that Art Rousseau and Reino Tulonen were doing at Keene in the late forties. In Readville days the big cars were astoundingly fast while safety equipment of any substance had not yet been considered. RA Silvia recapped in Vintage Racer magazine the report of a typical incident: "DRIVER KILLED AT AUTO RACES… Four other racers seriously injured at Readville Park as cars tear into machine of Wesley Johnson which had crashed into a pole and blocked the track. 5000 spectators horrified as two ambulances rushed to the scene and sped off with two of the victims. Only then it was discovered that Johnson had been hurled to the infield. A hose truck from the fire department was pressed into service to take him to the hospital where he died."

Oscar Ridlon winning a big car race at Topsfield Fairgrounds. *(Bob Miour photo)*

Oscar in his midget in 1941. Even at rest, he appeared to be moving forward. *(Clint Lawton photo)*

Ridlon, increasingly committed to driving, faced these dangers week in and week out. At Dracut he crashed big time in his midget, breaking his shoulder and numerous other bones, rendering himself unconscious for ten days, and losing several teeth. At Readville he swung wide to avoid a spinning car and drilled the fence, tossing himself right out of the track into a cluster of trees. His face was so badly fractured that doctors wired his jaw very tightly, allowing only limited usage for the rest of his life. And one the railbirds still talk about came at Thompson in 1941. Remarkably Ridlon was uninjured in a more-than-sensational ten-time end-for-end flip.

Those who knew Ridlon said such misadventures were just nuisances to him. Fear was a word with little meaning. True, he did have one or two superstitions. Early in his career a priest gave him a St. Christopher medal and he would not race without it. And, like many drivers of yesteryear, he considered peanuts bad luck. One night he knocked a guy cold for tossing peanut shells near his car. Any of Ridlon's thinking about luck, though, was much more focused on whether he would win than whether he would be wounded. And win he surely did.

"Cannonball" Ridlon on his way to the front, earning his nickname. *(Silvia Collection)*

Chief Charlie Sun Hawk was a full-blooded Cherokee and a feared open wheel competitor. *(Duncan Collection)*

He raced as often as he could, barnstorming at over 75 tracks, compiling over 100 feature wins. His prowess in the big cars transferred easily to the midgets and their bullring ovals. In the early forties he won 27 straight main events in his own outboard. He became so notorious for his take-no-prisoner charges to the front that he was called "Cannonball" Ridlon and he was in demand by promoters even outside of the country. By the late thirties he would spend winters racing in Argentina, where he was South American champion in 1938 and '39. Amazingly, he also earned titles in Cape Town, South Africa, and Sydney, Australia.

In later years Ridlon was fond of spinning the yarn about how he returned from Argentina with the tires of his winning midget stuffed full of gold. The truth is the gold was more important to him than the victories. Ridlon was quite different from most race drivers in this way. In 1935 he actually turned down a ride in the Indianapolis 500 in the Milton Marion Alfa Romeo out of Long Island. He calculated he could make more money racing regionally than he could sacrificing the month of May to the pursuit of the oily grail.

Ridlon's preoccupation with accumulating money in his race car had to harden him. After all, even apart from the interruptions of getting hurt, he had to match wits with legendary talents such as Joe Barzda, Dutch Schaefer, Dave Randolph, and Chief Sun Hawk. And all of this, of course, was happening right in those very difficult years following the Depression. Ridlon became fiercely self-reliant, doing things his own way, assuming always that everyone was out to screw him. The Oscar way worked for him, and by the mid-thirties he was already able to afford his own cars, something he always seemed to

Oscar in a flat out broadslide on the dirt at The Pines thumbs his nose at the infield photographer. *(Caruso Collection)*

Oscar and the ladies. *(Caruso Collection)*

prefer. He was simply not a team player; he was all Divide and Conquer.

It may well have been his desire to extract a few extra dollars out of promoters that caused the Cannonball to express his personality in another way. He became known as the consummate showman—not necessarily class act, but showman. His Elto-powered midget was famous for its exhaust system, so loud, old timers say, that with following winds you could hear it twenty miles away. And you could smell it, too. Oscar was quite the mixologist, brewing up exotic fuels, and he delighted in laying smoke screens as he roared down the straights. Back in December 1936 he won an indoor midget race at the old Boston Garden and, according to promoter Eddie Powers, nearly smoked out the paying fans with fumes. In this same midget he would confound fans and competitors alike by driving solo laps blindfolded—even allowing folks to tape bags over his head.

The Cannonball was the showman even when not racing. "The guy was just incredible," recalls Haverhill banker and veteran New England promoter, Ken Smith. "His hands were like gnarled steel, but he was an accomplished pianist, playing on cruise ships completely by ear." No doubt Ridlon enjoyed the extra income, but no doubt he also enjoyed the role and the attention he attracted from his largely female audiences. He had a strong appreciation for the fairer sex.

By 1940 at 34, Oscar Ridlon was at the top of his game and his fame. When The Pines Speedway opened that summer, he was an enormous drawing card.

Just in case racing the midgets was not hair-raising enough, the guys come up with a human battering ram stunt. That's Bob Blair on the hood and Oscar is beneath the hood. *(Blair Collection)*

Four thousand five hundred racing fans funneled into The Pines Speedway that opening night, Thursday August 29, 1940. Midget racing had blossomed in New England over the previous three summers, and the air was thick with excitement. However, the crowd had a different and much more local feel to it from the ones Westboro would draw a few years later. While Westboro was strategically located on Route 9, right near the Route 20 Boston Post Road intersection, and therefore quite accessible, The Pines was not. Groveland was then a small, sleepy village, a bedroom community to the factories in "shoe city," Haverhill, just across the river, and to the imposing industrial plants in Lawrence and Lowell. Tucked down in the Merrimack Valley, the town was simply hard to reach, especially in the days before the Interstate Routes 95 and 93, let alone 495.

When two years earlier businessmen John Smith, Paul Starta, Boz Orlando, Emil Short and attorney John Dondero met to discuss the possibility of a midget track in Groveland, they knew theirs would have to be a track serving the local communities. They also knew there was a definite history of recreation on the site they had in mind.

The fields, running North and West down to the bank of the Merrimack, once the Thomas Balch Farm, were transformed during the Gay '90's into an amusement park by the Bay State Railroad Company. There were benches, picnic tables, a pool and fountain, even diving horses and hot air balloonists. Folks from Groveland visited frequently on weekends and trolley cars delivered Haverhill residents in five minute intervals. In 1896 a sizeable and successful dance pavilion was constructed, only to be burned down by sparks from a popcorn machine. In 1912 another draw was attempted, this time

Bob White from Waltham was an early midget and sprint car standout.
(Caruso Collection)

a summer theatre. The productions were well received at first, but the stage eventually went silent.

By 1940 Smith and Dondero had launched their speedway start-up. Utilizing the natural half-bowl of the site, they carved out a 1/5 mile oval with the help of R. G. Watkins, capping it with copious loads of clay from a nearby pit. Midget racing writer Mac MacLeod observed that year, "This plant, located in a beautiful pine grove, provides the fans with fast, safe and thrilling racing and is also popular with the drivers. It is easily the prettiest and best laid-out midget track in this section, and the high bank overlooking the first and second turns and extending along the backstretch, gives the fans an excellent and unusual view."

Smith and Dondero's opening night audience was not disappointed. Some of the sport's biggest names were in the pits and they all engaged in thrilling broadsliding exhibitionism around the tight oval. Rufe Anderson, aboard his own well-funded car, had fast time of 17.2 seconds. He went on to be king for a night, sweeping the second consi and the feature over Tommy Simonetti and Dick Shuebruk.

Six more shows were anticipated for the fall of '40. They were well-attended and well-run. The Pines' management was professional and they brought in the legitimacy of the AAA sanction. Rufe Anderson did it again on the second evening and then Eddie Casterline, Hermie Delisle, Dick Shuebruk, and Joe Sostillio found their way to victory lane. The New England-based drivers were all humiliated thoroughly on September 13 when invading Wally Stokes towed into town and took everyone's lunch.

The real story of the year, though, was the seventh—and unscheduled—program. At the time, Watertown's Tommy Simonetti was already a wildly popular hot shoe. Just 20 years old when The Pines opened, the 5'2", 120-pound up-and-comer was already racing professionally, in a V-8 sixty he bought from Rufe Anderson, at tracks all

Frankie Simonetti in the Henry St. Ives car out of Fall River. *(Ken Smith Collection)*

over Massachusetts and at destination races at Thompson, Langhorne, and Castle Hill. His promising future, however, was snuffed out in a fatal crash at Union City, New Jersey.

In support of the Simonettis a benefit race was run at The Pines on Monday, November 11, the final show of the year and arguably the best. Before the feature taps was sounded, starter Mack Woolf dropped the checkered flag for Simonetti one more time. It was won by Concord's Lou Vigliotti after a stirring battle with Delisle in Nemo Russo's #22.

Amid growing concerns about the pending crisis in Europe, a thirteen-event season followed in 1941. John Smith was in control, buying out Dondero, while the AAA sanction remained in place. The year began poignantly when Frank Simonetti, Tommy's older brother, returned to car wars and conquered opening night. The rough and tumble Ed Eng, Bob Blair, and Ralph Purnell were also first-time winners. And then on September 25 the Cannonball, Oscar Ridlon, added to his medley of pre-war victories with his first ever feature at The Pines. The intimidating performer had already become notorious in Groveland. He liked the track. With his wry sense of humor he quipped that his outboard always ran well there because it was so close to the river.

For Oscar—and everyone else—war time was a time for introspection. He was lightning fast in 1941 when the races shut down and he was lightning fast when they restarted in 1946. But during those interim years he had begun expanding his personal horizons beyond just racing seats and piano benches. He was, after all, almost forty and even

The midgets blast away dustily at the Topsfield Fairgrounds. By today's safety standards, everything in this scene is unthinkable. *(Bob Miour photo)*

iron man Cannonball Ridlon had aches and pains from the ghosts of crashes past. And beyond his personal concentration on accumulating money and possessions, he had a family to feed, wife Tuck, son Terry, and daughter Barbara. He was smart enough to know he could not go on winning forever. Ridlon started buying up some income property and then he built up a moving company (often hauling pianos) located in a sprawling complex of garages in Jamaica Plain. They say he could carry a piano up a flight of stairs on his back by himself and he expected his employees to do the same.

Ridlon's orientation toward racing showed some broadening, too. By the beginning of the War he was President of Bay State Midget Racing Association, an unimaginable role for him five years earlier. Ridlon came to leverage this BSMRA post quite to his advantage. Johnny Whitehouse, a noted former Massachusetts sprint and midget driver, used to tell the story of one of the first midget races following the War. As BSMRA President, Oscar essentially put the show out to bid, available to the promoter who would post the highest purse. When the bids were all in, Oscar announced that Johnny Whitehouse had won, topping all others by a few dollars. Unbeknownest to the bidders, Oscar had made a deal with the Topsfield Fairgrounds to promote the race, using Whitehouse as a front man.

The scheming Ridlon knew full well that the event would be huge. He pushed it further by advertising bus service right to the Fairgrounds. On race day thousands showed up in Topsfield and soon Whitehouse was in the office telling Ridlon they were out of tickets. With a bark Ridlon had the sellers right back out there, selling the stubs.

Track conditions turned out to be horrible, as ungroomed dirt tracks often are by daylight. When the BSMRA drivers approached as a group to complain, Oscar dismissed them. "Screw you guys. Any of you who are too sissy to race, go home. I brought my own car. That just means more money for me."

The race eventually went off, but rather poorly with few cars, mostly invisible through thick clouds of dust. When it was all over, Ridlon was seen leaving the Fairgrounds with the rear of his road car weighted down with cash. Meanwhile, throngs of disappointed people were lining up waiting for the promised buses. They had quite a wait. The only buses coming were those on the scantily scheduled Portland-Boston route the next day.

When the BSMRA teams pulled into The Pines on the day of its opener in May of 1946, they were more enthusiastic about the facilities than they had been at Topsfield. John Smith still owned the track, but new promoters, Paul and Emil Starta and Len Short, had expanded the oval from a 1/5 to a 1/4, and it was paved. Two ambulances and all the track vehicles were nattily painted, all the attendants uniformed. It was a class joint. It was the dawn of two of The Pines' finest years.

The racers were likely not a lot happier with Cannonball Ridlon, though. Despite his expanding activities, he had lost none of his feel for the wheel. He dominated the first few shows. His streak was broken by Bob Blair on June 7 after the Cannonball jumped the first turn fence in his Elto #8 and rode the top of it for 100 feet before exiting the ballpark. In the same accident-ridden program, noted midget owner Johnny Carroll was struck in the infield by a spinning Johnny Black, his own driver. Carroll's sky-ride was missile-like, and no one could believe he was only bruised.

Nemo Russo's team arrives at The Pines on quite the trailer. *(Caruso Collection)*

Eddie Casterline is preparing for push off in the Koopman Offy. That's Rufe Anderson on the inside. The Pines was well presented after the war. *(Bob Miour photo)*

Eddie Casterline, Frank Simonetti, Bill Schindler, Bill Randall, and Ray Janelle were among the other victors that year. Even toward the end of this 21-program season, though, it was increasingly obvious that the nature of the midgets was changing. The expensive Offies were way too much for the outboards and cycles.

Offy domination was complete in 1947, beginning with Dedham's Bob Blair's romp the first Thursday night. His car, an Offy owned by newcomer Fred MacLeod, was rumored to have cost $10,500, a staggering sum for the times Joe Sostillio was also a factor in the Koopman Special, as were Bud Tatro (the Stone Offy), Ted Tappett, Al Keller, Randall, Schindler, and Johnny Bernardi, all blue chip names.

The season showcased spectacular competition before swelling audiences. There were new stands in the first and second turns and enlarged parking areas. The races were even broadcast on radio

Dick Shuebrek fights for control outside of Ray Jannelle in the #15. Johnny Thomson in the #21 and Frankie Simonetti follow, all eyes. *(Silvia Collection)*

The Cannonball took no prisoners in his Elto right after the war. *(Duncan Collection)*

WHAV, but it was gritty stuff. The ambulances were not just busy with drivers. Two starters, Bob Bullock and Lee Hiltz were hit and injured, Hiltz' accident seemingly just practice for his misadventure at Westboro a few years later. The most sensational incident, though, waited for the final night. Mac MacLeod called it this way. "Fran Magurn ran into Al Mitcheson's crossed-up car, and the Magurns' mount, the Haynes #77 V-8, went end-over-end and flipped sideways twice, ending up in the first turn infield. Fran was thrown out on the last flip when his seat belt broke, but by the grace of God and the Guardians who protect midget drivers, he escaped with only a severe shaking up in what appeared to be the accident that everyone hoped would never happen to anyone."

Just like down in Westboro, the off-season of '47-'48 was the winter of discontent in the Merrimack Valley. With BSMRA threatening

Starter Lee Hiltz was as tough as they came. *(Caruso Collection)*

to strike, Paul Starta and Len Short once again negotiated a sanction with the National AAA. The lid-lifter was postponed to June 10 and went to Joe "Fat Boy" Ross. Top guns Chet Gibbons, Bill Randall and Bud Tatro were lightning quick, but it was Lowell's Johnny Thomson who would most dominate the fields as they began to dwindle over the season. Thomson was soon to sit on the pole at Indy, and win the East Coast Championship, only to be killed back on the dirt in a sprinter. After a few weeks BSMRA was back. By August yet another new group, the United Car Owners Association, tried futilely to bring back stability. Crowds were in free fall; the future of the once-mighty midgets looked bleak. The Pines shuttered for the season on September 16, its earliest closure ever.

(left) This jolly scene in Portsmouth, New Hampshire, is the BSMRA crew after a rainout. From the left, engaged in his chug-a-lug, is Joe Ross. Mr. and Mrs. Bob Foss are behind them, while at the table are the Ed Casterlines, the Bob Bullocks, Lou Giuliano, Joe Sostilio, an unknown happy face, and the Johnny Blacks. *(Caruso Collection)*

(right) Art Abbot and Johnny Black (#89) go for a ride while Joe Sostilio finds wide-open spaces down below. *(Silvia Collection)*

Smith, Short, and Paul Starta Sr. were midget types, unprepared for and unfamiliar with the more uncivilized stock cars that were filling pit areas. They decided to reach out to Harvey Tattersall and they booked his United touring modified coupes and coaches for a brief twelve-show season, June to September 1949.

Given the novelty of the rock' em, sock' em hard tops, crowds were initially very strong. Fans were treated to the appearance of legendary racing figures. Former open-wheelers included Al Keller, Chet Gibbons, Carroll "Iron Hat" Sleeper, Ted Tappett, Ray Brown, and Hank Stevens. They pitted against a wave of new modified speciaists, Dick Egan, Sparky Belmont, and Charlie Gattalia among them.

The universally respected midget veteran, Bill Randall, proved Prince of The Pines by racking up during July and August a streak of five stock car wins in six features. Over the summer, though, the shows lost luster and fan following. One reason may well have been that the locally based fans in the Merrimack Valley simply preferred watching

Bill Randall was among the most popular wheelmen ever at The Pines. He was a master in the midgets and excelled in the United Stock Cars. The music died with him in a midget at Lime Rock in the sixties. *(Berggren Collection)*

local competitors. At The Pines the more professional, national AAA shows were never as popular as the more edgy, regional BSMRA events. In this respect United had an unfortunate start in the isolated Groveland with outsiders Johnny Rogers of Charlotte, NC, Ernie Gessell from Hollis, Long Island, and Ed Gauvin out of Bristol, CT starring the first four nights. The only two local winners were talented Dick Ford, a home builder from Topsfield and Ernie Gilbert. "Crash" Gilbert closed out the year with a Pines win on September 15. He was an ultra-aggressive, take-no-prisoners warrior from Manchester, NH who had just won the Medford Bowl championship.

By 1950 the once hopping riverside raceway was in serious financial straits. John Smith retired the operation to the authority of the courts, and a familiar figure, Johnny Whitehouse, stepped in as track manager. From every corner it seemed Whitehouse had his hands full; everything was in flux. Race dates were often Friday nights, but then there were programs on Tuesdays and Saturdays as well. Likewise, there were sanctioning bodies du jour. The New England Stock Car

Babe Stein won in the midgets and later in stock cars. *(Silvia Collection,* left; *Tibbert Collection,* right)

Racing Association was in for the first three nights only, replaced by the National Jalopy Association on June 18. Two UCOA midget shows, both going to the soft-spoken Johnny Thomson, were mixed in for good measure.

People in the know raised their eyebrows when they noticed front man Whitehouse in place in 1950. Especially when they began to see more and more of Oscar Ridlon. The Cannonball was himself a featured component of the show on July 9. He bested Waltham's Earl Anair in a match race between Anair's coupe and Ridlon's midget. Oscar did little without purpose. He was hanging out at The Pines because he was negotiating. Before long the newly prospering businessman/racer had purchased the speedway from the court.

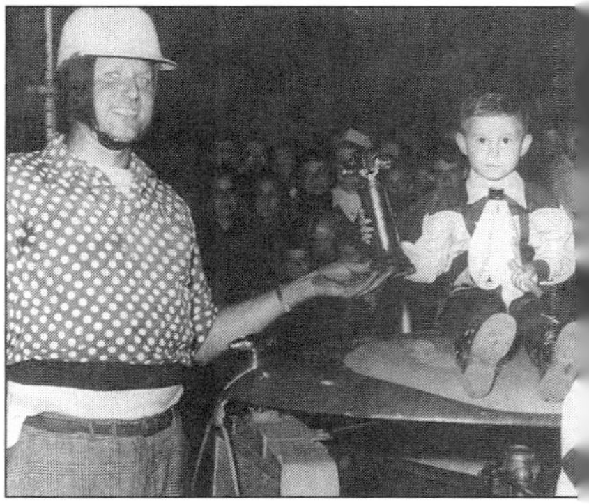

Manchester, NH's Ernie Gilbert. *(Spence Collection)*

Although fan attendance was hovering around 1,000, far south of the throngs during the midget boom, Ridlon must have liked some of the things he was seeing. First, the jalopies were cheap to build and so they did not require high purse payouts. Second both NESCRA and the NJA featured cars and stars from the immediate vicinity. Rollie Bishop of nearby Manchester, NH (the home of Manchester Motordome) was top dog opening night in his familiar #92, while Amesbury's Harry Harriman launched a credentialed Pines career with a romp on June 8 in the #130 Colonial Garage Ford. Another North Shore wheelman attracting renown was Ralph "Trigger" Watson. The Trigger pulled off two wins at the Pines in 1950 in the East Lynn Garage #193 and over the ensuing decade established himself as one of the era's greatest.

Oscar began working this local base of drivers immediately. Predictably, his means of soliciting loyalty was in no way to offer large purses or perks for the whole field. Rather, he built his alliances quietly and individually. Divide and conquer. Such was the case when

Manchester Motordrome was packed during jalopy days. It was a fifth mile, smaller even than Hudson, requiring a rear-end change for competitive teams. *(Berggren Collection)*

Casterline

Eddie Casterline was one of the finest open wheel drivers to come out of the Northeast —and surely from The Pines Speedway. At the end of the 1946 season, the BSMRA Champion went to California for the winter to race and planned to come back to New England following the Indy 500 on Memorial Day. All of New England watched, but unfortunately his ride was not ready for time trials at the Brickyard.

Casterline's much anticipated return to The Pines was on Thursday, May 27, 1947. Lew Walberg wrote in *Speed Age* magazine about an incredible performance in the heat race that night, demonstrating Casterline's Herculean physical strength as he actually held the rear end of the car in place. "In four laps he fought his way from the back to the front, and it was evident that he had not lost any of the ability he had shown the previous year. He had a fairly comfortable lead built up by the fifth lap and looked like a cinch to start breaking some old records. On the fifth lap he did break something. However, it was not a record but a radius rod on the rear right hand side of the car. The rod, hanging down from the rear axle, threatened to dig into the track and possibly flip the car. Aware of his plight, Eddie reached down with his right arm and caught the rod in his hand. Having to lean over to his right with his body, while making left turns and using super strength to hold the rod, Eddie managed to speed on, driving with one hand. However, he was having plenty of trouble in the turns and Bob Foss, who was driving the Stone #3 Ford, bore down on him. For the last three laps, Foss stayed right on Eddie's tail, threatening to overtake him if he slid in the turns. On the straightaways the more powerful Offenhauser managed to pull away from the Ford. In the turns Ed had to do some fancy handling with his left arm to keep the car under control and Foss from passing him. When the checkered flag was dropped Eddie and his broken radius rod were scarcely half a car length ahead of Foss. The applause that followed spoke to the approval of the fine job done by Casterline who actually held the car together and won the heat."

As fate would have it, Casterline would not get back to either Indianapolis or The Pines. Just two weeks later he was killed in a devastating crash at Seekonk Speedway, one of the three fatalities that haunted Anthony Venditti's new track its very first year.

On September 14, Bill Randall, Bob Blair, and Joe Ross were podium finishers at The Pines in a major Casterline memorial race. It attracted the largest crowd ever to see a midget race at Groveland.

Eddie works the midgets at Ted Koopman's garage area, affectionately known as "Gasoline Alley." *(Caruso Collection)*

This haunting Bob Miour photo shows the attendance line at Casterline's funeral. *(Caruso Collection)*

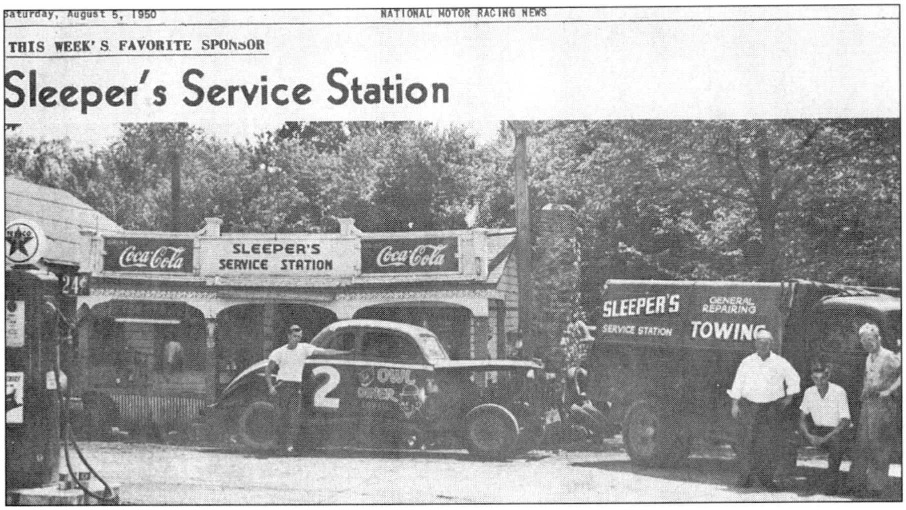

The National Jalopy Association picked a favorite sponsor of the week. The crew at Sleeper's Service Station in Chelmsford looks quite pleased in this classic period photo. *(National Motor Racing News)*

an uncommonly brash and brave kid from Wilmington pulled in with a '32 Ford coupe late in the year. Racing illegally at age 15, he crashed fiercely in the feature, piercing his head with the shift lever. His name was Don MacLaren.

Over the next few days, Ridlon made several trips to the hospital and crafted a deal with the wounded youngster. Oscar would go along with a fib to the insurance company about Mac's real age if Mac would agree to run The Pines—instead of Norwood—full time in the future. Thinking about the whole affair today, the Flying Scotsman sums it up saying simply, "I loved the guy." Guys like Ridlon and MacLaren do tough love. Mac continues, "Of course, we had moments. One night years later I didn't get what was coming to me in the payoff. I just punched Oscar out, took the money, and left him unconscious on the floor. The police came to my house and got me, but Oscar placed no charges when I promised to be back at the races the next week."

In 1951 Whitehouse and Ridlon switched the racing back to Thursday nights once again. Eastern Massachusetts and Southern

For a short time in 1950, The Pines and West Peabody Speedway actually cooperated. In front of a huge crowd, it's Al McKennon (#298), Danny Sullivan (#300), Ray Hudson (#94), Ralph Flannery (#201), Don Heath (#83), Happy Gath (#416), and Neil Hansen (#21) in West Peabody action. *(National Motor Racing News)*

Jackie Dodge in the office of Ray Farnell's #702. Ray, an ex-midget owner, says they could race this car seven times a week at the height of the jalopy craze. *(Farnell Collection)*

New Hampshire were awash with active stock car tracks and new, competing racing associations, and Oscar did make, at first, some attempt to get along with others. As the summer passed, his chosen sanction, Mystic Valley, merged with the Merrimack Valley Racing Association and schedules were further complicated. The fiercely independent Ridlon's frustrations about such outside influences were mounting daily. He struggled to achieve self-reliance as a local, self-contained, destination track, not prey to anyone from the outside. He first booked added attractions. He ran the Speedway's first Powder Puff in June, snagged by the wife of Don Heath, a journeyman jalopy driver from Malden. He even staged races for a few house-owned Crosleys to spice the show. Then, noticing the new-car fad at Westboro and Thompson, he promoted an event for 1948-1951 model cars for his final event. As would be expected of the Cannonball, however, he did not reach out to NASCAR for cars. Rather, he attempted to go it alone, rustling up his own roster. Some outsiders such as Reino Tulonen with his Henry J. did show, but a car count of 15 was too low

That's Oscar outside his moving facilities in Jamaica Plain. At this point he had not planned to compete in the Ford coupe. *(Slater Collection)*

Tiny Thompson was very fast in his six cylinder. One night he got pretty banged up in a crash and was loaded into the ambulance. As it left the track, Thompson came rolling out the back door, still on the stretcher. At that point he declined to get back in, saying the track was a safer place to be. *(Slater Collection)*

for the 150-lap grind. Oscar urged anyone to run and he picked up the glove himself. He raced a 1950 Ford to a second place finish behind Kazzy King. Oscar's Ford had the benefit of only three wheels for much of the race. Even more remarkably, Bennie Bernstein was third in a Crosley. It must have been painful to watch.

The Thursday night jalopy shows did go reasonably well, and Ridlon progressed toward his goal of Pines-only stars. Buddy Salsman, Hank Dodge, Don Lawler and Red Castor were all victors and all would cut many laps around The Pines in subsequent years. So, too, would a crowd-pleaser named Tiny Thompson who was up front on July 26. Thompson was one of the few not to use a Flathead Ford, and it is said that his six cylinder flew around The Pines, never changing its speed or level of RPM. Fans in 1951 also cheered on a colorful five-car team: Wally Spenser in the #41, Ed Skofield in the #42, Don Yeo (#43), Lenny Hamel (#44), and Bill LoGerte (#45). Team founder, Eddie Skofield, soon rose to shining star status in the cut downs. Nothing was too crazy for Skofield. One of his other "part-time" jobs was with Lagasse Amusements—as a circus trapeze artist, juggler, and backup volunteer for the guy shot out of the cannon into the net.

Eddie Skofield in the #42 is anxious to get out of town for obvious reasons. *(Aramian Collection)*

By 1952 Oscar Ridlon had taken a set with his new speed plant. For better or worse he had in place the business plan he would follow over the next twenty years. He was now the acknowledged top dog, owning and running the track himself. Motoring on with full Ridlon conviction, he switched to Saturday nights, coupling with Hudson Speedway (which he would soon also own) on Sundays. He formed a mini-Merrimack Valley circuit, in so doing boldly severing himself from the outside racing world. The rift with the successful West Peabody Speedway—also a Saturday night track—would grow deeper. Intense competition brewed between the two nearby facilities over the next eight seasons before Peabody was closed.

Ridlon still worried about the fickleness of the jalopy associations. He did headline jalopies and bombers as his key drawing cards, but he peppered the programs with weekly big car shows and midget stock (Crosley) competition. The big car races did not bring many entries. Oscar himself, now nearing fifty, won opening night. He flashed his old time showmanship with a drama on July 4th weekend when he flipped the #99 open wheeler clear over the starter's box, landing upside down in a smoldering heap. Somehow amidst the dust and smoke of the crash, he crept out, undetected, and watched from the concession stand with a coffee as the track crews searched wildly for the car's driver before an anxious crowd.

Jerry Russo, Art Rousseau, and other hot shoes appeared from time to time, but The Pines' own Hank Dodge was the real big car dude.

An early entry from Merrick's garage in Haverhill. It was pretty, but it weighed too much. Buddy Merrick cut it up. *(Bud Merrick Collection)*

Leo Richard and Hugh McGovern (in "Ray's" helmet) earn trophies. Marty Harty, the car owner, remembers all the cards and phone numbers the handsome Richard would receive from ladies. "I just can't understand why my brother Johnny and I never got any," laments Marty. *(Harty Collection).*

Stock car fields, however, did begin to swell, fueled by interest from local teams. Lucien Foote, one hard-driving customer from Seabrook, dominated opening night and won the season point race over the talented Hal Carrick of Lynn, Newburyport's Art Nicholson, and Johnny Dodge. Known for cars—including the Dudley Diner yellow #59 from Salisbury, that often seemed to smoke, Foote's only setting was flat out. Typical was the night he rolled over several times, landing right side up, motor screaming. He kept right on going, never taking his foot off the hammer. Foote's style was in direct contrast to another newcomer's that year. Jerry Dolliver, the New Hampshire State Ice Racing Champion, soldiered to his first asphalt feature win on August 26, with his calm, measured approach behind the wheel. Other winners were Speed Sullivan, Don Yeo, Earl Bentley, and the great Paul Finlayson. "Cowboy Jack" Lovering of East Hampstead was very quick in a pickup truck-bodied racer, #1/2, crewed by Buddy Merrick, Ron Sylvester, and Deacon Vencis.

As a promoter Ridlon would need that toughness he had learned as a driver. On September 13 jalopy chauffeur Bill Flynn threw a wheel that soared high above the catch fence and landed in the grandstands, injuring two spectators. Most upsetting to everyone involved, however, was an incident on July 1. Snooks Wentzel of Reading, PA was performing a roll-over stunt during the Joie Chitwood Thrill Show. The jalopy feature was all lined up on the backstretch. All the racers watched, along with a sizeable crowd as Wentzel crashed to the ground upside down and his car burst into flames. The 32-year old was trapped inside and burned to death.

Just as at Westboro and Norwood, there were pressures at The Pines over the rules in the early fifties. Some constituents were clamoring to go in the direction of the chopped-and-channeled early cut downs, bolting on multiple carburetors and all the new speed equipment then becoming available. But Ridlon was shrewd enough to real-

This is Jerry Dolliver's first asphalt car. Pictured with him are Bob Merrick, his neighbor and long time mechanic, and the great Art Sprague. *(Dolliver Collection)*

Paul Starta Jr., son of The Pines former promoter, became a journeyman jalopy man. *(Slater Collection)*

ize that over a few years he could use the rules to his advantage and end up with a field that could compete only at his Pines-Hudson circuit. By 1953 he was policing the cars carefully, allowing just a minimum of body and engine modification for his own nearly formed United Race Drivers Club.

URDC's technical inspections stirred up friction between management and the competitors. Ridlon responded with his usual approach of buying individual loyalty. He purchased the allegiance of another promising teenage driver, just as he had with MacLaren, in classic Ridlon fashion. After suffering through a season or two of poor performance and savage wrecks, Roy Eldridge finally found himself up front one night. When the tech man announced he wanted to see Roy's motor, Roy fumbled around saying he had no tools to take it apart. He knew he was illegal and he loaded up and went home with no money. During the week, Oscar quietly paid Eldridge in full, making him promise to race at The Pines and not to tell anyone what happened. Eldridge, everyone's favorite, raced on for Ridlon for years.

Roy Eldridge first ventured to The Pines in 1950 at the age of 15. Other than some time off for the service, he ran for the URDC each year up to the 1965 strike. Today he runs a restored super on the vintage circuit. *(Lowes Collection)*

The spring of 1953 saw the arrival of another Ridlon ally in The Pines, and she was to remain his constant companion through thick and thin. Originally a "temporary supervisor," 27-year old Florence Hudson of Lawrence was publicly anointed track manager on June 13. Over the years she acted as a calming social interface for Ridlon the Gruff. John Smith, a standout modified driver from Wilmington who began driving under Flo's watch, says succinctly, "She was the Matron Saint of racing."

As The Pines' local roster expanded, another arrival on Memorial Day was even more noticeable to the spectators. It was a storybook-handsome speedster by the name of Ollie Silva, on his way to rewriting racing records

A racing motor pierced the air one weekday afternoon in 1953, and Ken Smith, then a eighth-grader, hopped on his bike and boogied down to the track to see what was up. There was Ollie Silva, all by himself, new to The Pines, testing out a red #1 coupe out of Tommy Tidd's Georgetown emporium. Smith was thrilled that Silva talked to him – in fact, he asked him to go buy some oil for the race car. Smith's impressions remain crystal clear today. In his omnipresent sunglasses the tall, dark athletic-looking driver was cut from a different cloth from the usual Pines competitor. He was pleasant enough, but at the same time carried an air of quiet intensity and the seriousness of the ex-soldier he was.

Born to a Portuguese farming family in Topsfield, one of nine girls and seven boys, Silva was no stranger to hard work. He labored endlessly, growing vegetables and trucking them to the Boston markets until the farm was claimed in the early fifties to make way for Route 95. The rigors of farm life contained his aspirations even after a couple of years at Tampa State University in Florida studying mechanical engineering. In later years Silva would tell Russ Conway, "All a guy needs is a nice car, nice clothes, and a little jingle in the pocket."

Back from an Army Corps of Engineers tour in Europe, Silva was at The Pines intent upon continuing the racing he had started earlier at Dracut in the Mancuso Garage car. This time he wanted to do it well and he was willing to commit any necessary effort. He would often be seen at The Pines over the years, all alone, seeking some small advantage. More Saturdays than not he would quietly pull in in his uptown road car at noon, long before the fray. No one watching, he would sweep all the pebbles and loose rubber off the second groove, often helped by idolizing local kids. Asked years later by Wes Pettengill why he spent so much time at it, Ollie responded, "I made my living on the outside." He commented to Dick Berggren that, "You get exactly out of racing what you put into it. You've got to be sharp and

Ollie Silva bangs up the #94 Mancuso car out of Lawrence at Dracut. It was not a happy experience. *(Slater Collection)*

to believe you can do it. This is one rough business." He knew full well that for stock car racing to provide for even his simplest wants in cars, clothes, and cash, he would have to excel. Big time.

It was also Silva's nature to slide out when the races were over. It was off to the Arlington Diner, rather than hanging around telling tall tales and drinking beer, the normal post-race activity even at The Pines, which had no beer stand. Silva was considered a loner even by some of those who worked with him most closely. Ray Farnell was central to the #1 car, the #99 that followed taking Silva to his first wins, and then the breakthrough Little Beaver coupe. Farnell tells how Silva would come over to Georgetown each afternoon, thoroughly focused on the car, polishing it religiously every week. But all the

They say the Little Beaver was the car that really started Ollie Silva. It had already won big time at Norwood. *(Slater Collection)*

Jim Slater Jr. and Sr. border Ollie Silva in the pit meeting at Manchester. (Slater Collection)

while he had little interaction with the crew. He seemed shy and mysterious, almost unto himself, opening up only in long conversations with Ray's wife Mary.

Farnell, Tidd, Teddy Belanger and all Silva supporters even then would agree, though, that on the track it was a very different matter. After one lap you could feel his "attitude." His natural talent was enormous. "I always kidded him about not being able to see with those sunglasses he wore even then. But the truth is he could see an accident two laps before it happened. He was that good," says Farnell.

Hal Carrick, Dick Sewell, Johnny Dodge, and Jerry Dolliver made it difficult for the determined Silva to reach the front that first year. However, on the last night, August 29, he was not to be denied. He manhandled the #99 to a popular victory. It was precursor to the hundreds more Ollie would earn over the next 25 years, almost always to applause from both the stands and the pits. The better announcers would incite the enthusiasm, chanting "Hi Ho Silver" over the PA system. The Pines announcer, Danny Wilson, eventually nicknamed him "Quick Silva" and that mention would create an instant buzz of electricity among the fans: "There he comes out of the pits, Ladies and Gentlemen, Quick Silva in the Big O!"

Silva was, of course, not the only one to seek advantage by extra effort. Ridlon's increasing technical control over the cars forced good teams to go to extraordinary lengths in pursuit of speed. Jim Slater's guys worked under-the-table relationships with local hospital employees to get ether supplies, which, mixed with aviation fuel, gave the old flathead engines quite the pop. Freddie Borden, a decisive jalopy winner on the North Shore before going to Westboro and Norwood, sighs today about the countless hours he spent polishing the inner workings of his 85 horsepower Ford to make it "frictionless." Groton pilot, Lee Hurd, like his twin brother Art a winner at The Pines, did setups without locking the rear end in an effort to make his car completely "free." A totally successful owner/driver in 1953, Hurd entered 130 races (prelims included) and won 110 of them in a pretty—and apparently "free"—#00 Ford square top coupe that he saved and has since donated to the Smithsonian Museum. Much like Oscar but unlike most drivers such as Silva, Hurd was also serious about business. He soon won a bid for the concrete form work for the famous Levittown housing development, a project he leveraged brilliantly, bringing him great financial reward.

When Hurd was hurt in 1954, it is not altogether surprising that Ridlon hired him to be tech man and to bring some technical order to The Pines pits. The hostility had become steamy. Hurd's approach was no nonsense. He claims to have eventually established some respect for the rules after sending a number of stars—including Silva—packing for infractions. One year was enough, though. In 1955 he returned in part to his driving exploits, but more completely to his thriving business interests.

Even the tension in the pits was outdone in 1954 by high drama on the speedway itself. Twenty-four cars would usually start the feature that 12-event summer. The action went over the top on July 17 when Dick Ford, charging for the lead in Buddy Merrick's #8 with a lap and a half to go, had one of the worse wrecks ever in the history of The Pines. Tom Stone wrote "The starter's stand was completely demolished, two light poles sheared off, and starter Wally Faulkner cheated the Grim Reaper with a last second leap." Ford's legs were both severely cut after going right through the firewall. There was no motor left in the chassis when it was over. However, the same car and the same driver won the heat race at Manchester the next evening. "We didn't do much sleeping then," comments Merrick with a smile. The race was won by Plaistow's Woody Woodchuck. "He was one hot

(left) That's Buddy Merrick inside his flyweight #8 coupe usually driven by Dick Ford. The car sure looked differently when it got home the night of July 17, 1954. *(Bud Merrick Collection)*

(right) Red Castor in the famous #191 coupe. The LaBonte family and their East Lynn garage welded up some of the finest cars in the history of The Pines, and their #181 and #191 cars became central to its folklore. *(Slater Collection)*

Ollie Silva called him "Good and Mean." Harry "Hurry Up" Harriman drove this car for Dick Jaffarian of Haverhill. *(Conway Collection)*

driver," remembers Red LaRoche, "but a wild man. He would cruise around in that coupe with his head hanging right out of the window".

The year turned into a dramatic race for the URDC point championship. Although Woodchuck, Trigger Watson, Dick Sewell, and Johnny Eaton all tasted triumph along the way, the real contest matched Red Castor, Hal Carrick, Jerry Dolliver, and Ollie Silva. Castor and Carrick, teamed in the #191 and 192 cars from the East Lynn Garage, were that year considered high buck outsiders by the provincial Groveland fans. Haverhill's Silva and nearby Kingston, NH's "Doll" were considered little guys and clearly the crowd favorites. And, as if it were a promoter's dream, it all would be resolved on October 2 when Oscar had scheduled a 100-lapper.

The highly anticipated century grind ran under green for 44 laps, allowing the hot dogs to motor through the pack toward the front. Suddenly, any semblance of order evaporated. Harry Harriman and Dick Sewell, who was about to be crowned Hudson's champion, tangled on the second turn after several laps of high-stakes bumper tag. Harriman jumped from his car and pummeled Sewell. The fracas turned into High Noon, as the pits emptied onto the track to do combat. Equilibrium finally restored, a dramatic four-car race ensued with Carrick and Castor running one/two. Gentle Jerry Dolliver's third place finish was enough, however, to earn him The Pines title for the year.

It's easy to understand how a couple of winters in Florida at engineering school would make a big impression on Ollie Silva after spending his younger years battling the vagaries of New England weather on a truck farm. By 1954 Ollie was going south each winter often with

Bob Cloutier whom he had met at Manchester. Ahead of his time not only with motors and springs, he was also a very early Sun Bird. Based in a modest garage in St. Petersburg, he became a well-recognized star at tracks such as Hialeah, West Palm Beach, Golden Gate in Plant City, and Sunshine Speedway in St. Pete. He competed against such stalwarts as Frankie Schneider, Pancho Alverez, Larry Brazil, Bill Ronyon, Frank Riddle, Dave Scarborough, and Bobby Allison.

When Silva headed back North on a Friday in May of 1955, he must have been eating nails with anticipation. After selling the Little Beaver #3, Ollie and the Georgetown boys had put together a shortened, black #0 square top coupe. It was fast. And now on the trailer Ollie had another little square top to try. Again #0, but this time nicknamed "Super Cat." Everyone assumed he would be red-hot, and he was. But Silva was not the only one with a good ride that year. This was the height of the transformation of the jalopies to the cutdowns, and there had been a lot of cutting and welding done during the winter months.

Forty year old Archie Archambault, forsaking for once his trademark #54 cars, was driving the Taffy's Luncheonette car out of Newburyport, a clean #425 coupe Archie built for Registry officer Gordon Little. The two made their intentions perfectly clear by winning the first two weeks. Hank Kiazim of Goffstown in the Bardahl Special #50 was hot. They say he could adjust the timing of his pancake distributor from the seat. Also upfront were Don Lawler in the #162, and Larry Seidel wheeling the Mal Hallett Special. Chet Kauns, Dick Gadsby, Wes Taylor, Barney Atherton, Cy Parlin, and Wally Chapman were also factors.

Bigger fields and somewhat bigger crowds were pulling in on Saturday nights, but it was not tea and crumpets. Oscar's insistence on defining (sometimes quite capriciously) his own rules plus his

(left) By the time Silva built the Super Cat in St. Pete over the winter of 1954-1955, he was totally committed to racing. It showed. *(Smith Collection)*

(right) Car owner Gordon Little's wife, Bertha, was a big Powder Puff winner in this car. So was Archie Archambault. He was good at The Pines, but at Dracut one year he won every race they entered. *(Caruso Collection)*

(left) Jerry Dolliver in his #24 with the Morton-Welch Flathead that likely won more races than any other motor in New England. *(Bud Merrick Collection)*

(right) Hank Kiazim, always a strong runner in the pretty Blaine Special in 1956. *(St. Hilaire Collection)*

grumpy reluctance to dish out purse money the racers considered reasonable seemed a foil to what was going on right down the street. West Peabody Speedway was at the height of its popularity with the fans. And it paid the racers better and had a much more tolerant rulebook.

Quite a few folks had already left for Peabody, but the situation was really highlighted when good guy Jerry Dolliver, The Pines' track champion, defected in 1955. In April of that year Oscar's boys checked over the Dolliver-Merrick #24 and its Morton-Welch flathead. It was okayed, and the team won a few shows. Then at midseason, the officials suddenly took exception to the Denver heads on the car, and they sent an infuriated Dolliver packing. On his way he went. He continued winning, thank you very much, at Westboro and Oxford Plains, as well as West Peabody. Over the next five seasons he won nearly 100 features using the same engine.

New drivers, of course, were coming along, most usually starting out in rather understated circumstances. Jimmy Martel, legendary racer from Ipswich, most definitely was a poster child of the inauspicious beginning.

Jim and Barbara Martel had just married in 1955 when the upstairs neighbor in their apartment building, Leo Comeau, came bounding into their flat, full of beans, because he had just purchased a Class A race car. For $40. And Jimmy, who had never seen a race, was tasked with getting it to that track in Groveland. Over to The Pines they went in a hay truck and it took just one warm-up lap for Comeau to decide forever that he was not born to drive a race car. In Jim's words, "I was concerned about how we were going to pay for the hay truck ride. Phil Roy, the handicapper, told me to take the car out and go one lap. I'd get tow money. Then, wouldn't you know, he put me on the pole. My right foot was shaking uncontrollably when Kenny Small did his dance and waved the green. I floored it, hooked

the shifter up in second, and never lifted. All over the track for sure, but still ahead after four laps. Every lap, though, I was going higher and higher, faster and faster, and finally I sucked into the sand between three and four, flipping big time over the bank and down the other side. Everything broke and the seat flew out from between the floor boards with me still strapped in. What a mess! Then I was sitting there next to a crashed car and everyone was running up to me and saying, 'Hey, did you know you were leading?' Well, with all those pats on the back, I figured I had to fix the car and go racing." He sure did, though it would take "Gentleman Jim" four more years to begin his long list of feature wins.

(left) Bobby Edwards, "The Alligator", drove this cutdown. It has been beautifully restored by Lloyd Hutchins in Barre, VT and now runs the vintage circuit. *(Hutchins Collection)*

(right) Hal Wilcox in an Ed Bowley machine in 1956. Note the drive shafts used as nerf bars doubling the exhaust collectors. *(St. Hilaire Collection)*

Other first-timers in the summers of '55 and '56 included Al Riley, the great Buzzie Bezanson, and Bob Cloutier, while first time-winners included Artie Young in a Haverhill-based #42 car called "Chilly Willy." It was crewed by Buster Hamel, Ralph McKinnon, and Ray Abbott. Also winners were Parky Parkhurst of Wilmington, Bobby Edwards, feisty Charlie Sullivan, Hal Wilcox, Porky Kinsman, and Smokey Boutwell. Wilcox and Kinsman were closely watched as they piloted cars campaigned by noteworthy owners. Wilcox, a forty-year old former midget and Medford Bowl runner, was at the helm of the #5 Tewksbury Auto Parts entry fielded by Ed Bowley. A tough, no-nonsense figure with little to say about anything, Bowley grew a robust business in scrap metal. His time off was dedicated to quarterbacking a world-class race team, first with the cutdowns and then the super-modifieds. Sequin, Boutwell, and a host of others would wheel "Flying 5s," though likely not with the prominence, success, or notoriety of Bentley Warren.

Hard-partying Porky Kinsman, who years later would toast merrily to his twilight successes at Westboro, drove the #444 in 1956, built and owned by Andy Cote. Cote was savvy and industrious with a lim-

Big Starter Small

When Oscar Ridlon first took him to the races to help out in the pits right after the war, family friend Ken Small was hooked immediately. Before the season was out, he was behind the wheel of a midget and in later seasons a big car.

The driving part did not go well, and by 1954 Kenny had yet to win a feature. However, his passion for the oval still ran wild. His answer was to do something even more dangerous. Working mostly for URDC and then NESMRA, he became a colorful, highly recognized starter who flagged more than 10,000 races from Florida to Canada over the next thirty years.

Kenny Small's style was that of the old time matador. Very much respected by the competitors, he would send them off on their parade lap with a friendly tap of the flags on their hoods. He would say, race after race, "Okay, boys, it's time to roll 'em out." He would then size up the field from right on the straightaway and leap high into the air waving the green. Hardly anyone would take a full breath until the whole pack had passed him.

Over time, Small paid dearly for his abandoned approach to his duties. He was hurt many times, the most serious of which was at Hudson the Sunday before the 1965 URDC/NESMRA strike. He was hit in a figure eight race in an accident that many thought was fatal. Ruptured spleen and broken bones healed, he was right back at it.

In 1976, the race papers carried the news that Kenny Small had died. He was driving his tractor trailer on an early Monday morning through a toll booth near Hackensack, NJ, when he slumped over with an apparent heart attack. He had come off a double header of flagging for NESMRA on Saturday and Sunday nights. He was the last of a brave breed.

NESMRA selected Harry Harriman to assume the Chief Starter position at Star. Harry did not have to "hurry up" off the track when the field went by, however. He wisely stayed right up there in that elevated flag stand.

Given where he started the races from, Kenny Small had to be very quick on his feet to miss the growling pack. Most of the time he was. *(Conway Collection)*

Ed Bowley and Bentley Warren attempting to conjure up yet another super modified win in the eighties. *(Berggren Collection)*

itless bag of tricks up his sleeve, some legal, some not. He is said to have been the type who simply expected his hot rods to win.

The Pines' Bombers also had an influx of talent. Over the next decade, the complexion of the division would evolve dramatically from six-cylinder non-Fords to wild, overhead valve V-8 powered creations with steamroller slicks. Wheelmen ahead of the curve included John Hendrickson, Froggy Kneeland, Don MacLaren, Brice Haskell, Frankie Carter, Sully Sullivan, Choppy Baldwin, Carl Perkins, and Al Duff.

The overall health of The Pines slowly improved over the summers of 1956-1959, but promoter Ridlon's standoffish style meant there was constant tension with his URDC membership. Sometimes there would be rumors of an impending driver strike, and Oscar would hurriedly schedule a midget or a pleasure car special for the next week, just in case. Jerry Russo, Ray Burke, and North Reading's Bill Randall were hot in the little jobs at the time. It was on such a midget night in 1956 that Russ Conway first came to The Pines. The seven-year-old's dad was a midget fan from way back and he brought his boy over to watch Bill Randall. It would be a hard call whether The Pines ended up having a bigger impact on Russell Conway—or visa versa.

Russ was snagged hook, line, and sinker by the lure of the oval that first night. Now Associate Editor of the *Lawrence-Eagle Tribune* in North Andover, he was apparently of the persuasive type from the get go. Before long he had organized the kids in his Haverhill neighborhood to race soapbox-type hill runners, all painted and lettered like A-cars at The Pines.

In 1957 Oscar tried something new. Building upon his occasional pleasure car races, he initiated weekly "spectator races" in which fans

Russ Conway with Ernie Gahan on his right. *(Berggren photo)*

in registered street cars would compete as the final race of the evening. "From the first night they were pretty wild," Conway recalls. He's right. On June 15, Tom Doucette, a high school football player from Haverhill, flipped his family sedan near the starter's box. The seventeen year old was thrown from the car, which continued flipping right over him. Luckily, Doucette escaped with only arm and shoulder injuries, but his parents were likely unimpressed with the appearance of their car the next morning.

Years later Conway himself drove in a spectator race in one of his trademark Corvettes. All was well until suddenly his rear view mirror was filled with the front bumper of Paul Richardson. Not good. As a track official Russ had had Paul black-flagged in the previous event. "Fast?" laughs Russ. "You cannot believe how fast I got off that race track!"

New winners included some of the area's greatest, Parky Parkhurst of Wilmington in the #212, Buzzy Bezanson in the #64 from Plaistow,

(left) Here's Smokey Boutwell in the cab of Paul Abbot's #11, ordinarily driven by Carl Perkins. Harry Hansen drove the #111 team car, while Sonny Perkins was in the #71. *(St. Hilaire Collection)*

(right) Bobby Dean was a successful racer from 1959 right through 1973. In Kendall Smith's words, "Nobody messed with Bobby Dean." *(Lowes Collection)*

Art Young, Doc McKenzie, and an infrequent visitor from Foxboro, formidable Freddie Schulz. Choppy Baldwin, Charlie Sullivan, Harry Hansen, Len Shuster, and Moe Bolduc were Class B victors.

Crowds in the 2500-3000 range were reportedly becoming commonplace, and now and then Oscar really went home with a stash. One such night, August 11, 1956, a throng estimated at 7,000 watched Archie Archambault scamper off with the main. The show was so well attended that earlier in the evening heat races had to be delayed to allow everyone to park and find a seat.

Certainly the competitors were aware of Oscar's increasing ticket sales and they were also thinking about the increasing costs they faced. Overhead engines were working into the local scene, and the cars were becoming lower and lighter each year. It was update or be beaten. Updating was expensive.

Still Oscar clamped his iron fist around the rules—and the purse. He kept his rules a little behind those of West Peabody and other area tracks, attempting to keep his cars at Hudson and The Pines. Saturday nights were often not happy times for Amesbury's Phil Roy, a former driver who became tech man. Jim Martel tells how guys would literally bang into Roy's wooden officials' tower, shaking it with their bumpers, expressing their anger over technical inspections. It was during the summer of 1958 that the strength of Oscar's conviction and authority really became obvious.

Ollie "Quick" Silva was by now at the top of his game, as he would be for another twenty years. In 1958 he made the switch to Andy Cote's #444 which had been vacated by Ernie Gilbert. Cote sometimes painted the car black with a zero with respectful reference to his new driver. With Lowell's Mike Pappas turning some wrenches, the team was a terror and a definite fan favorite.

On June 7 the drivers, Ollie and Art Young as spokesmen, approached Ridlon for a bigger purse. Ridlon refused bluntly and

(left) "Hurry Up" Harriman in the Hardy Auto Body coach out of Rowley. Red MacDonald, now the owner and promoter of Lee Speedway, remembers pulling the motor out of a hulking '49 Oldsmobile for this car. *(Charles Hardy Collection)*

(right) The Merrick Brothers' last car. The creature on the side is a reference to Sonny Merrick who was quiet as a mouse, but invaluable to the maintenance of the car. Sonny never went to the races. *(Bud Merrick Collection)*

defiantly. However, as the owners began hooking up their trailers to pull out, Oscar is said to have relented and to have offered a 50-50 split of grandstand receipts, up from 40-60. He had a deal.

Beware the wrath of Ridlon, however. The very next week Silva and Cote were suspended by URDC for running at an Atlantic-sanctioned show at Westboro. In a split second the hyper-popular Ollie was out the door, off to West Peabody.

The absence of one of their key players made the natives no less restless, especially when Oscar allegedly began monkeying with the purse again. Over the next few weeks the drivers organized further and formed the Twin State Drivers Association under the leadership of Leo LaRochelle out of Plaistow. LaRochelle was the high profile owner of the very fast "Lakeside Special" #9, built by Buddy, Sonny, and Kenny Merrick and driven by Dick Ford. This time Oscar didn't wait for threats. He took quick action, tossing the stock cars out of The Pines on their ear and bringing back the NEMA midgets for the July 4 weekend.

The midgets remained in town for the next month with Maury Dumas in the announcer's booth. Bill Eldridge in Gibby Parmenter's V-8 60, Dick Brown in the Al Monast Offy, and the rain played starring roles.

By the second weekend in August the Cannonball had shelled and destroyed Twin State's spirit. Most all of the cars meandered back. Some guys were reasoned about the whole thing. Archie Archambault said philosophically, "You know, Oscar was a businessman. Like everyone else. Things aren't always good. One night at Dracut I ran four races and got paid $3.00." Smokey Boutwell hustled the Bowley #5 to laurels in four of 1958's seven remaining shows. Parky Parkhurst took home two and a surprising Al Riley won the last night. Leo "Tippy" Byron, Carl Perkins, Paul Bergeron, and Don MacLaren topped the bombers.

(left) Still Water's John Hendrickson was a good runner. His orange and white spit fire got it done at both Westboro and The Pines. *(Balser photo)*

(right) Tippy Byron of Haverhill had a good career in bombers and cut downs. His son, Dick, is a pro stock racer today. *(Hurn Collection)*

Saturday April 25, 1959 was a history maker, much to the delight of a good but chilly opening night crowd. The two starring chauffeurs could not have been more different in temperament.

As Kenny Small unfurled the feature green, Eddie Skofield and Parky Parkhurst entered a lead-swapping duel that lasted until a restart when Parkhurst blew a tire. On lap twenty Bedford, NH's Al Riley sneaked into the lead driving his #50 cut down. Riley had started out right in the A division back in 1956. He produced well-tooled cars and was known as one of the cleanest, smoothest drivers on the URDC circuit. His style was so smooth he sometimes seemed to be holding back, but he had turned heads with his win the previous fall.

Almost immediately Riley was challenged by Frankie Carter, a nine-year veteran from Tewksbury. Given the cast of characters at The Pines over the years, rating the most hammer-down among them would be no easy task. Carter, however, would most likely end up near the top. One evening in May of 1958 he flipped wildly out of the ballpark and into the pits during a bomber prelim. Then in the A main he performed a spectacular triple end-for-end over the fourth turn bank and down onto pit road.

When Carter caught Riley, he went to the high side, and the two roared to the only dead heat feature finish ever at The Pines.

Opening days were big for Frankie. On the Easter Sunday opener at Hudson the next year, he was hospitalized with serious injuries when his seat belt broke in a horrifying crash, demolishing his A car. While recuperating Carter decided to concentrate on the B class. This he did with a series of rugged white #20 coupes and coaches. He kept his same right foot, however. He once told Judi Boutwell, "I can't even

Al Riley, left, and Frankie Carter, right. *(Hurn and Conway Collections)*

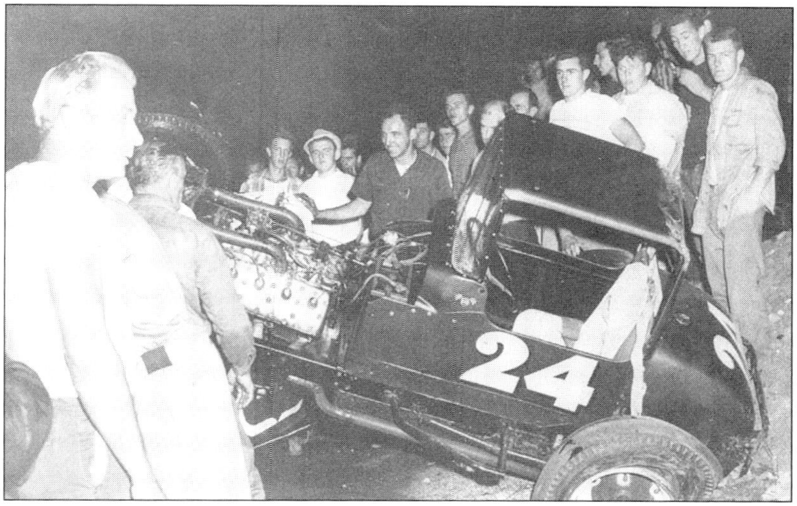

(left) Junior Prescott built this pretty little cut down for Jerry Dolliver in 1959. It, too, housed that same Morton-Welch flathead. *(Dolliver Collection)*

(right) Brian Dolliver tries it out. He runs a limited super today with Skip Armstrong who used to help his dad. *(Dolliver Collection)*

count the number of times I've rolled them over. But I have improved with practice. I was the only class B that didn't roll over in 1962."

Because the stands were more populated in 1959, Oscar opted for a twenty-seven event schedule, and the year rolled on less emotionally than the one before. Boutwell, a visiting Silva, Roy Caron, Archie Archambault, and "Cigars" Olsen were additional winners over the long season. Ridlon's late close on October 17 gave outsiders the chance to tour The Pines, and on that night the lion roared. Leo Cleary, Hall-of-Famer from the Norwood area, attacked Groveland in Andy Smith's #99 and snarled at the locals on his way to victory. Sully Sullivan, Len Shuster, Paul Bergeron, Lee Allard, Bobby Dean, Al LeCerte, Choppy Baldwin, Dick Wendell, and Red LaRoche won 1959's bomber shows.

Like his friend Ollie, LaRoche was just an occasional racer at The Pines these days. He'd sometimes run West Peabody, load up right

Lowell's George "Choppy" Baldwin drove this coupe with great success as well as a number of "LL" cars in subsequent years. He was the URDC Class B champ in 1957. *(Hurn Collection)*

The Mayor of Randolph

You can take this to the bank. When you ask any old Pines fan about the guy they nick-named the Mayor of Randolph, you get a great big smile in return.

The diminutive Al Crockett began racing in the mid-fifties at the suggestion of the Randolph, MA Police. They thought it better for the refuse business operator to wreck cars at a race track rather than the previous locations he had chosen. He turned into a gutsy Norwood ramp racer.

Perhaps with the arrival of NASCAR and its "high hat" approach to racing at Norwood, Crockett decided he should tow all the way up to The Pines and Hudson. They were surely more his style. The spunky, unkempt Crockett became an immediate hit on URDC, typically wheeling enormous, black Chrysler product sedans numbered 94. His best year was 1962 when at 43 he won The Pines Bomber championship and was second at Hudson. His 12-year old son, Alfred Jr, was his top wrench.

Forty years later:

John Spence: "What a showman! He'd get spun out and he'd keep his leg in it. If it meant going backwards down the chute till he hit the turn, he would and then snap it around like a Chitwood driver. When he'd go through the corners, his head would come out the window. Down the chutes he'd pull it back in. He was a real character. I hope Oscar threw him a few because if he didn't he should have."

Mike Sargent: "He was the clown prince of racing. I swear that every week he showed up with a different car. When he knew he wouldn't have to, he just left one in a barn in Hudson for the next weekend."

"Nasty" Neil Murray: "Some say he just crashed and never won. That's not true. One time he bought an old Haskell coupe from me. He came to my house in Woburn to pick it up. What a scene that was, but you should have seen the roll of hundreds he had in his pocket. Wow! He put a Hemi in that car and he trucked the freight. He won a lot of races."

Russ Conway: "Crockett became a cult hero. He was always smiling, always showing his one tooth. And, I'll tell you this, he had the all time record for number of flips—anywhere."

Paul Wellington: "Maybe he got accustomed to flipping. I saw him turn a car over in the pits at The Pines one night to work on it."

Joe LaRochelle: "One night Al flipped going across the line at The Pines winning the feature. Oscar Ridlon really liked that. He and Crockett became good buddies."

(top) Al spins in front of Dick Edgerly and Don Monaghan at the Hudson opener, March 31, 1963. Water from the melting snow was running down the fourth turn banking. *(Boyd Collection)*

(left) Rocket Crocket poses with Miss Norwood Arena in 1959. *(Balser photo)*

(left) Red LaRoche was a fine driver in the fifties and early sixties, who has endeared himself to all of the racing community. For many years, Red has been a selfless aid and support system for Ollie Silva following his horrible crash at Monadnock in 1978. *(Balser photo)*

(right) Bob Cloutier poses in Joe Fisek's cut down. Cloutier was a fan favorite who became heavily involved in the launch of NESMRA. *(Hurn Collection)*

after his feature, and hustle up to Groveland, hopefully in time to fall into the back of the feature lineup at The Pines. On September 19 he won. Another autumn evening was not as perfect. Red's #00 coupe broke and came to a stop next to the starter's box. Lee Allard drilled him full-tilt boogie. A pipe running from the cab of the #00 to the back bumper dislodged and smashed through the driver's seat, through the firewall, cleaning off the carburetion and flying into the sand bank, LaRoche was fortunate to just "lose a chunk of flesh from my side."

Things had not worked out so luckily in an incident on the Fourth of July. Robert Pederson, crewman from Melrose, fell from the rear of a bomber being pushed back to the pits after the feature. Pederson, 28, was rushed to Massachusetts General Hospital in Boston where he died.

When the points were tallied for the year, the flying florist, Ed Skofield, was crowned champion of both Hudson and The Pines. Skofield and his wife Barbara had over time become among the most popular and respected players at The Pines. His accomplishment was particularly significant in that he pulled it off in a flathead-powered car, a #30 fielded by Don Donovan of Haverhill.

When Oscar Ridlon woke up in the dawn of the sixties, he was feeling chipper about his URDC circuit. With good reason. 1960-1965 became what can only be considered the Golden Age of stock cars in the Merrimack Valley. There were many reasons for this crescendo of interest in racing, some under Oscar's control while some other factors were entirely external.

The most obvious change over these years related to the construction and appearance of the cars. Fans came to follow with new excitement who would show up with what equipment. The main cat-

(left) Ed Skofield is ready to wake everyone up in Eddie Blaine's infamous #110, the Stove Pipe car. *(Hurn Collection)*

(right) Billy Murphy stuck with the flatheads longer than most. He was aggressive—the type who'd grind you, but not actually bang you. Don MacLaren considered Ollie Silva and Billy Murphy his biggest competition. *(Hurn Collection)*

alyst was the powerful overhead engine, the noisiest example of which was Ed Skofield. Following a brief lapse after his 1959 title in a flathead, Eddie took over the controls of a #110 cutdown owned by Eddie Blaine that had previously been driven by Mark Gazaway. It was called "the Stovepipe Car." Much to the thrill of the fans, its potent overhead engine would literally explode out the king-sized exhaust collectors, echoing for miles, each time he backed off for the turn.

An exceptionally capable bomber graduate, Lee Allard from Hudson, NH, was also leading edge when he came through the gate in 1960 with a pretty '32 coupe with a thundering overhead engine. Strong runner Bobby Edwards responded by carrying on the winning #444 tradition with style. His copy was "The Ace Express Special" wrenched by Louie Mechalides. Jimmy Martel appeared with the famous Andy Smith A-frame car, renumbered #14. Mike Murphy, Woburn's popular phys-ed teacher, parked the Edwards Welding coupe when the Woburn gang downsized to a tiny pink overhead-powered unit. Essex marina owner Eddie Perkins, a standard-setting builder, designed one of his beautiful creations, a '32 square coupe for

Phil Roy, the techman standing on the left, scratches his head about Lee Allard's trendsetting "Lil Wonder." Allard was a talented driver who became a noteworthy owner fielding potent modifieds for Geoff Bodine. *(Hurn Collection)*

Eddie West takes Mike Murphy and followers into the turn. *(Conway Collection)*

Billy Murphy. And Sammy Sanborn was back with a new #"?". His car had a musical seat, and some of the players were Parky Parkhurst, Dick Wolstenhume, and Sammy's son, Roger Sanborn.

By 1963 the pits were also dotted with so-called "rail cars," a kind of Pines hybrid of the space frame design. Forrest Dame built such a rocket, leaning on what he had learned the previous summer out at Oswego with Don Maclaren. Johnny and Hank Duggan welded up two, the #1/3 and #2/3. Several very brave men would sit in the 108 inch orange and white #1/3, but none as often as Nathan "Smokey" Boutwell who steered it to fifteen victories. A less frequent but formidable runner was the great Bud Crotty, then in the blue #41 Jr. rail job out of Stoughton, MA owned by Dick Mann and sponsored by Simonds Chevrolet. Crotty was especially fast at Thompson, CT.

The new focus on technology led for the first time to multiple cars with the same design. Pioneer builders in this part of New England were Frank and Bill Barthell. Former drag racers, in 1964 they turned out five beautiful chasses in their Dracut shop, the first of which was

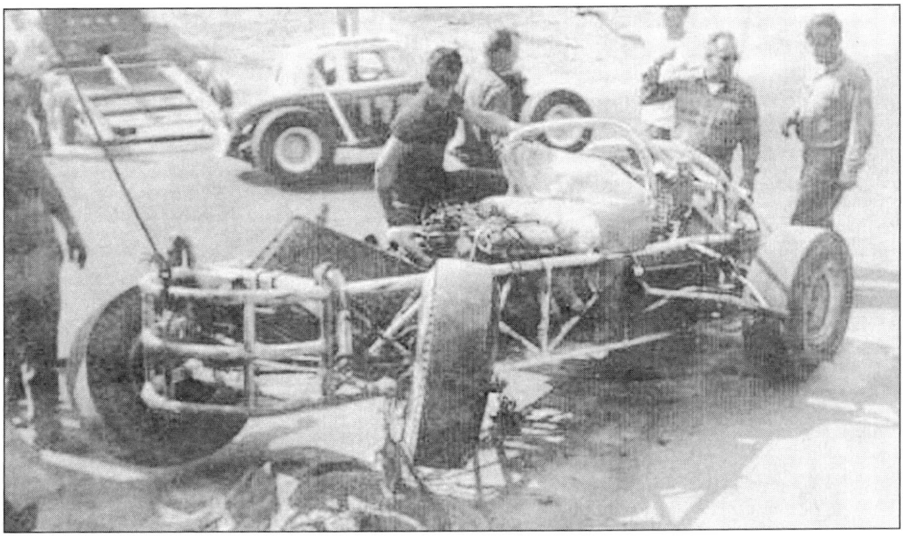

Smokey Boutwell with the Duggan/Wilmington Ford 1/3 railcar—and the car after a Cloutier crash at Hudson. (above, *Pettengill Collection;* right, *Conway Collection)*

(left) Eddie West started at Westboro in some sub-standard equipment. He was smart enough to know it. Two years after he came to The Pines, he was prepared. This Barthell chassis may have been just 289 Ford-powered, but the boys surely took notice. *(Boyd Collection)*

(right) Candy Allard probably had some words with Lee this night. He flipped his Barthell "twister" car big time down the Hudson front stretch shearing the roll cage right off the car. Remarkably, his injuries were not life-threatening.

Ollie's smile inside that coupe is clearly contagious. Could it be he is psyched about his new fuel injection system? And how about that box over the top of it! *(Hurn Collection)*

Lee Allard's # 1/4 , "The Twister." Their most famous one may have been Eddie West's high-winding, cobra-powered #61 Jr. that propelled the personable Westie to many of the early wins in his Hall of Fame career and earned him the dual-track URDC championships in 1964.

Everyone was in the equipment craze, and leaders had to stay a step ahead. In 1962 Ollie Silva returned from Florida with some wild looking tubes between the valve covers of his #0 coupe. He caused quite the stir. It was one of the very first fuel injection systems seen in the area. It would have been a good thing if injection had been more available a couple of seasons before.

⁘ ⁘ ⁘ ⁘ ⁘

During this rush for technology the number of carburetors on a motor seemed a measure of masculinity. Two became three, became six. In

Whitey Hoyt poses in his own car. He started in the fifties and won a few in his low-key way. The Concord, NH driver was real tough at Lee. *(Conway Collection)*

retrospect, it rings pretty silly. Fact is that many of the cars, especially in the initial laps of a race, were bogging way down from too much fuel. But there was a more serious side to it. Fitting up a linkage that will precisely and reliably control the gas/oxygen flow in multiple carbs is no easy feat, especially when exposed to racing conditions. A common result of a linkage failure is that it will not close. If that happens on a racetrack, almost by definition it means that the car is stuck wide open.

In the 1960-1964 timeframe URDC Class A cars often flew out of the sand-banked ball parks with their hapless drivers having no time or way to react. The seriousness of this situation became obvious back in 1960 when popular Hank Kiazim was killed at Hudson.

Kiazim was a veteran admired by many young drivers. That summer he was driving the #D3 offered up by Wilmington's Forrest Dame. Older than most in the sport and looking that way in his overalls, Damie had a long history in racing, deep into big car days. He was sharp as they come. He was unprepared for the tragedy, however, when the butterflies on the triple carb setup jammed, fatally launching Hank into the trees. The situation was especially poignant. Hank's wife, who had persuaded him to quit racing because of her

(left) Hank Kiazim, still with his Bardahl special helmet, sits in Damie's car (right) Don MacLaren then took it over, after sending his family down to Damie's garage to say it was okay. Damie fortified the rollcage on the same car, and Mac was off to many wins. (left, *Berggren Collection;* right, *Hurn Collection)*

concern about the danger, had recently passed away. Fighting depression, Hank had decided to return to his passion.

Four years later, on a cold September evening in 1964, the scene was rerun at The Pines. Charlie Coffin, a 23-year old friend of Howie and Maxine Brown from Epping, shot off the fourth turn, arched through the air and a chain link fence, and flipped wildly into the parking lot. His #117 Class A car landed broken, its jammed carburetion system on fire. He died of a fractured skull in the Lawrence General Hospital with his bride at his side.

In between the Kiazim and Coffin markers, there were many similar incidents—some injury producing, but none fatal. Jimmy Martel remembers it as, "So bad that I don't think anyone didn't have it happen at one time or another." Carl Tiberio, Archie Archambault, Ollie Silva, and Smokey Boutwell had particularly spectacular sky rides. And then there was world-class talent Bentley Warren, hands down 1963 URDC Class B Champion with 18 wins in Ernie McKay's Ford. Over the winter he and buddy Jimmy Carter struggled to produce a spiffy-looking #707 cut down. On his very first hot lap in warm-ups he went aerial. Long time crew chief Pete Hurn was right there. So were Eddie Skofield and Russ Conway. "A couple of us were walking down to the pits and varoom—Bentley goes flying right over us. We thought it was a plane. He finally landed, bounced and crashed over toward the Merrimack. We ran over, thinking he was dead. He was getting out, shaking himself off, and muttering, 'I just lost every penny I've got.' " Meanwhile, Ollie Silva was watching the whole thing. Hearing that Bentley was unhurt, Silva commented in his understated way, "The only thing that lies between that kid and Indianapolis is the river."

By the next week Bentley was back with a rebuilt car. By 1970 he was in the lineup at Indy.

(above) Forrest Dame was respected by all, because he had seen it all. *(Boyd Collection)*

(below) This mob scene surrounded the #117 of Charlie Coffin when it landed. Rescue efforts in racing have become massively more organized and effective. *(Pettingill Collection)*

Bentley at the Brickyard. *(Indianapolis Speedway photo)*

If Oscar was being uncharacteristically open with the Class A rules in the early sixties letting so much new stuff in the pits, he was even more so with the old bomber division. By 1960 the class had developed into a novel mixture of racy six cylinder coupes and coaches spiced up with some later model A-frame sedans with flathead V-8s. By 1962 many of the top cars sported overheads. By this time they were going very fast.

Just as Roy Eldridge, Dick Noel, Hank Duggan, Parky Parkhurst and the old guard in the A Division now squared off with wide-eyed newcomers like Lee Allard, Gonic's Jim Landry, and the parachuter from Chelmsford, Frank Conway, the seasoned B-car runners had a swarm of eager young throttle jockeys right in their face. The result was some of the most colorful and outrageous racing ever in those parts. Given the big motors and tires, the high center of gravity of most of the cars, and the varying levels of driver experience, anything could happen. Well-recognized stars like Brice Haskel shone. The long-time competitor from Nashua piloted blue and white #213 coupes labeled "The Bonnierick Special" to honor his two eldest kids. Howard Brown, a former Golden Gloves boxer, was a huge winner. His "Woodchopper Special" #069 coupes often appeared unmercifully beaten up, but they gave him all the training he needed to excel immediately in the cut downs when Bentley Warren offered him a ride. Zany, fun-loving Bob "Barn Rat" Devaney also did his bomber time—some days in victory lanes, some days rubber side up before moving to the A class. Haverhill's Bob Bixby, Jeff Arnold of Lawrence, Ipswich's Wally Buzzell and Don Monaghan, Bill O'Brian from Hamilton, Doug Henderson, and Jackie Whelan. One of the most outrageous acts was a three-car show presented each week by Bob Morin of the Brandy Brow Junk Yard in Plaistow. The hulking sedans, called "the

Frank Conway seemed to have found some cheap square tubing when he built this car for 1964. *(Conway Collection)*

A bundle of bombers: (ltop left)) Butch Tiberio; (top right) Dick Edgerly and the "Triple Nickel"; (middle left) Howie Brown; (middle right) Don Monaghan just before he went cut down; (bottom left) Brice Haskell who started driving at The Pines for Mun Cody of Dover; (bottom right) Bill Aramian, Buzzy Bezanson, Art Young, and Brownie Duchemin. *(Hurn Collection, Conway Collection, Hurn Collection, Lowes Collection, Lowes Collection; Hurn Collection)*

Untouchables" and numbered #24, #25, #26, were wheeled by John and Phil Beauvais, Froggy Kneeland, and Dick Edgerly.

The loosening of URDC's Class A and B rules in these years was in no way attributable to some softening of Oscar Ridlon, now approaching sixty. Instead, the reasoning came from the outside. The once-thriving West Peabody Speedway was in trouble; it was in fact going out of business. The winds of change were blowing.

When Jack Peterson moved to Peabody in 1955, he remembers it as a rural area, spottily marked with mink and chicken farms along Route 1. When his dad took Jack and his brothers Dave and Freddie to the races to watch Jackie Dodge or Red Sequin, in the family's # A21 cut down, they visited a quarter-mile West Peabody oval that seemed miles out in the boonies. Not so just five years later. Urban sprawl already lapped at the sides of Sam Magarvaro's track. It did not take many Saturday nights for the new neighbors to squawk about the noise and unruliness. Never mind that the race track had been there first.

What pushed the tension level over the top was an unfortunate decision on the part of track management. Anxious to milk a little more revenue from their facility, they began hosting go-kart races on Wednesday nights. That might not sound too bad right now, but apparently it did then. Powered by deafeningly loud McCulloch chain saw engines, the tiny karts drove West Peabody into the ground. By 1961 it was essentially covered over.

For The Pines, of course, this was huge. With no other Saturday night venue as close, Oscar's crowd had the potential to more than double over night. Today Lenny Maughan, son of Leo "Doc" Maughan who drove the overworked ambulance at The Pines for years, is running annual Pines reunions with Dwight Lowes, owner of the popular Checkered Flag Raceway, a slot car track in Merrimac and Claire Walsh of the Groveland Historical Society. Lenny recounts what happened in the early sixties, how traffic on Routes 113 and 97 would be backed up by mid-afternoon on Saturdays as new fans tooled into Groveland in their big-finned cruisers.

Ridlon had been wearing long pants for quite a while. He knew to make hay when the sun was shining. He ran lots of shows. Some of his endeavors today seem like logistical suicide, but he pulled them off. The prime example may have been what he came to do with great success on Columbus Day. He would jam up the town with a fourth

Byfield's Jackie Dodge towers over an injected DeAlmeda cut down, late into his long racing career. He was agressive and intense. It is said that one night at the Pines, he agreed to a match race with Ollie Silva during intermission. He was so upset when he lost that he loaded up and went home. *(Hurn Collection)*

quarter championship in the afternoon. People would then have to leave and re-enter for a 100 lap open competition that very night.

The mobs of excited fans, the new horsepower of the cars, and the wave of young drivers—and experienced ones from West Peabody, all contributed to The Pines' continued tradition of feistiness. Stock car tracks were not sophisticated environments in the fifties or sixties, especially not Oscar's. The pecking order in the pits was established according to the right foot, sharp wit, and closed fists. Weekly brawls were as much a part of the show as in the early fifties, still very much encouraged by "Showman" Oscar. As if to maximize the excitement, Ridlon appointed an incredible announcer named Danny Wilson.

According to Russ Conway, "Danny was absolutely the one who put the plug in the socket and brought the electricity. He had a colorful nickname for everyone. He was the dude with his little handkerchief around his neck. Just like a Brit. One night a bomber flipped and caught fire. Danny saw the driver escape, but he repeatedly screamed over the PA for the fire truck to quell 'the burning inferno and save that poor guy.' Later that night I was sitting in Ollie's car having a beer with Danny. A woman came up and slapped him one hard, right on the noggin. "You monster," she yelled. "That was my husband. What did you think my kids and I were thinking up there in the grandstands!?"

On June 20, 1964 the 50-lap Oilzum Trophy night presented Wilson with a storybook opportunity to get the fans stirred up. That year Skofield was in a brilliantly quick #18 owned by Jack and Tony DeAlmeda. Eddie, normally the gentleman through and through, was in seething mode about an earlier incident with Big Daddy Don MacLaren at Hudson. Following a spirited race, Skofield slammed MacLaren (in his own #30) and pushed him T-bone style through the first and second turns. Mac jumped out of the car, ripped off Skofield's visor, and started swinging. Wilson, meanwhile, was in his element, winding the crowd up like a fiddle string. Wes Pettengill, now a major vintage race supporter on the North Shore, remembers being

(left) West Newbury's Dick Noel was among the most liked of Ridlon's drivers. His owners have included Ed Hamel, Lenny Caron, Milt Holland, Eddie Vandercaster and Sam Sanborn. *(Hurn Collection)*

(right) Steve Newman's bomber is loaded up in Gloucester ready for car wars at The Pines. Steve progressed in to the supers and even competed at Oswego in a radical rear-engine machine. Today he runs a web site, www.thepinesspeedway.com, from his business, Speedway Welding Supply. *(Newman Collection)*

Jack DeAlmeda, left, bee-lines for Don MacLaren. It took Police Chief Shanahan and his "Tiger Taming team" a bit of time to calm this one down. *(Conway Collection)*

flipped out. "I was just an innocent kid. I couldn't believe what I was seeing. It looked like a guy was being strangled in front of 5000 people and the announcer was throwing fuel on it!"

It worked. Everyone went nuts. In a flash the DeAlmeda Brothers—and half the pits—came running out to take on Big Mac. Finally everything settled down through the efforts of two Groveland cops, Hector Grazio Jr and Sr. (Grazio Jr. used his experiences at The Pines to his advantage and is now a Massachusetts State Policeman). Tony DeAlmeda and Big Daddy were arrested. The following Monday the hellions appeared in Haverhill Court, below the bench of crusty old Judge Arthur Thompson. Mac pled "guilty." "$25.00," snapped the Judge. When asked how he would plead, DeAlmeda, a Rowley pig farmer still in his dungarees, said "Your Honor, I did hit him. I am guilty. But I want you to know that, if I had known it was just gonna cost me $25, I would have really whaled him."

(bottom left) In 1964 Mac shoed his own rig, an advanced #30. He was also a master constructor. Racing ran in his family. His dad used to race at Rockingham. *(Conway Collection)*

(bottom right) The #18 Jack DeAlmeda car was state-of-the-art, built by Ray Harmony. It was metallic blue with a chrome front axle. Billy Murphy drove the #8 owned by Tony DeAlmeda. *(Lowes Collection)*

Despite the shenanigans Saturday nights, by the next week tempers had usually cooled. In fact, in 1962 an interesting sociable side of The Pines' racers was brewing.

By this time Ken Smith and Russ Conway were well known in the pits. After a brief fling behind the wheel, Kendall married and dedicated himself to his promising career as a banker. Almost as a way to keep his hand in racing, he began to write results for a local paper, the Haverhill Gazette. It was something welcomed by fans and competitors alike. There had been only minimum newspaper and radio attention to The Pines. Oscar's attitude was the media was an enemy, intent only on selling him an ad or running a negative article. Russ Conway, ten years younger than Ken Smith, had picked up on the same void. Just a teenager in the early sixties, he would hitch a ride to the races with the Skofields, hurry home to peck out the results on an ancient typewriter, and rush them off to the Journal, the competitive local paper. Fortunately, there was some photography available. Dick Yemma snapped shots from the mid-fifties to the mid-sixties. John Halloran, owner of Victory Tool and Die and sponsor of Ollie Silva in later years, was also active with the shutter.

Smith and Conway, both articulate and extroverted, became buddies. They started attending informal Tuesday night get-togethers at the Heidelberg in Methuen, long a favorite hitching post for thirsty racers on the way home from Hudson or The Pines. At the outset the meetings were entirely sociable. There was no agenda other than beer and bench racing. Attendance grew over 1962-1965. The two organizers Silva and Cloutier would be there and Tiberio and Westy. And flamboyant Big Daddy would frequently pop into town and buy all the drinks.

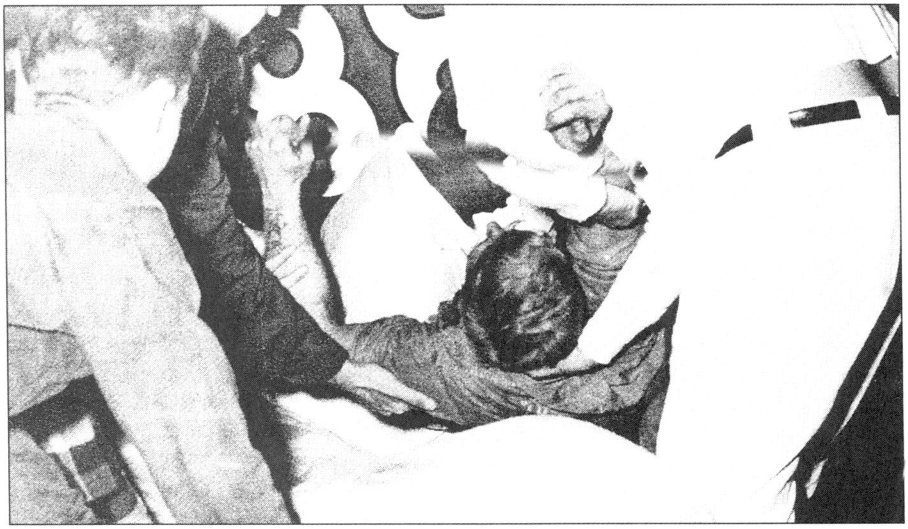

An unconscious Bob Bixby is loaded onto a stretcher following a flip at The Pines. Many say Bixby didn't have a bad bone in his body, but for all the daredevil division driving he did, they surely were bruised. He died in a riding mower accident in the nineties. *(Boyd Collection)*

THE PINES

A Fan's Perspective

By Wes Pettengill

It's difficult to relate to those who weren't on board during the early 1960s just how strong an emotional pull The Pines had for us Baby Boomers. Looking back, we can see all the components that made that Saturday night bull ring our Fenway Park.

Way ahead of his time, the announcer played the villains and heroes hype to what can only be compared to a modern day wrestling promotion. Danny Wilson brought us to our feet with our fists shaking and enough noise to leave us hoarse on Sunday morning. We wouldn't have expected to see the professional image of a first class starter at our local track, but Kenny Small's showmanship (and leatherette bow tie) were yet more ingredients. Scores of guys in high school spent many a boring history lesson daydreaming about the coming weekend. A doodle of a slanted "O" or the crude image of a certain blue three window coupe got us through the class. We would donate our allowance to the family's newspaper subscription just to be able to jump off the school bus and grab Thursday's edition. The walk up the driveway meant that Russ Conway's article was half read before reaching the front door. Oscar had what he must have envisioned all along—entertainment with a hook. Our level of passion is verified today whenever there is a reunion. Beaming fans share countless scrapbooks, photos, and vivid memories. A testament to just how fortunate we really were. Danny Wilson was our Curt Gowdy. The Tiberio Brothers were the visiting Yankees, and Ollie Silva was everybody's Ted Williams.

Ahh, the memories:

One of the grandstand vendors would bark "Ice cream here. Make your liver quiver, make your bladder splatter!"

Danny Wilson's favorite song for intermission? "Under the Boardwalk."

Follow your nose to the restrooms and you would find signs reading "Guys" and "Dolls."

Remember the call to the photo and novelty stand? A wave of the checkered flag from the stand would acknowledge Danny's announcement.

Dusty parking lot? True, but we had to be cool driving in on Saturday afternoon. That meant polishing the cruiser, knowing full well it would be a mess on Sunday morning.

We'd drive home from the track believing that we could have won the feature. The West Newbury cops were ready. "Whaddyathink, you are at Pines Speedway or something?" Well, yeah…?!

The Silva-MacLaren rivalry began at The Pines and lasted for years. Silva's cars benefitted by the engineering - savvy John Yellard. *(Conway Collection)*

Ron Hebert started with a nail-head Buick, but switched to a Chevy. He was third in points in 1964. *(Duncan Collection)*

"Man Mountain" Moe Farmer was a definite factor in Bob Bouchard's potent supers out of Salem, MA. *(Bouchard Collection)*

Whether in Bombers or cutdowns, Bob "Barnrat" Devaney was a lot of action. *(Lowes Collection)*

Bruce Parkhurst's square top was just as fast as it was pretty. *(Lowes Collection)*

URDC had a weekly news flyer in the early sixties. Paul Richardson was cover boy this time, parking Chet Richardson's bomber vertically next to a 4th turn pole. Chet, no relation, went on to field the infamous "Cyclone 5", driven by Jim Cheney and Paul's brother Ken. *(Conway Collection)*

By 1965 the level of humor at the Heidelberg was dropping. It was obvious that Oscar was doing real well. Yet there were these persistent stories such as the one with Ridlon, Carl Tiberio, and the light socket. And Oscar had recently been playing a tiresome diversionary tactic. Kendall Smith smiles as he tells how The Cannonball purposefully delayed releasing any money until the wee hours, saying that he had to "figure out the finish." Lots of guys opted to go home and to see if they could collect the money the next day at Hudson. This time lapse is just what Oscar wanted. It took attention from skinny payouts.

Then came the crowning blow. By the spring of 1965 Oscar had purchased Arundel, an inconsequential asphalt track on Route 1 near Portland and Beech Ridge Speedway. His plan was to bump his URDC weekend to three nights, Arundel on Fridays. Trouble is, good guy Charlie Elliott was running Friday night races right down the road in Dover, NH. Everyone liked Charlie, and he paid, it seemed, two times as much as Oscar. On Sunday night June 19, Phil Roy announced at Hudson that anyone who ran Dover on Fridays would not be allowed into The Pines or Hudson. That Tuesday night the Heidelberg was abuzz. It was time to confront Ridlon. There was a lot of back and forth about who would be spokesman. Bentley Warren was selected, but he declined. He did not have the heart to do it because Oscar had just had a whole string of tickets fixed for him. "Then I put my young little hand up," says Conway. "I figured, 'Hey, I'm just a writer. I'll just tell him what the boys want.' I knew he wouldn't be happy, but I didn't really think it through."

By 6:30 on Saturday evening June 26 lines of fans at the ticket windows were stirring. Something was wrong. The weather was perfect, but there were only B cars in the pits. The A's were all down the street, all lined up, still on their trailers, Silva and Cloutier acting as leaders. As Flo Hudson tried to deal with the fans, Conway supported by Carl Tiberio sought out Oscar and told him the boys had a demand. It was

Bob Cloutier and Johnny Duggan. *(Conway Collection)*

simple, one sheet of paper, saying "Summer Pay Off—$400 to win, $300, $200, $150, $100." Oscar looked at it for all of one second, threw it on the ground and stepped on it. He grabbed Russell by the ear and dragged him over to two cops. "Take this kid out to the front gate. I never want to see him in here again".

This was the most dramatic moment in the history of The Pines Speedway. The strike was on. This time it would not be broken.

Bentley Warren always had a way with the lassies. *(Pettengill Collection)*

With Smith and Conway acting informally as coordinators, the strikers formed a loose-fit group called "The Supermodified Club." Even the name was significant. It pointed to a new day. The A cars were no longer just "cut down" coupes and coaches; they were now totally custom built creations, hand-crafted from the ground up. Kendall called around and booked as many shows as he could. Seekonk bought one, and Faulkner obliged with some Wednesday specials at Westboro. "It was short money," says Kendall. "The winner got $100 and everyone else $50." Charlie Elliott, however, was consistently supportive at Dover, maintaining his generous payoff and keeping the Club alive.

That winter Smith, Conway, Silva, and Cloutier, still fully committed to independence from URDC, formed a corporation, the New England Super Modified Racing Association. NESMRA then signed for a season at Bob Bonser's triangular Lee Speedway on Route 125 in New Hampshire, right next to his nudist colony. It was a barnburner lift-off season with NESMRA's first year end classic event paying a stunning $2000 to win. Carl Tiberio was the first NESMRA champion.

NESMRA had taken from Ridlon the top twenty or so teams. One of their most important new assets, though, was a huge and very public rivalry that was heating up between "Quick" Silva and "Big Daddy" MacLaren. The socially retiring, but charismatic Silva with his friend Bob Cloutier were now intent on racing full time and they strove to build the professionalism of NESMRA. Ollie insisted that even his crew be properly presented in white shirts and black pants. He would win 179 NESMRA features. Meanwhile, Mac remained Mac: Quick-tempered, irreverent, aggressive and upfront. For nearly twenty years these two New England greats could not start a motor without firing up the other. This on-going tension added much drama to the field of fire-belching supers. It was a marketer's dream.

NESMRA used it well. Over the next twenty years under the sleepless guidance of Smith, Conway, and new partner Charlie Elliot, the organization produced over 1,000 promotions from Canada to Florida and eventually owned Hudson, Star, and Lee Speedways. Along the way it turned its Merrimack Valley cut down drivers into nationally known figures in supermodified racing.

(left) White Hat. Ollie Silva was committed to taking racing uptown, so he sought to look presentable. Personally that is. Sometime in the seventies his cars looked kind of shabby. Until he passed you! *(Conway Collection)*

(right) Black Hat. Big Daddy was committed to not much else than hammer down. *(Berggren photo)*

Meanwhile, Oscar stuck to his guns. "He never thought we would make it," Smith recalls. "It's just that we were young enough to be energetic and not smart enough to know how difficult it would be." But the fact is Oscar had taken a hit from which he would never recover. A full complement of B cars did keep him going through 1965. Over the following winter he tried to pull in more Class As with some result. Jerry Dolliver returned to The Pines from an unsatisfying run with NASCAR at Norwood with Junior Prescott. Jerry drove a pretty little #29 cut down coupe owned by Butch True and "Deuce" Dusseault. Mike Murphy in the #28, Al Riley in his Prescott built #50, Frank Presutti in Damie's Blue Streak, Sully Sullivan in the Bob Edwards #444, "Man Mountain" Moe Farmer in the Bob Bouchard #297, and Bruce Parkhurst in the #250 all decided to stay at The Pines. Paul "Ricochet" Richardson was just up from the "Bs" and he won right off the trailer in his #5 cut down, formerly an Al Rileymobile. His brother, Ken, who brought Paul to racing, opted to go with NESMRA. Over time outsiders would straggle in, but fields were hurting. Often the same cars would run more than one heat.

There was a particularly tense moment in the Memorial Day show in 1966. Tinker Progin tried out the banking near the pit gate in a '29 Ford-bodied cut down built by Vic Kangas. The car flipped and blew up, Progin stuck inside. Scrappy Artie Rousseau from Ipswich broke

(left) The year of the strike, Silva drove the challenger #191 for the LaBonte's of Lynn's East Lynn Garage. Ed Duncan, a researcher for this book, was a crewmember. Ollie later bought the car and renumbered it #0. *(Hurn Collection)*

through the faltering rescuers, jumped into the flaming wreckage, and pulled Progin out. Progin was taken to Hale Hospital and treated for multiple burns. An unappreciated Rousseau had to be bailed out of jail by Ridlon. Apparently the police had not liked the way he broke through their ranks to reach the fire scene. In the end the race was won by Dover's Lou Harton, a journeyman performer who was killed in a late model at Lee in the seventies. Dave Grantz won the "B" feature, followed by Rick St. Onge, Brice Haskell and his inadequately funded "Bonnierick" #213, and Ken LaPointe.

Once back from the slammer, Rousseau, dramatically younger than most of his rivals, continued his dramatic racing pursuits. Sons of a jalopy driver, Russ, all three Rousseau boys, Charlie, Artie, and Stevie, have been racers. Artie began in 1963 in a bomber owned by Gene Trask. As well as showing his stuff behind the wheel, Rousseau proved himself to be a master constructor. By 1967 he was Class A champion in his own machine.

(below left) Butch True and Deuce Dusscault glued up this "Red Devil' for Jerry Dolliver. It was a big winner. Butch and Deuce subsequently went NASCAR modified racing, working with Ernie Gahan and Lou Austin. (Duncan Collection)

(below right) Teaming with True/Dusseault/Dolliver was Georgetown's Paul Richardson. Paul came through the bomber division like a meteor and won the in the A's immediately. Butch True says, "Paul was a natural and he simply had no fear." *(Duncan Collection)*

Same Start, Different Tracks

They were typical baby boomer kids, born right after the war on the North Shore, and they would soon be neighbors on Rt. 97 in Georgetown. They became great friends, each driven by boundless energy and captivating personalities. They chased girls together, they drank beer, and they discovered The Pines Speedway in the early sixties. Paul Richardson and Jim Cheney were also to become two of the greatest supermodified drivers in the Northeast.

Paul Richardson scored his first car by inheritance. His brother Kenny gave him a bomber when Kenny was asked to drive Chet Richardson's (no relation) cutdown. The bomber was a clapped out 1957 Chevy that Paul promptly parked on its nose at The Pines, inflicting serious damage. After Cheney, clever with a torch and welder from the start, pieced it back together, Paul was again in the hunt. The very next year, 1965, he hawked everything to buy Al Riley's "Little Princess." Paul chuckles about it today. "I had a wife, my first kid, and we lived in my Mom's house. We had nothing. Not even a road car. But I'll tell you this: I had the fastest race car around!"

Jimmy, too, started in a bomber, in his case a derelict 1950 Ford. Despite the interruptions of his early fun-loving ways and a call from Uncle Sam in 1966, his natural ability did catch the attention of some owners. In fact, it was Chet Richardson who first promoted him and assigned him to the chair of the Barthell-built Cyclone 5.

Both Paul and Jimmy were competent enough to catapult from URDC to the tougher level of Smith, Conway, and Elliott's NESMRA. Also winners there in a flash, the two buddies began frequent jaunts out to Oswego Speedway, the fabled home of American supermodifieds. They both had good rides, and it seemed nothing could stop them. In 1977, however, Jimmy had a sickening crash and fire at Oswego in the Holinski roadster. He was trapped upside down, and his burns were widespread and horrible, especially on his hands. Supported endlessly by his family, he endured months of painful rehabilitation. Then, in one of the most dramatic moments in racing history, he won the Thompson Ice Breaker opener the very next spring.

Over the years that followed, to those who knew him, it almost seemed that Jimmy's healing stopped—especially psychologically. He told me that he hated the physical look he had after the fire. It was somehow more noticeable to him than to others. He was also frustrated to be struggling financially despite the fact that he knew he was talented. He could do most anything he put his mind to, at one point building a fleet of winning V-6 supers from scratch with his partner, Bobby Witcom. Eventually, working as a truck mechanic for Bentley Warren, the color must have drained completely from the world he once knew. He quietly took his own life.

Jim Cheney *(Berggren photo)*

Cheney in Chet Richardson's Cyclone 5. *(Pettengill photo)*

Paul and Joe LaRochelle *(Bouchard Collection)*

Paul Richardson *(Lowes Collection)*

Paul Richardson's career involved modifieds and late models in addition to supers with hundreds of attendant victories. In an incredible coincidence, however, with scary similarity to Jimmy, Paul stuck a throttle at Star Speedway. It was a 100 mph wall shot in the infamous NAPA Auto Parts Supermodified. With a broken back, foot, and multiple miscellaneous injuries, Paul, too, spent a full winter in hospitals and rehab and family support. Just like his neighbor he was back at the track opening day the next spring. So was the NAPA super. Incredibly, he also won.

Richardson took a successful fling with the BUSCH North Tour around 2000, but eventually withdrew from competition. He had other things to do. He had a large and very engaged family. He had been buying and selling residential property, and working his garage and used car business. His wife Maryann runs a busy salon and day spa. His favorite saying is something poor Jim Cheney would have had trouble following. "I'm gunna pack everything I have into every second I've got. I have learned this for sure: life is no dress rehearsal."

(left) Mike Murphy stuck with the URDC for a couple of seasons before moving on to NESMRA. He continued racing well into the nineties, mostly in late model sportsman and pro-stock cars. He may well be the all-time feature winner at Hudson. *(Duncan Collection)*

(right) Tinker Progin had multiple wins after the strike in the Vic Kangas tooled #0. On Memorial Day of 1966, however, the car got too hot to handle. *(Lowes Collection)*

(left) Somerville's Bobby Powers checks the watch, following a carb test run with Jerry Chaille. Powers was one of Oscar's top bomber guys in the late sixties before he left for NESMRA and the Super Modifieds. *(Berggren photo)*

(right) Dave Grantz was a bomber specialist, one of URDC's best. In future years, he became a support division star at Monadnock Speedway near Keene, NH. *(Conway Collection)*

Over the winter of 1965-66, Russ Conway received a surprising phone call from Oscar, who was definitely concerned at this point about a declining fan base. "Hey Kid, when you are not off with NESMRA, how about doing those write-ups for me?" URDC/NESMRA friction aside, Conway was a race enthusiast. He accepted.

The next winter Ridlon reared up again. In March of 1967 he invited Ken and Russ for an evening at the place he shared with Flo Hudson in South Lawrence. It was a long night. Florence ended up

Young Ronnie Bouchard ran at The Pines briefly before taking on the A-frame cars at Seekonk in 1968. *(Lowes Collection)*

getting out of bed at 5:00 in the morning to make the three bleary-eyed guys breakfast. With whiskey.

Ridlon had come as close to baring his soul as he may have ever done. He talked of his own racing career and he banged out a few tunes on the piano. The aging Cannonball even arm-wrestled Russell, forty plus years his junior, and won. Oscar urged Russ and Kenny "not to spoil things. Just pay 40% of the front gate. All the back gate is for the promoter. And don't run those huge year end classics. In the end big buck races will hurt you."

During the wee hours an honest friendship developed between the three. It grew to the point that a series of URDC-NESMRA challenge races were held—three at Hudson on Friday nights and one at The Pines. (Ollie won The Pines feature, his last in Groveland, in clever Dave Kane's #01). For whatever reasons, the shows simply did not draw fans. The friendship did not become a collaboration, and the NESMRA crew did not alter their course. Neither did Oscar.

At NESMRA's opener at Star Speedway in 1968, Don MacLaren was unusually frisky, even for Don MacLaren. After not being allowed to leave pit road late for a race, Big Mac once again climbed from his car. This time track official Ronnie Sylvester and long-time friend of Ollie Silva was recipient of the punches. The two rolled down the banking of the track fighting in front of a packed grandstand. The police broke it up, and Mac was tossed out of NESMRA for the year. He ran The Pines and blistered them. Later in the summer Ed Bowley appeared asking that the suspension be lifted. A committee of Buster Taylor, Dick Batchelder, Russ, and Kendall decided to let him back for the

Kendall Smith hams it up as host of any early NESMRA function. *(Berggren photo).*

Woburn's Dick Cail drove, crew chiefed on a number of cars, and campaigns a Pro Stock today. *(Berggren photo)*

Classic. Wouldn't you know it, Big Daddy won in Bowley's car, snatching the checker from the late Gary Whittier. The $2500 first place money was at that point the most ever paid in comparable racing history.

Still seeking to pump up his devastated "A" lineup, Oscar was soon back to the side deals. Artie Rousseau had left The Pines to run Star on Saturdays in 1968. For 1969 he needed a new car. One winter day Oscar called him and summoned him to Jamaica Plain. He opened one of his garage doors and there sat a storied car, the Bud Shirk Offy Sprinter, complete with spares. "I didn't know what he was doing or why he seemed to like me, but I took him seriously. He wasn't that big. He just had that square jaw and voice of authority," says Rousseau. He told me "take this car. It's a four cylinder, but you will win. Give me half of what you make and at the end of the year you will own it. But you have to run The Pines." Ridlon was spot on with his prediction. The time-honored car served Artie well for the next two years. In 1970 he was a four-time Class A victor, surpassed only

Artie Rousseau at speed in Oscar's sprinter. Artie's dad took one look at the car and said, "Arthur, if you're gonna run that car, you're gonna put a cage on first." Arthur obeyed. *(Berggren photo)*

Paul Wellington. *(Lowes Collection)*

by seven impressive wins by John Parkins. Parkins was driving the last Forest Dame car, previously shoed by Woburn's Dick Cail. The car had been parked following a ghastly accident at Hudson. Beverly's Frank Presutti, Big Daddy, Dick Cline, and Connie Yanuszewski were also winners.

The B division, temporarily called the Modified-Sportsman class, was dominated by Vic Brokvist, Paul Matthews, Eddie Santisi, and Bob Luz. A popular captor of two checkers was Billerica's Paul Wellington in his #470 Buick-powered Chevy coupe. Bobby Dean, Bob Bixby, and Ken Smith (of Wilmington's Smith family of racing) showed the "Daredevils" the way around.

Remembering the South Lawrence all-nighter, Kendall Smith often repeats what Oscar had to say—"The worst thing that can happen to a race track is to look successful."

The Cannonball surely felt it when his boys scoped out the big crowds and went on strike. But it wasn't just the racers who had noticed the big mid-sixties attendance. It was the town, too. Additionally, Oscar had come up with a deal to ship gravel from The Pines to the construction site of the Logan Airport extension. It took load after load. Artie Rousseau tells how Oscar hired him to stand at the gate with a counter to make sure that Oscar wasn't getting cheated. All these trucks and all this dust became the Groveland equivalent of the go karts in West Peabody. In Kendall's words, "by the end of the sixties the neighbors just plain wanted Oscar out."

As the negative sentiment grew around him, there was little motivation for Oscar to reinvest. The whole facility began slipping quickly into disrepair. The seat boards, lights, plumbing were at this point pretty much used up, and Oscar's low-cost patch-ups only brought more complaints. It was a bleak picture. With writer Russ long gone on

Sheila Hayes started at The Pines in Powder Puff racing. She advanced to URDC cutdowns and NESMRA supers. She was on the gas. Here she has flipped right out of the Park at The Pines, landing on Dwight Lowes' ramp truck. *(Lowes Collection)*

his NESMRA pursuits, there was little media attention at all given to the URDC circuit. Oscar certainly wasn't out there wining and dining the press. Little of the racing community even knew that for the 1971 season he quietly dropped his once proud Class A division completely. Racing was reduced to whatever machines The Pines could pull in for a Late Model headliner and a Daredevil division backup. A pretty motley group showed up. Paul Wellington summarized what a lot of the racers were thinking: "I wasn't about to spend any money at that point. I simply took the body off my coupe and slapped on a '57 Chevy shell." Charlie Rousseau, Artie's brother, won opening day. Bob McCarthy, Bob Gagne, Davey Grantz, Don Wilson, Brice Haskell. Frank Rzasa, and Warren Johnson saw checkers. However, the top dog for the year was Bobby Dean who won the last four in a row. Don Blanchard won four in the Daredevil class.

The stands were empty at The Pines compared to the new Star Speedway, just up Route 125 in Epping, shining bright with the NESMRA supermodifieds. One night Oscar got to see it for himself when the old showman accepted the limelight one last time at Oscar Ridlon Appreciation Night at Star. Put together by Charlie Elliott, Ken Smith, and Russ Conway, it was an outstanding evening of NEMA midgets and NESMRA supers. It sealed the friendship between old school URDC and the young and racy NESMRA. Both sides were acknowledging symbolically that time was going by. "In

Wally Buzzell was quick in Ron Marcorelle's coupe. *(Lowes Collection)*

looking back at it all now," reflects Ken Smith, "it is amazing to me to realize how much of what Oscar had to say was actually true."

From a competitor point of view anyway 1972 was looking a little better at The Pines. Herb Simpson, Russ Nutting, Jeff Stevens, Howie Lane, Al McClure, promising Mike Weeden, Roger Sanborn, and Dave Simard ran there. Two future greats, Dave Dion and Peter Fiandaca, were new winners. John Smith won the first two Daredevil mains.

Something about the summer, however, seemed way off. A short 14-show season was over following an August rainout. "Fireball Joe" LaRochelle, a long time contributor to Val LeSieur's *Speedway Scene* newspaper, was for fifteen years an important—and varying—Pines player. He was a driver, a flagman, he worked on the track crew, and he did all kinds of odd jobs for Ridlon. In thinking about 1972 Joe remembers that Oscar just didn't seem to be around as much, and nobody knew why. It was only by chance that Joe learned that Oscar was undergoing dialysis.

The Cannonball was quiet about his illness. It was his style. Showmen usually are about their own affairs. Apparently, however, he

Charlie Rousseau has been winning for an impressively long time. *(Newman Collection)*

Standing left to right, Charlie Elliott, Butch Walsh, Kendall Smith, Lou Fray, Oscar Ridlon, and Dave Humphrey at Oscar Ridlon Night at Star Speedway. *(Smith Collection)*

had every intention to soldier on and he opened in 1973, though late, on June 8. Herb Simpson and Dave Dion, both of Hudson, NH, and Bobby Dean won the three shows that were run off that rainy summer. The local papers carried just box scores; the racing papers received no releases. Oscar was really hurting. Soon he was admitted to the Lawrence General Hospital for an extended stay. In June he took a turn for the worse, struggling for several weeks. On July 17th he suffered a heart attack from which he did not recover, and Cannonball Ridlon passed quietly away.

Hobart Esty had as long an involvement with The Pines as anyone. At 15 years of age he cut and trucked the lumber from the site to make the early fence boards. In midget years he learned to score from Lenny Poe and he served as URDC's handicapper for years.

By 1973 Hobart was a Groveland selectman, as well as a principal of Esty Lumber. Knowing the long tradition of the site, he negotiated on behalf of the town, a purchase of the property from Oscar's estate for "recreation and future town development." The entire 38 acre river front property went for $110,000, a tiny fraction of what it would now be worth.

Today a few town buildings dot the rolling site, but it is largely dedicated to ball fields and well-groomed open space. It is amazing how much the area has changed. Road and railroad construction have made commuter access to Boston possible. Just down the banks of the Merrimack towards West Newbury, some of the most lavish, expensive homes on the North Shore have been built. It is SUVs and Volvo wagons. On Saturday evenings in summer, natty party boats cruise lazily on the river over cocktails.

It is hard not to think what would happen to those gin and tonic glasses if a good pop from the old Stove Pipe Car came reverberating up the valley just one more time. Or better yet, the untamed thunder of the Cannonball's Elto.

The Old Showman. *(Conway Collection)*

This photo shows the Norwood Arena tucked in behind US Route 1, between Boston and Providence. *(Norwood Historical Society)*

NORWOOD

Racing on the Auto Mile

MY GOODNESS, THINGS SURE WERE ANOTHER KIND OF SMOKE DOWN at Norwood Arena. Right from its conception and siting in 1947 and its construction in 1948, Norwood was very different from any other New England speedway.

Norwood Arena was located a dozen miles south of Boston, not far from the old Readville dirt track. It was built on an abandoned sewage disposal facility alongside US Route 1, that guitar string of a road weaving through coastal towns and cities from Key West, FL to Caribou, ME. In the forties this stretch was known as the Boston-Providence Road. It was good highway for the day, punctuated only by the occasional gas station. But given its proximity to Boston and direct convenience to Providence, it was only a matter of time before commercial creep connected the dots. Today the heavily traveled highway is crammed with stores and businesses, right near a famous strip of lavish SUV and foreign car dealerships known as the "Auto Mile."

You'd think such an accessible site at the edge of significant urban population would be the perfect spot for a speedway, certainly much better than the valley-locked site of The Pines or even than Westboro Stadium out there near Worcester. Historically, however, this has not always been the case for race tracks. Over the years in the United States stock car racing has tended to be much better attended where the corn grows. It might be that rural areas simply have had fewer entertainment options. At any rate, there was always a level of tension at Norwood about its real estate. As it turned out, that was for good reason.

Norwood was different, too, in the way it was built. This was no rerun of the Turgeons scraping deals together with friendly contractors at Westboro. Or Starta and Smith planning with the Esty Family to use the wood on the site of The Pines for seat boards. Norwood's approach was more thoroughly funded and uptown. A Board of Directors including Wes Plummer, Herb Anderson, John Peterson, Pat Toye, and Harry Butters offered shares in the facility that would be managed by Art Forrest. Over three hundred people invested, and right from day one the press releases spoke of "the new $1,000,000 Norwood Arena." That was a princely sum for the forties, even if significantly exaggerated. *Illustrated Speedway News* described the plush new arena with "every facility for the comfort and convenience of its patrons," including over 13,000 seats completely surrounding the track and infield area, special box seats, paved walkways with shrubs, an open air terrace, and even an elongated bar and lounge beneath the offices and tower. The ISN story carried on about the modern "lighting and public address systems laid out under Westinghouse supervision."

You have to wonder what in the world was the Board thinking by investing anything close to a million dollars in a race track. All said and done, it does not seem that Norwood shareholders were actually betting on a 'speedway'. Their vision was an 'arena'. In the welcome message in an early fan program, the first Board president, Dr. Francis Burns, wrote, "The Norwood Arena has been constructed for the purpose of presenting the finest in all types of outdoor amusements... Nothing has been spared in making this arena the finest in the country today." Norwood's management surely did intend to go after a broad agenda. Promotions in the opening years included weekly football, concerts, wrestling, model airplanes—and even barbershop harmony. Very tuned to the number of people going through any turnstiles, though, the Board knew they could ride the tail of that red hot post-war phenomenon, the midget craze. By no means did they expect the midgets to dominate Norwood's future. Truth be known, the real desire was to bring in the dogs. Most all of the original shareholders were actually gambling that Norfolk County would vote in pari-mutuel betting. Norwood, so well appointed with customer convenience, would become dog racing's flagship facility.

Just about any $2000-a-day management consultant these days would have a belly laugh about Norwood's strategy. Every business book preaches the importance of focus—knowing your subject inside and out, concentrating on it passionately, and offering the very best products possible. Here in Norwood the Board was going to lead with auto racing, something they knew very little about and hoped would be temporary.

Well, so much for the management consultants. Norwood Arena, opened the year after Westboro opened and closed the year before The Pines closed, consistently outdrew them both. Norwood became among the most famous short tracks in the country, launching a number of New Englanders to stardom as national champions. Its 25-year run lost steam only when the Directors—still uninformed about the business of racing in the sixties—made a series of poor decisions. It left the property fully exposed to the relentless reach of urban sprawl.

The first racing show went off at the million dollar arena on Monday night, June 14, 1948. Mother Nature rained on the track's parade that

Reading's Wild Bill Randall in Harry Hull's #15. *(Bob Sheldon photo, Silvia Collection)*

summer. The two previous Monday nights had been complete washouts.

Already the Board had more things to worry about than just the weather. That winter had been the time of the midget competitor discontent. Fields and crowds were down everywhere in 1948 in contrast to the boomer summer before. And, good times or bad, Monday has never been a good race night. But there was no other opening on the weekly midget circuit for the brand new Norwood facility.

With these problems and the recurrent summer drizzle of 1948, the season went by with just modest success. Attendance was approximately 4,000 per night. Just as at Westboro and The Pines, the well-funded teams took all the bacon, leaving the struggling local racers hungry. The great Bill Randall set the pace winning the first heat opening night, Norwood's very first race. Framingham's Johnny Bernardi, Johnny Thomson, and Joe Sostilio blocked him from a podium finish in the main event.

Jerry Clark (#82) and Milt Henry battle it out in old style uprights. *(Signal photo, Silvia Collection)*

Bernardi, a former motorcycle racer who developed over the years into one of Massachusetts's finest open-wheelers, leveraged his win at the opener with four others, earning him the first Norwood point championship. Bill Schindler was second with three wins. Dick Shuebruk and Frankie Simonetti also copped three each.

There was an unusual promotion that summer that certainly spoke to the cooperation between the area tracks that shared the midgets' weekly tour. He said he wanted to offer "the owners and the public... a greater understanding of the dangers the drivers face." So, Norwood's General Manager, Art Forrest, challenged Westboro's owner Roland Turgeon to three five-lap match races in midgets. Forrest prevailed in the first, held at Norwood, but Turgeon evened things out at the next show at Westboro. The final clash came on Labor Day night at Norwood. Apparently the two neophyte chauffeurs got into it big time. They flashed by the white flag, one to go, flat out and side by side. Turgeon crashed in a thrilling finish before an animated grandstand, giving the contest to Forrest. Happily, Westboro's owner was not seriously hurt.

Not being passionate racing people, the Norwood Directors were disappointed with the '48 season. As it turned out, a perkier promotional possibility was not that far away. Only twenty or so miles to the south was Lonsdale, RI, the site of the Northeast's first stock car races that had made such a big impression on Bill Welch and anyone else who had seen them. By 1948 Lonsdale was packing them in beyond belief. Fields were for a time limited to the first 200 jalopies through

The midget boys' night out. (left to right), Babe Stein, Bill Randall, Oscar Ridlon, Bob Blair, Ted Koopman, and Eddie Casterline. *(Webber photo, Caruso Collection)*

Johnny Black receives a trophy from widow Pat Casterline. In later years his salvage yard would be the source of many parts for racing scavengers. *(Caruso Collection)*

the gate while crowds swelled above 20,000. Lonsdale ran Sunday nights, so Saturdays were available.

At most tracks those days an owner such as Oscar Ridlon would also operate the show. At a few places such as Westboro, the property owner would lease the facility to a promoter. Knowing that they were inexperienced in matters of racing, Norwood's Directors hired racing clubs that could come in with the cars and the officials and make the races happen. Norwood management would sell the tickets, run the concessions—and the bar. At night's end the club would get the purse money to pay the racers. The formula was ordinarily 35-40% of the front gate, though some details seemed a tad sketchy. With the disintegration of Bay State Midget Racing Association, for midget racing the Board signed on in early years with the United Car Owners Association. UCOA was managed by Bucky Haynes, Bob Bullock, Ashton Cox, and Lenny Poe.

The Board quickly secured a stock car club anxious to deliver the slam-bang hard tops for the '49 season. Ed Stone, the pioneering speed parts entrepreneur, had backed down a peg from his own racing career. Himself a former big car driver, he had recently campaigned a world-class midget, the Stone Offy. It was wrenched by Bill Welch and exercised by the era's finest, including Billy Tibbert, Bill Randall, and Johnny Black. Observing the coming crescendo of stock cars, Stone held a meeting in the basement of his Belmont home with Bud Tatro and Andy Anderson for leading competitors and officials. They formed the New England Stock Car Racing Association, and Stone was installed as President and Business Manager. By opening day of '49, the energetic president had all his ducks lined up. NESCRA was at Hudson, NH on Tuesdays; Wednesdays at Avon, CT; Thursdays at both West Peabody and West Springfield; Fridays at Westboro;

There is little activity about the birth of stock car racing that did not involve Sammy Packard. *(Tibbert Collection)*

Saturdays at Norwood; and Sundays at Lonsdale. An appealing benefit to Stoney's endeavors, says Billy Tibbert, is that he was able to make sure that all competitors were properly insured.

Given all the organizational work the NESCRA team must have faced putting their circuit together, what they came up with for opening day on the Auto Mile was astounding. It was the longest, most difficult, and most innovative event ever held in the young history of the sport. Paralleling Boston's internationally famous April foot race, Norwood and NESCRA promoted a marathon of their own. It was a 24-hour stock car team race starting at noon on April 18 and ending up at noon the following day.

Twenty four cars barked at Lee Hiltz' green, each driver (save one) backed up by a relief driver waiting in the pits. The lounge area by the bar was lined with cots for rest. Downpours that gray April afternoon made the grinding competition vastly more difficult. Then during the night there were snow showers. Although there were few accidents, pit stops were frequent due to tire wear. Mac MacLeod reported that "everything was thick with rubber powder." It was pretty bleak. Some teams really went for broke, such as Joe Ross who brought Longy's #515 in for an extended stop during which the entire rear end was changed. Sammy Packard, a New England Hall-of-Famer, was known to have a twinkle in his eye. He showed up with a sprawling 4 door Lincoln sedan, displaying lavishly the colors of his sponsor, Elsa's Lodge in Pawtucket. The car had a radio to ease monotony. More significantly, perhaps, it was the only car to have operating windshield wipers. The most remarkable tale of the time was, no contest, Ralph Gurney. The New Bedford pilot proved beyond question that he was just as tough as he was fast. When his teammate Jug Menard took ill and was temporarily out of the picture, the Herculean Gurney earned

Ralph "Iron Man" Gurney and Tom Gifford. *(H. White photo, Silvia Collection)*

Ed Stone, with tie presents the spoils to Frank Litwin (left) and Red Cummings while Ed Flynn looks on. *(Gendreau Collection)*

his tag line "Iron Man" by soldiering through the entire event himself in his #60 Ford.

Three thousand five hundred and seventy two slippery laps and 893 miles later, Wenham's Harold "Red" Cummings motored across the line first in the Dynamite Special coupe. Cummings was teamed with Red Keizer. They beat out Billy Tibbert/Johnny Black and Sammy Packard/Dick Shuebruk and won a 1949 Ford sedan for their efforts. It was donated by area dealers including Paul Clark Ford.

The Norwood/NESCRA combo wrote up a busy schedule for the balance of 1949. There were over 40 stock car events, spread over Thursday and Saturday nights.

Because so many folks wanted to run at the plush new facility and because Saturday was usually the week's best race night, fields were overflowing right from the start. And, significantly, lineups were sprinkled amply with name drivers, many of whom were converts from the midget ranks. The Marathon winner, Red Cummings, was the most revered among them. The reigning New England champion, nicknamed the "Yankee Red Head," had entered 35 shows in 1948, winning 19. At Norwood he was teamed in the #42 and #43 cars fielded from the North Shore's Frank Litwin. A character in his own right, Litwin tooled his cars in a garage right in Salem center, out of the same building from which he broadcast his popular musical "Polish Hour" radio show Sunday. Neither Cumming nor Litwin considered second place in any way an acceptable alternative.

Cummings continued his romp after the Marathon and was the big winner in the first half of the season. However, other ex-midgeteers were all over him. One was George "Wild Man" Lewis, a loud and husky speedster the fans also called "The Boogeyman." Lewis alternated between Jimmy Costello's car, Joe Davidson's "Jackrabbit #22," and his own #17. One night before the races he announced to all who

"Wild Man" Georgie Lewis adapts a culinary look for his sponsor. *(Tibbert Collection)*

would listen that he would set a new track record. He did just that. By the end of June, Billy Tibbert, in the office of the Wentworth-Jennings #10, also found his way to the front. Tibbert had gone to school with the Simonetti boys and had won many midget races with Johnny Carroll and Ed Stone. Towards July and August he really got hooked up in the stock cars and threatened Cummings' point lead. A heated, fan-pleasing competition between the two developed as the weeks clicked off. The point race became so intense that, when the Wentworth-Jennings mount began to fail, Ralph Moody offered up his Norton-based #28 for Tibbert to keep up the chase. Despite some good showings, it was to no avail, however, and the Yankee Red Head was champion in 1949. Again. Tibbert was second, followed by Nashua's Stan Woods. By year end Norwood's roster had shown great depth as well as breadth. Legendary names took checkers such as Bill Randall, Long Island's Ted Tappett, and NASCAR-bound Ralph

(left) Billy Tibbert was quick in anything he drove. *(Toombs Collection)*

(right) Ralph Moody was among the very first Northerners to migrate South. Although a much celebrated driver, his more lasting fame would come from his car-building business, Holman and Moody. *(H. White photo, Silvia Collection)*

Moody. Bill McNutt, Dave Daab, Jim Styles, Bob Harper, and Melvin "Red" (or "Heavy") Foote were right on their bumpers.

Good racing was not all the fans were seeing at Norwood. The early modifieds brought slam-bang action often not for the faint of heart. On June 11 in the severest accident to date at Norwood, Joe O'Neil and Pete Horne clobbered the third turn wall and were both hospitalized. Likewise, Joe Ross got caught between Gavin Couper and the fence while leading and was launched high into the air, landing with a thunderous crash on the car's side. Drivers never want such a lateral blow. Always in the limelight one way or another, the Fat Boy was removed to the Norwood Hospital suffering fractured ribs and multiple injuries. His car owner, legendary Adolph "Longy" Blomberg took the piece home to Beverly in a basket.

Word about the excitement at Norwood got around like wild fire, and the sparse crowds were gone with the midgets. By mid-summer the Directors were grinning ear to ear, welcoming record crowds one after another. The race release of August 6 reported that the fans "taxed every available seat here at the Arena."

In the early days of the oval tracks fans and competitors were never too worked up about driver injury. It was expected—even downplayed. In fact, a common ritual for a driver coming off of a bad wreck was to climb right back into a car, just as soon as healing would allow. It was thought that re-engaging immediately saved a guy's "nerve"—and "nerve" was a highly valued commodity.

Despite this prevailing devil-may-care attitude, some racing incidents were over-the-top, sobering reminders of the often fatal dangers of the game. In a horrible example that summer at Norwood, a stock car threw a wheel coming off the fourth turn near the pit area. It

Three of Longy Blomberg's Flathead chariots in 1950. Jug Menard, Joe Ross, Red Cummings. *(H. White photo, Silvia Collection)*

soared high over the catch fence and landed, sickeningly, right in the middle of the grandstands. Emily Arden, the 52-year old wife of Boston surgeon Carmi Arden, was killed. Helen Littlefield and Joan Nielson, both of Chestnut Hill, were badly injured. Arden's family sued for $100,000; the Littlefields and the Nielsons for $20,000 each.

One of Norwood's draws was that it attracted the best of the young stock car guys, as well as midget graduates. The best of breed was from Rhode Island. New England stock car racing was arguably born at Lonsdale and on the dirt of Kingston, RI Fairgrounds. In Fred Luchesi's words, "We were the young ones who didn't care. We were up and coming. The midget guys didn't like us a lot."

Among the first Narragansett wheelmen to make his presence known on the Auto Mile was Gavin Couper. Some presence it was. A small, powder-packed firecracker of a man, Couper was bright and equally irreverent. His hands never stopped moving, nor did his mouth. A speed parts peddler much of his life, he could talk to anyone and sell anything, constantly rocking back and forth on his feet, his arms swinging together. At the track he was the epicenter of activity, frequently doing handstands and jumping jacks in front of the crowd. His driving was equally colorful and beyond courageous. Especially in his learning years he spent a good deal of time doing jumps and flips in his race car as well. One of Norwood's scorers of the era, Doris Toombs, remembers, "Gavin was the consummate entertainer. He thrived on attention. He'd crash and crash. Finally, he'd be in a big one and we'd think, ' this is it. He's all done this time'. Then he would come crawling out of the wreckage, waving his hands and screaming at someone. One thing for sure, it was never his fault." Doris got to know Couper well, since for a time he was her brother-in-law. When Gavin married Doris' sister, the former Audrey Maher, on October 1, 1949, a splashy wedding reception was held right at the track. There was a torch-light procession around the oval with sixty cars, a gift presentation, and even fireworks. It was certainly not understated. Nor was Couper.

Couper brought others North to Norwood from Rhode Island's Interstate Stock Car Association, including Luchesi, and Hop Harrington (the 1949 Interstate Champ who had started on Luchesi's pit crew). Red Bolduc and Don Hall followed slightly later. Like Hop, Luchesi was already a credentialed performer. Placing second (first New Englander) in the final championship race at Kingston in 1948, he had been named the first New England NASCAR champion. He spent so much time with Couper that the two became known as the "Gold Dust Twins" for their win-or-flip mentality. They took every opportunity to do either. Luchesi chuckles about a night at Kingston

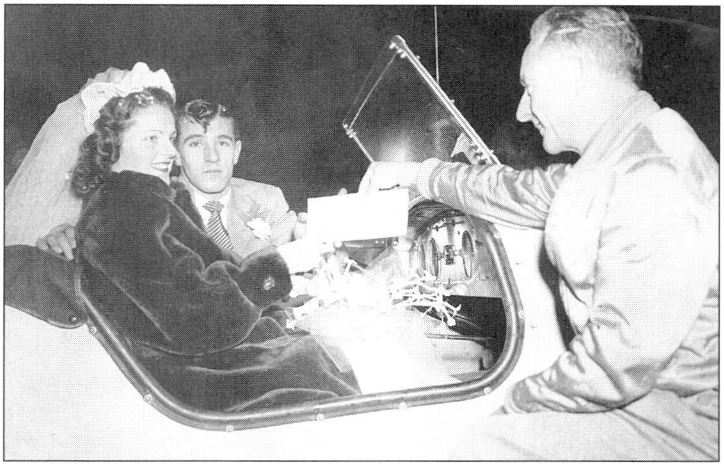

(left) Ed Stone sends Gavin and Audrey off to a New York honeymoon with a bit of purse money. *(Toombs Collection)*

(right) Freddie Luchesi, Cromwell helmet, white socks, no fear. *(Silvia Collection)*

when he crashed. Gavin came along and offered him a lift on his running board back to the pits. Wouldn't you know it, they flipped. Right then during the red flag condition. Luchesi scrambled out just in time as the huge coupe came tumbling over. An elderly woman came up to him after the incident and said, "Fred, sure is a good thing you have lead in your foot and not in your ass. Otherwise, you'd be a goner!"

As Spring approached in 1950, everyone was psyched about what promised to be a banner year at Norwood. All winter the press releases peppered the media with news. A Thursday/Saturday schedule was set, totaling an astounding 50 shows for modified cars alone. The occasional jalopy or midget program was also thrown in for good measure. And, very significantly, it was announced that the Saturday night races would be captured on film and broadcast on WBZ Channel 4 TV the following Friday at 10:45 PM. The shows were sponsored by Boston's James Hanley Brewing Co.

The Arena opened once again with its innovative 24 hour race, and this time Patriot's Day offered up much warmer weather. Thirty-three teams competed, with 21 still plugging away the next day. The winner was Foxboro's Art Clark who, with unstoppable co-driver Bobby Sprague, hammered out 3521 laps. With a half hour to go, the Yankee Red Head was in the lead looking for his second win, but he broke an axle and limped home to a fifth place finish.

Most all the regular features that year were barnburners. By the end of June, 15 different drivers had won, including Ralph Moody, Jug Menard, Ray Janelle, Paul Veracka, Babe Stein, Gordon Martin, Tommy DuPont, and Iron Man Gurney. A thrilling 25-lapper on May 6 finished in a dead heat between Cummings and Tommy DuPont out of Harrisville, RI. Several up-and-comers were already developing the

NORWOOD

A View from the Top

You can only imagine how difficult scoring must have been for the 24-hour marathons. Bill Welch, NESCRA's lead scorer, had to reach out for lots of volunteers. Gavin Couper suggested his future sister-in-law, Doris Toombs, and, though she had never even seen a race, Welchie hired her. She was immediately hooked by the thrills of the Arena. Welchie was hooked, too. He said she was the only one who got her scoring sheets right. He asked her to stay, and she joined NESCRA's multi-track official team.

From up there in the tower Doris had a bird's eye view of Norwood around 1950. She recalls vividly the camaraderie of the drivers, even though they raced against each other several times a week, most often as their living. She also remembers the enormity of the crowds. "The number of spectators was tremendous. It was not a rowdy crowd. There wasn't a whole lot of drunkenness. Norwood was the big thing. People from Needham (her home town) couldn't wait for Saturday night. It was the best entertainment around."

A sociable and very attractive woman, Doris soon ventured down to the pits whenever she could to meet the racers. One night just after she stood up from Mike Favulli's handicapper's stand, a wheel flew over the fourth turn fence and smashed her chair to smithereens. "That was it for me," she says, and it was back up top she went.

Her career as an official came to an end when she moved to the Midwest in the mid-fifties. These days, back in a pleasant apartment in Needham, she has not forgotten her enthusiasm for the sport. She laughs at the thought that she is the only senior in the complex whose television is glued to NASCAR's 200 mph broadcasts. Her son Kenny did not forget about the racing thing, either. After his return from Vietnam, Kenny went to work for Bob Melnick in Gasoline Alley, welding up race cars. He even took a fling at competing himself at Westboro, before moving to Florida.

In an interview back in 1950, Doris was asked what she would think if Kenny, then a pre-schooler, ever wanted to drive a race car. Her answer was fabulous—and completely noncommittal. "That's too far in the future for me to say. Anyway, maybe stock car racing will be too slow for kids growing up in a world where all the talk is of jet planes and atomic power."

Doris with Junior Pooler before his midget fire and starter Chris Mello *(Toombs Collection)*

That's Rolly Turgin, announcer, Bill Welch, Doris Toombs, and Art Sprague. Following his career-ending injuries in 1949, Sprague was frequently an "expert advisor" up in the booth. *(Toombs Collection)*

(left) Few would ever match the long Seekonk-Lonsdale-Norwood-Westboro record of the pioneering—and playful—Bobby Sprague. *(Rudloph Friewald photo)*

(right) Roland Fruzetti and Hop Harrington enjoy a win—one of many—in 1950. *(H. White photo, Silvia Collection)*

tools that would propel them to prominent roles in Norwood history. There was Red Foote, the hard-driving, hard-partier from Meriden, CT who won his first on April 22. So, too, there was Pawtucket's Ralph "Hop" Harrington who climbed aboard the Fruzetti #74 for the 1950 campaign. They were looking really good. Whenever this owner-driver combination came together over the years, there was magic.

Mid-way through the summer a journeyman Providence driver named Slim Ingalls wheeled into Victory Lane in a 20-lapper carried over from a rainout. The shiny #1 coupe was originally owned by Connecticut's Ralph Legendre.

Late on a Saturday afternoon in 1949, a young Carl Merrill from Newton was driving down Route 1 when he came upon a great big traffic jam and a sign saying "auto races." Curious about the commotion, he pulled in and watched the show. "I didn't know a screw driver from a 9/16, but I liked what I saw so I kept going back," he recalls. One night, noticing a ton of Newton residents in the crowd, he got an idea eerily like the attention to "NASCAR dads" in the '04 presidential election. After the races, Merrill went down to the pits and walked up to the owner of the most conspicuous car, an aluminum-colored coach driven by Foote, owned by Legendre. Merrill, who was running for office, asked Legendre to letter "Merrill for Alderman" on the car for the sum of $10 per week. Legendre was quick to agree, a friendship developed, and by autumn Merrill was co-owner in the car.

In 1950 Merrill wished to keep the connection to his town so "Miss Newton" was lettered on the new blue and white racer Ingalls would drive. Interestingly, that was a little too racy for some of the old guard such as Longy Blomberg. Merrill and Legendre were asked to remove the name. Apparently, even the mention of women—let alone their physical presence—was deemed inappropriate for the pit area.

Billy Tibbert at the helm of the famous Fish #M-1 car sailed away on July 1 before 7,000 fans. Johnny Black, Ken Dayton, Joe Ross, Fred Luchesi, and Red Bolduc were also winners. Natick's Porky Kinsman, one of the few victors at Westboro, The Pines, and Norwood,

left with a trophy at a special jalopy event held on a chilly Wednesday evening, October 4.

The long season was punctuated by crashes and wild action. No fatalities were reported. It must have been sheer luck. An incident not considered that unusual involved Jim Lees, a freshman driver from Needham. With his own car #99 on the fritz, he hopped into Reggie Bullock's #93, with disastrous result. He sheered off a light pole, bringing down the lights and the catch fence in his aerial gyrations. Lees eventually recovered from his injuries and fielded a sprint car for his neighbor Jack Malone.

(left) Starter Emil Janelle celebrates Slim Ingalls in the Legendre-Merrill #1. *(H. White photo, Silvia Collection)*

(right) One of the most storied modifieds of the era was the Fish Carburetor Special, #M-1. Billy Tibbert drove it at Norwood. He was even in it on the old beach course in Daytona. So was Fireball Roberts. *(H. White photo, Silvia Collection)*

(bottom) Red Bolduc races by while Andy Anderson grabs a look at Jim Lees' flight. *(H. White photo, Toombs Collection)*

An unknown amateur photographer clicked this haunting sequence of Junior Pooler, on fire, exiting his midget. *(Toombs Collection)*

Probably the most frightening incident, starred Junior Pooler, an immensely popular speedster from Quincy. Definitely the happy-go-lucky type, Pooler was known to repaint his stock car each time he added to his family. Pink or blue. When ARDC and UCOA came to town on Thursday June 6, he accepted a ride in a midget and seemed to have a good finish in the bag. On the very last lap, as Johnny Thomson took the checkers, the car exploded and Pooler incurred serious burns. The track held a benefit for his family a month later.

For fans and competitors alike these were good times. The Board also had to be pleased—and they acted that way. Acknowledging that Norwood had already become a "hub" track with top-shelf racing and huge purses, they posted a "jackpot" bonus increasing each week to any outsider who could come in and take the regulars' lunch. As the bonus grew, hopeful invaders towed into town. No one would win the extra gold.

The jackpot promotion was curious because it came at a time when the Directors seemed to be backing down from really energetic involvement in the Arena. There was less miscellaneous activity. Far less attention was spent figuring out whether football, wrestling, or other attractions might bring in some folks. Pari-mutuel betting had

There were definitely more laps than fans at the second marathon. *(R. Micklay photo, Gendreau Collection)*

not been passed into law and it was not going to be. The Directors and other stakeholders appeared to be settling into a future of stock cars.

Meanwhile there had been some changes within the racing clubs. Ed Stone and Bud Tatro's NESCRA had by 1950 become NEARA, New England Auto Racing Association. It now provided cars for three Massachusetts tracks: Wednesdays at Seekonk; Thursdays and Saturdays at Norwood; and Fridays at Westboro. A cooperative arrangement was worked out with Interstate in Rhode Island. Although Ed Stone kept his club involvement for a time, car owner Ed Gendreau of West Roxbury and Frank Litwin were beginning to take over the organization.

The advent of NEARA saw a decrease in the number of special shows. For example, the 1950 24-hour "annual" marathon was the last. Although the Arena had boasted of total attendance of 35,000 for the 1949 event, the figure was likely a gross overstatement. 1950's crowd was also mediocre. In terms of risk-reward, the regular shows had more punch.

Norwood and NEARA did try one more innovative event, the last show of the year. It was Armistice Day, November 11. Bud Tatro had spun off to launch a group called the Racing Corporation of America that featured 1946-1951 pleasure cars. The 150-lap RCA event, heralded as the Norwood Arena Grand Prix, was a flop. Waltham's Gordon Martin from the great Martin racing family out of the Watch City, won the yawner in a 1946 Ford over just 11 other starters. Barely 1000 fans huddled on a chilly afternoon to endure the show. Surely this disappointment added to rethinking about Norwood's future. It seemed best to back down a peg and to stick to the knitting. The Directors decided to stay with a good club that could deliver cars and build on a good thing. Over time they faded quietly from the daily picture, showing up just for the races, watching from the special room, reportedly going through a great deal of alcohol with their guests.

Gordon Martin was the patriarch of a wave of Waltham racers that flowed for 25 years. *(H. White photo, Silvia Collection)*

The year 1951, became the most "regular season" to date at Norwood. Attendance, both in the stands and at the pit sign-in, was good, and no serious injuries were reported.

Hop Harrington leveraged his successes of the prior year and became a big favorite of the fans. He began by posting an impressive win streak in the Spring, beaten finally in late May by Concord's Andy Anderson in the Owens Motors Special. By the end of the year Hop had all but replaced the Yankee Red Head as the Auto Mile's top dude.

It is interesting that the Directors offered up no changes for 1952, but Litwin and Gendreau did. They held a number of off season meetings for the club in Norwood and Lynnfield. They sensed the winds of change blowing over the pit areas at Norwood, Westboro, and The Pines. The members agreed that, since they sanctioned Lonsdale and Norwood, marquis tracks of the region, they should stay right in front of all technical trends. The hot issue of the day was how far and how fast racing would move away from the full coupe modifieds to the more racy, expensive, and dangerous cut downs. Litwin and Gendreau went a good eight or nine yards. They put forth a Sportsman division as their lead card. The rules were pretty darn loose: in terms of engines, if you can't see it, it's legal; in terms of body/chassis, chopping and channeling was okay.

They were equally gutsy in reinventing the support division. They ushered in non-Ford rules, adding huge momentum to that movement in the Northeast. The non-Fords became a weekly mainstay of the program. But, there was a kicker as well, known as the Merry-Go-Round Feature. Every third lap the non-Fords were required to run over (all four wheels) three 18" ramps located in the infield just off the front stretch. This wild, flip-producing concept was an instant hit with the fans. It was copied immediately on Friday nights at Westboro.

(left) Ed Gendreau Sr.(L) and his driver Bob Harper look pretty happy, all considered. Their #31 coupe doesn't look so chipper—and it was only one night old. *(Gendreau Collection)*

(right) Paul Veracka brings Ralph Gurney, Hop Harrington, and Tommy DuPont down for the green in 1950. His car—its "Little Beaver" lettering unchanged—would do a lot of winning up North in later years with Ollie Silva in the cab. *(H. White photo, Silvia Collection)*

(left) Jim Holt *(Tibbert Collection)*

(middle) Ray Janelle. Now he lives just across the street from Bugsy Stevens in Edgewater, FL. *(Tibbert Collection)*

(right) Fred Luchesi, Andy Anderson, and Joe Ross (back to camera) relax in the bar. *(Toombs Collection)*

As if to symbolize the seriousness of their changes, Litwin and Gendreau also changed NEARA to NARA, North American Racing Association. Newt Fowler became steward. The new rule book had a long-lasting impact on racing at Norwood, which once Lonsdale closed in 1956, was the area's undisputed destination track. The cut downs and non-Fords would grow and mature in as orderly way as could possibly be expected until the end of 1959.

Seekonk resident, the great David Humphrey, Red Cummings, Ray Janelle, Tommy DuPont, Eddie Hoyle, Jim Holt, Jug Menard, and Gavin Couper were among the Sportsman trophy winners for 1952, but they were somewhat incidental. The year could be properly summed up as a Pawtucket piece of time. Led by Hop Harrington on his hurried hunt to another Norwood crown, the Pawtucket posse of Fred Luchesi, Red Bolduc, Red Barbeau, and Roland Banville pretty much dominated the new division.

As more trickier cars were constructed in pursuit of the healthy Norwood purses, there was talk all over the state about an owner by the name of Joe Davidson. By any account this guy was one intriguing personality. In Luchesi's words, "he was the craziest man in the whole world, but bright as the day is long." An active businessman, Davidson ran an auto salvage business in South Attleboro called Goldbug. An enthusiastic aviator, he had interest in a nearby airstrip where in the thirties he held races as Interstate Speedway Park. He was also a shareholder in Norwood. A man of his own opinions, Davidson had a disarming way of communicating. Billy Tibbert, one of his many drivers, says "He would talk to you very slowly, as if feeling you out. He was always testing you. Finding the limits. People got mad."

Davidson's opinions about race cars were radical and futuristic. He was watched closely by owners from the North such as the Harty

(left) Concord's Andy Anderson, best man at Gavin and Audrey's nuptials, was as successful as any stock car pioneer when he decided to hang it up for family reasons in the mid-fifties. *(H. White photo, Silvia Collection)*

(right) The Cleary Family rampmobile. *(Balser photo)*

Brothers. He experimented with all manner of things—from running tiny diameter Crosley wheels to moving the radiator to the rear of the car. His most lasting obsession, though, was with weight. He used only the skimpiest of materials, never mind the issue of safety. He would put a tomato can where the starter went, never mind that you had to push start the car. He told Andy Anderson once that he would love Andy to drive for him, but he was simply too hefty. Even his more pint-sized picks such as Gavin Couper were told to drive in sneakers, not shoes. Wallets and watches needed to come off prior to competition. Couper once told Dick Berggren that Davidson had read in *Hot Rod* magazine that top drag racers thought weight was the key to the strip. He brought the approach to Norwood's oval aggressively. A Goldbug car, said Gavin, "was a terrible, evil thing. You could get killed just sitting in it."

Davidson had Cy Yates and Art Lee in his #61 mini-coach, but he knew these Pawtucket guys were quick and he put Fred Luchesi in his #12 car in 1952. Fred did not disappoint, snatching his first win of the year on June 7. For the other Goldbug Special #22 Davidson had selected Luchesi's buddy, Arthur "Red" Bolduc, a skilled, full-time racer whose name would become associated with Norwood Arena forever.

In 1952 Red Bolduc was half of the only known father-son racing duo in New England. His Dad, Omer "Pop" Bolduc, was one of 22 children born to a Canadian family that moved down to Pawtucket. Pop had raced beginning in 1919 at Narragansett Park in Cranston, Rhode Island. The competition sounded pretty treacherous. "We had plenty of tricks those days. We used to blow our horns at each other or turn off the ignition to make a backfire so the driver in front thought you had a blowout and would move over. We had a gallon of kerosene we could mix with the gas with a petcock so the driver could make a good smoke screen." Asked about his son, "You can't teach someone

to be a racer, but I have tried to point out his mistakes and I've always told him to keep all four wheels down. I've had a couple of spills, but I've never been hurt racing. If you've got the skill, you don't get hurt." Red would turn out to have the skill, and Pop would turn out to be very wrong.

Pop was driving a yellow 1933 Buick, #22, in the non-Ford and ramp races. In truth, at 52 he was no longer fast and was the target of a good deal of ribbing. The same was not the case for his son and the Davidson #22. He was red hot and won two of the first three nights, setting a pace the Goldbugs would maintain all year.

The weather was threatening on Saturday night April 25 when the Arena lit up for '53. Still the largest opening crowd just kept flowing in. According to the release, "Directors Pat Toye, John Peterson, and Herb Anderson had to pitch in to help handle the overflow attendance. Later three subatomic bombs rocked the stands to celebrate the new season." Three drivers, Billy Tibbert, Bridgewater's racing family patriarch Joe Rosenfield, and Jim Holt then rocked the stands with a stirring three-abreast feature battle. Tibbert won.

Swelling crowds watched Art Chase, Don Perry, Shorty Melinus, Cliff Dunn, Cy Yates, Eddie Bean, and Roland Lapierre build names in the A division that year. Bomber standouts were Augie Walackus, Bobby Sprague, Ray Harling, and Don Green. A lot of eyes followed a Bomber newcomer, Mario "Fats" Caruso. He towed in from Shrewsbury, just down the street from Westboro.

Given a pit area jammed with 130 or more cars each week, it is surprising that one entry could have stood out as much as Hop Harrington. By mid season he had snatched ten of the thirteen main events. Toward the end of the long season, Red Bolduc did give Hop reason for concern with a gutsy Fall charge. Harrington's own personal parade was then interrupted on October 3. Early in the main, Hop shot to the inside of the pack to pick up a couple of spots, but his

(left) Lincoln's Wally Silva had a stellar Norwood career. Here he is in the early fifties. Summers he hired college boys to help with his garbage business. After the races, they would have quite a time with the ladies down in the lounge. They identified themselves as "G-men." *(H. White photo, Silvia Collection)*

(right) Hop Harrington #74 missed this one, but on October 3 he was not so fortunate. *(Hathaway Collection)* gamble misfired. He rode a wheel, did five tight flips across the track, crashed through the guardrail, and landed atop the hurricane fence. It was called the most spectacular mishap of the year. The popular speedster was hospitalized with severe abrasions and other injuries. He was able to return the final night, October 24, to clinch the championship. That night will long be remembered for the straightaways' long series of end-over-end flips and fire of Rue Karner, riding a '32 Ford coupe. He suffered only a scratch on the cheek, but his daredevil days were done. His wife Josephine said it was time to have kids. The Karners ended up with five, and their friend George Summers ended up with their car number, #77.

One special event the Board opted to try was labeled the "International 250." Sanctioned by NASCAR and promoted by Ed Otto and Captain "Red" Crise, it pitted late model stock cars against foreign cars including Jaguar XK 120's steered by major stars Frankie Schneider and Nicky Fornoro. 8000 fans saw NASCAR short track ace, Jim Reed of White Plains, NY, prevail in a 1950 "police Ford."

A more regular race that was probably much more special was scheduled for Labor Day and was billed as the New England Sweepstakes. Reinforcing Norwood's hub status, all cut down (or hot rod) teams were invited to compete with the Auto Milers. It was quite the night. Right off the bat there were six flips in the first four qualifiers. Eventually, thirty-three cars lined up in eleven rows of three for the 35-lap go. Fly-weight cars, few if any nerf bars, three deep. Surprisingly, though the race was stopped five times, it was for little more than spinouts. Not surprisingly, the Norwood drivers took no prisoners. At the end it was Bolduc clipping Harrington and Ralph

Howard White, author of so many of the images in this book, and his wife are joined by Hank Dyer (right) and his wife at the novelty stand. *(H. White photo, Silvia Collection)*

"Trigger" Watson. Trigger, known as the Clown Prince of New England Racing, had forsaken Peabody and The Pines for Norwood that summer. No slouch for sure, he had won on the Auto Mile by August 15.

The NARA boys figured they would be attracting fields approaching 150 in 1954. They were right. Norwood's unusually large fan base, so much stronger than Westboro or The Pines, translated into the highest weekly pay-offs in the area. NARA decided to divide the cut down division into two, the A and B classes. The only difference related to the size of the motor. It worked well.

Fred Borden, future king of Westboro's banks, beat out 22 Class A hot rods on Saturday, May 1 after a sizzling duel with Dave Humphrey and Hank Stevens. A near-capacity throng of blanket-wrapped enthusiasts saw Quincy's Danny Ambrosio wheel his #100 Ford to victory in the B main. Red Hill, Wally Silva, Reino Tulonen, Norm Duquette, Bob Valliere, Joe Jackson, Cy Yates, Red Barbeau, Larry Antonellis, and Fred Schulz were all victorious over the course of a thrilling season. Historian RA Silvia will tell you about the sensationalism of these mid-fifties cut down programs. Coordinated with drama-building announcing, most all the lights in the Arena and on the midway would be shut off for a few parade laps before the feature. Then, at the unfurling of the green, 24 very brave men would blast off turn four, side by side, twelve rows deep, in a explosion of light and sound.

The year 1954 will be known also for the real emergence of the Lion. Leo Cleary, of Quincy and later Hanover, a future NEAR Hall-of-Famer, just plain had the stuff. Given his groove-inventing technique behind the wheel, his well-deserved fame as a car constructor, and his bouncy, Irish personality, many consider Leo Cleary to be Mr.

(left) Hughie Mattie works on his brother Barney's first car. The shot was taken by another of the Mattie crew, Bill Balser. Balser has taken quite a few more pictures over the years. *(Balser photo)*

(right) Red Bolduc shows what's meant by a cut-down. At its side is Johnny Phillip Morris. *(Volante Collection)*

Trigger and the Thing

In 1949 Longy loaned a seriously beaten-up jalopy to Ralph "Trigger" Watson to race up at The Pines. It must have been quite the sight being flat-towed up the road from Beverly. Watson, soon to be known as "the Comic of the Speedway," painted a huge bull's eye on the trunk. Out of its middle came a piece of flex exhaust pipe, feigning a tail.

Jokers usually aren't taken too seriously at the races, but this guy was different. He was fast. By the very next year he was described by Mike Gibbons as, "the tousle-haired, devil-may-care champ of all jalopy drivers." He flashed his flare very publicly one night after winning a 100-lapper at Medford Bowl. Jumping out of his car, he told his crew to unbolt the body and remove it, and he then auctioned it off to the hollering fans. All proceeds went to racer Ray Hill who was recuperating from one of his mishaps.

By 1953 Trigger was a full-time racer with lots of rides. He may have been humorous, but he took no prisoners. One Sunday at Manchester he rolled a car owned by Lee Spaulding and Bill Welch nine times, sending him to the crash house with a concussion, serious facial lacerations, and internal injuries. Wednesday night he was right back at it at Dracut, winning the show for Andy Cote.

In 1954 Trigger was off to Norwood Arena in Buck Monies' #516. They fit in perfectly, despite the Emmett Kelly clown head on the roof. In no time they were track champs.

His most memorable car, however, was of his own manufacture, built for the 1956 season. Labeled "The Thing" by the fans as soon as it showed up, the tiny little coach, like all Trigger's cars, initially went to the track in primer. "I never lettered them until I won a feature," says Trigger. "Well, The Thing cleaned house the first night, so I had to mix up some paint the next week. Wouldn't you know it, it came out pink." To complete the picture, Trigger installed curtains in the back and painted on the occasional flower and slogan.

His best weekend came that fall when he won Westboro, Norwood, and the 75-Lap Canadian-American Classic at Pinecrest Speedway in Toronto for a cool grand.

One Saturday a couple of years later, Trigger was having problems getting a motor together for the weekend. A North Shore friend said, "Oh come on, Ralph, let's just go fishin'". And so a grand cut down career was over, just ten years after it started. Trigger's car and all his kit went to long time helper Bob "Nemo" Alexander, who subsequently fielded the #16 for the Freddies, Borden and Luchesi.

Even though only in his early thirties, Trigger never looked back. He was looking ahead—for tuna. He got so good at it that he soon had a plane and was chief pilot and spotter for the National Marine Fisheries.

That's Bob Alexander leaning on the right rear of "The Thing" at Pinecrest Speedway. Red Sequin leans on the left of the infamous # Circle Two cut down. *(Watson Collection)*

Trigger clowns around next to the #193 out of Art LaBonte's East Lynn garage. *(Watson Collection)*

Trigger was taken to the hospital with serious injuries. The Spaulding–Welch #42 likely went to the auto graveyard that Sunday. *(Watson Collection)*

The next Wednesday was for winning. Note the bandages over Trigger's eye. That's Andy Cote with the flag. *(Watson Collection)*

Some nights Leo seemed to drive half the cars in the pits. This evening he was on his way to some bucks. *(Silvia Collection)*

Norwood Arena. And the fact is that what actually got the whole thing started was a pain in the neck.

Leo came to racing and adulthood early. He married young. He and Charlotte had already started on a family when he and buddy Joe Gerrior began following Bernie Barrows to the races. One day at Lonsdale in 1951 Bernie had a nagging boil on his neck. The leather of his Cromwell helmet simply did not want to close around it. The car owner, Ray Leach, asked Leo to drive. Leo knew Charlotte would not be pleased. She wasn't, even though he won the feature. She was in the hospital, busy having son Jim, the eldest of their six kids.

By 1953 Leo, Joe, and Leo's brother, Pat, had become fixtures in the Norwood pits. Leo was a starter in almost every lower-division race. It was obvious that he could wring the most out of a car, and so Leo attracted rides to supplement the Cleary Auto Body non-Ford. Soon he was also performing in the Sportsman division and in the late models whenever they came. He was jumping in one car after another. Leo says, "I was getting a lot of experience and the money was really good. I could make a couple of hundred a night myself, but, I tell you, I tried to hide some from myself in all my pockets. That bar at Norwood was real good at taking the money back. And in those days we'd be down there for hours after the races—every week." Sometimes the scene after the races was not only alcoholic, but aggressive as well. At 23 Leo had quite the temper and was not to be messed with. All of this would ease away over the years, but as late as the mid-sixties, Leo was known to weld the number of a competitor on his front bumper before going to Norwood. Leo Cleary's front bumper is where no race car driver wanted to be.

Pat, Joe, and Bernie were bothered that no one would entrust a good cut down to the combative Leo. Their answer was to build one for 1954, which is exactly what Pat did in Leo's shop in Quincy with the help of former standout driver, Bob Harper. The slick little machine, #2, was finished by late June, and just three weeks later the Lion roared by Hop Harrington and Red Hill and grabbed the mid-season championship. It was a big night. Overflow race cars and the fattest crowd in two years ballooned the purse to over $4,000. During the rest of the year, the Lion bit off two more cut down mains. He won in other divisions, too, especially consistently in the Lucia Brothers #0 non-Ford Hudson. He still beats himself up about never capturing all the features in one night.

Just as at Westboro and The Pines, 1955-1956 were the first of a few softer years at Norwood before the noticeably brisker sixties at all three tracks. In Norwood's case, there was no great downturn; there were no great changes. More than anything the flattening was likely caused by management complacency.

That should not suggest that there was any falling off in dramatic incidents at the track. One involved Newton's politically minded Carl Merrill. Following a year or two with Ralph Legendre and drivers Slim Ingalls and Bob Hersey, Merrill had to leave the partnership in 1952 when he was transferred down South. Moving back North to Newton the next year, he also returned to Norwood. This time his focus was as an official, an activity that has taken him over the years to

Occasionally Fred Astle wandered north to Norwood from his Seekonk base. This visit was a warm one. *(G. Grant photo, Silvia Collection)*

Rudy Kingma's Bomber slid down the front stretch before erupting in flames on July 31. *(Silvia Collection)*

almost every track in New England. Today he directs the show at New Hampshire's Monadnock Speedway.

By 1955 Merrill had been involved in most all aspects of officiating and was a key man—often the disciplinarian—at Norwood. His insistence on protocol sometimes put him at odds with the guys in the pits, but one night he raised everyone's eyebrows with admiration. Rudy Kingma, a veteran of Bomber wars, flipped his #5 coupe coming off the fourth turn. Suddenly the car flashed up in a ball of flames, Kingma still inside. Merrill, claiming to respond "completely out of instinct," scrambled right into the fire, wrenching out the still conscious driver. Both were lucky to escape really serious burns. Kingma was able to race again, and Merrill received a plaque honoring his actions at the Fall banquet.

Unhappily, another Bomber mishap was just what everyone dreaded. Freddie Gross of Attleboro ventured up to the Arena for the very first time in September 1955 to pinch hit for his partner and the usual driver, Bob Dionne. Freddie had won the heat but on lap three of the main he got crossed up between turns one and two. He was launched high over the guardrail in a ghastly scene of devastation. He died with massive head injuries. A collection was taken for Mary Gross and their two children two weeks later. Fred's fellow Marines played taps followed by a three-gun salute.

Fans were further saddened by tragic news from way up on Bean Mountain in East Lempster, NH. A motorist noticed a small plane with a sputtering motor that made a sudden course change and plunged into the mountain. Dead in a fiery wreckage that looked from afar like the Northern Lights was Stan Woods, 35, of Nashua, one of Norwood's finest open wheel and hard top racers.

There was also Carroll Sleeper, the guy, says Doris Toombs, all the gals came to Norwood to see. He went off with Uncle Sam and the Marines. He was on leave down South and was badly hurt in a racing crash. He spent the rest of his life in a wheelchair.

(left) Stan Woods surveys the damage with track officials as they prepare to right his coupe. It took rescuers much longer to reach him when he crashed his airplane in the White Mountains.
(H. White Photo, Silvia Collection)

(right) The man with the million dollar smile. Carroll Sleeper's brilliant racing days sunsetted way too early.
(Toombs Collection)

And then there was Billy Tibbert whose brilliant racing career was nipped off mid-stream by the biggest health concern of the day, polio. There had been no motorized thing that the talented Tibbert could not do. He'd won everything up North. He had raced in Florida and even run down South once or twice for Longy. He had tested M&H tires for legendary Hall-of Famer Marvin Rifchin at Darlington and now in 1955 he was thinking of moving that way to work with his friend Ralph Moody. It was all to no avail. Although Tibbert attempted a comeback at Seekonk in the sixties, his grand drives were essentially over.

On April 28, 1956 spring rain dampened Norm Duquette's masterful conquest of a 26-car starting field. Rain and mist continued to be a factor all summer long, trimming crowds and slickening up the track surface. Freddie Luchesi found it to his likeing and he parlayed two late June wins to the season championship in his own Gershkoff Special. It was no cakewalk, however. Woonsocket's Henri "Red" Barbeau was banging on all eight in the Roy Devereaux/Lou Auclair #L-1 cutdown. He added six feature notches to his belt. Four came in a row at the season's end, and he fell just short of Luchesi, 437 to 446 points. Borden was third.

The story in the non-Ford Bombers was Larry Antonellis with nine wins. He beat Leo Cleary rescundingly, 583 to 436 points. Bobby Sprague was third in Joe Spagnola's car. Big Joe Rosenfield also had another great year. The non-Ford division always seemed to have its complement of characters. There was a feisty young driver from Needham named Jack Malone the fans were beginning to watch. He was getting fast with his #78 cars. On August 25 the fans moaned when, looking really fast, he was knocked out of the heat. They broke out in laughter when he climbed through the window of the steaming

(left) Jimmy Lynch needed a lot of new parts—and some welding rod as well—after this warm up wall shot in 1955. He had won in this Sportsman car on July 16, the last of a special series of Friday night shows that year. *(Silvia Collection)*

(right) That's King Hop with more hardware still. The presenter is Louis Giuliano, former driver, owner, announcer, and steward from East Providence. *(Volante Collection)*

coupe, completely topped and tailed. He had spent the afternoon at a wedding. No time to change out of his tuxedo. As the sixties came along, Malone matured into a deeply respected driver and, quite successful commercially, he helped and mentored no small number of racers from the Needham area.

There was a major reorganizing and ride-hopping in the cut down ranks over the next couple of years, and a newcomer just out of college was smack in the thick of it. Brighton's Dick Volante had bought some street parts from affable Gavin Couper at New England Speed and decided to take in a show at Norwood. He was blown away, most especially by the talents of Dave Humphrey in the blue and orange #257 Sportsman and the Perry #3a cutdown. Volante knew he had to be a racer. He wanted to drive just like Humphrey.

That night Gavin introduced him to Paul Doody of Dedham, Couper's car owner. Before long the two were friends, and Doody taught Volante to weld while resurrecting an old cut down from out back of the shop. A standard-width, dropped-body #163, the car had been driven by Malone. Bolting in a flathead engine and numbering the car #33 (Volante's father's number when he entered Ellis Island), it was off to Norwood and Westboro for the 1958 campaign.

Volante surely had world-class help and advice for his initial motorsports foray. Associated with Doody's slick #0 was mechanic Jim McGee from Stoughton. McGee's talents would be well rewarded in the future as he became a top Indianapolis crew chief. He was part of the 500 winning team of Clint Brawner and Mario Andretti.

A car closely matching Doody's #0 was the #1 car owned by meticulous engineer, Dick Carmen, and driven by Eddie Hoyle. The loose fit team of Couper and Hoyle got it done. Both were winners.

So, too, were Henry Rufo's Red-haired Cummings and Hill, at the wheels of dark gold #53 and #51 cut downs. Hill heated the subfreezing evening of April 26, advancing from deep in the pack of 24 starters to the front over Watson and Harrington. His work was made a little easier when late in the race Fred Borden and Granite State visitor Ernie Gahan tangled. Gahan flipped viciously and slammed into the guard rail with such force that his helmet flew out of the car. He was hospitalized with head injuries.

Another going combination was Leo Cleary and Longy Blomberg. Pat Cleary and Bob Harper's cut down had, in fact, allowed the Lion the time he needed to strut his stuff. Longy's cars were highly desirable rides, and Leo took his new responsibilities seriously. When he was asked to join with Freddie Shultz in Longy's two-car team, "I had

(left) This midget misadventure was ridden out by NEMA rookie, Everett's Bob Bianchi, after tangling with Tony Bonadies. He survived, but that was it with the race cars. *(Silvia Collection)*

(right) When you talk about Dave Humphrey, talk to racing people in the know. Never receiving the accolades he deserves, the quiet man from Seekonk had one of the longest and finest records of anyone in the Northeast. *(P. Conley photo, Silvia Collection)*

(bottom) Standing next to Gavin Couper are Paul Doody and Cal Blout (R). Kneeling are Walt Nordstrom and Jim McGee (R). *(Volante Collection)*

(left) It's August of 1958 and Red Bolduc looks to be feeling good about that pretty little cut down. *(Volante Collection)*

(right) Freddie Luchesi in the Alexander #16 out of Beverly. *(Cohen Collection)*

to start thinking about winning races and keeping the equipment together. It was that or start looking for another ride. Longy had really good stuff." Leo's somewhat calmer style behind the wheel and his knowledge of handling were a perfect fit for Longy.

The Lion also had to learn some patience in the pits. Longy was not your average Joe. At 6' 8" the elderly Swede had often delighted the pit areas at Norwood and other tracks with impromptu wrestling matches with Andy Anderson, himself hardly a shrimp. Longy's cars went through the turns as smooth as silk and purred down the straights with Morton-Welch motors. Longy had his own ideas about design and maintenance. Pat Cleary says that Longy's idea of changing the spark plugs was to move them from one side to the other. Leo was talking to himself late in the fall of 1958—the height of the point chase—when they found a cracked block with three more races to go. "Longy just kept saying, 'Don't worry about it' while I was having a fit. He wouldn't let me warm up. After every race he would drain the water and oil from the crankcase. He wouldn't do anything else. But he was right. We made it." Leo and Longy were 1958 NARA champs. Bobby Sprague topped the Bombers in his #16, and Leo Comeau of Hull showed the Novices the way around.

There was a particularly sad evening at the track that June 7, 1958. It was a memorial for Basil "Jug" Menard, the 28-year old driver from Taunton. Menard had been a consistent stock car standout at the Auto Mile, winning a cut down show as recently as May 12, 1956. In 1957 he was unexpectedly absent. Then, in April of 1958 he came around the pits at Norwood to bid farewell. Within a month he passed away at Lemuel Shattuck Hospital of incurable cancer. Making the whole situation more difficult was Menard's own persona. Although definitely a lover of wine and song and definitely a track favorite, Jug was kind of a loner. In early days he spent every second he could with

In a happier time Jug Menard receives a non-Ford trophy from Evelyn Gendreau. *(D. MacKenzie photo, Gendreau Collection)*

his mentor, Ralph Moody. But, after Moody went South, Jug was most often alone. That was the case one night at Hudson. Jug flew off the backstretch, hit some trees, and was temporarily knocked unconscious. He had no crew with him and no one saw him. "Suddenly we were running down the backstretch in the feature," recalls Andy Anderson, "and slowly up over the banking into the lights comes this figure. We thought it was a ghost."

By 1959 the thunder of the overhead engines was shaking the ground in Norwood. As would be expected, the Arena took a more aggressive approach to bringing them in than Westboro or The Pines.

Several of the top runners opted not to make the switch from flatheads right away. The Lion was one, but his wins the first two nights were his only cut down triumphs of the year. Hop, too, stuck with the older and heavier motor style, but with a difference. Harrington's pretty little #9 car, owned by Frank Sgambato, allegedly housed a

Frank Sgambato Sr. owned the #9, but it was flagger Frank Sgambato Jr. who gave Hop the checker. *(Hathaway Collection)*

(left) West Roxbury's Don Casey in Liz Healey's #6-T. *(Tulonen Collection)*

(right) It's a Saturday afternoon in August, 1959, and Barney Mattie makes his Red Devil purr for Norwood, just as he would each Saturday for another ten years. *(Balser photo)*

"cross fire." A trick crankshaft designed to allow two cylinders to fire at once delivered awesome power and a very unusual sound.

Freddie Luchesi was first to deliver an overhead to victory circle when he wrestled the A-frames of Andy Smith's #99 "Impala Special" to the front on May 16. The car was on its way to becoming a winner at all three tracks, Westboro, The Pines, and Norwood. Gavin was racy in the Paul Doody car, beefed up with a 312 Ford, three deuces, and an Isky cam. Dick Volante followed Doody's lead and welded up a shortened, narrowed overhead-powered hot rod. He bolted fenders on his little unit for a SCODA sports car race at Norwood on Labor Day and swept the show. In a true "As-the-World-Turns" story, Volante sold his previous car to Brighton's Jim McGuire who raced it as the #37. Soon Couper and Doody had a spat of sorts, and Couper became Volante's driver. Meanwhile, Doody sold the #0 to longtime Norwood personality Liz Healey. Liz lettered it #6-T and put Don Casey at the helm. Doody then built a sprinter and went racing nationally with McGuire, who was showing enormous talent. McGuire won the 1963 URC championship, but it would all end on the dirt at New Breman, Ohio. There Jim, a draftsman by trade, lost his right arm in a savage accident.

By 1959 the non-Ford cars were also really trucking, having been allowed higher displacement engines. Joe Rosenfield, Barnie Mattie, Bobby Sprague, and George Summers were all noteworthy, but Fats Caruso was particularly fast in Greg Mills' #79 coupe. The Caruso/Mills combo raced Westboro, Dover, and anywhere else. They usually won; they were always the life of the party.

Throughout the year, however, there was an uncomfortable under-current at Norwood. There was tension about the spiraling costs of competition, only increased by loose rules of the cut downs, by the new overheads, and even by the beefier non-Ford engines. And crowds were not what they had been. Early that year track manage-

(left) Ned Dunn dumps on a busy non-Ford street in July of 1958. *(Balser photo, Caruso Collection)*

(right) The Leaning #2, proudly displaying its Independent decal, was one of Fred Luchesi's final rides. "I never went back after I quit", he says. "Off came my helmet; end of movie. But I'll tell you this, I'd do it again in a minute." *(Volante Collection)*

ment tried to mollify the drivers by posting a guaranteed purse of $3,000, regardless of fan attendance. It seemed to do little good.

As the season wore on, a splinter cut down faction cropped up. It was called Independent Race Car Owners' Association, and Carl Merrill joined in as the group's business agent. Independent's relationship with Norwood's Board was not good. There were threatened strikes over money. What really got the Directors' attention—and NARA's—was the final night. Every single car in the cut down pit area carried an Independent decal. This was war.

There was something about those black and white Independent stickers. As if red had been waved before the sleeping bull's eye, The Board seemed to wake up—angry—from a decade-long snooze. In no way were they going to tolerate competitor insurrection. They came down from their tower, determined to bury Independent. Problem is, they had learned nothing more about the dynamics of racing while they were asleep.

That winter Norwood's Directors began conversations with NASCAR. The fast-growing Daytona-based operation was intending to develop a short-track presence at the time and was creeping up the East Coast. They were strong in New Jersey and New York. In New England they had nothing in 1960 but Stafford, CT, a somewhat marginal dirt track known for good racing. You can bet the NASCAR big wigs wined and dined Norwood's Directors. Flattery worked. The deal was signed before the Directors likely understood the implications. The NASCAR Sportsmen and Modifieds would be the headliner division going forward at the Auto Mile.

Because NASCAR had national championships even for its short-track cars, by very definition Norwood would now be hosting point chasers from all over. Almost immediately Norwood shed its identity as a local, Massachusetts track, the direction a promoter like Oscar Ridlon wished to follow. Instead, the Board's course brought great renown to Norwood, especially as many Arena drivers would win national NASCAR honors over the next decade. The track soon allied with Thompson, CT and Stafford Springs, which paved in 1967. Both were also NASCAR sanctioned.

There's been a lot of debate over the years about the Directors' decision. Did they unknowingly do the right thing by bringing in NASCAR? Or did they, in fact, fence what could have been a promising New England circuit? If the advent of NASCAR coupes had not killed the local cut downs, is it possible that a broader, regional cut down collaboration could have started? Certainly Westboro, always a friend to Norwood, would have gone along with it. The Westboro folks in no way could afford a NASCAR sanction, though, so they ended up crafting their own retro flathead rules. Who knows, in his later years even Oscar Ridlon might have warmed up to some cooperation. There was Ken Squier up in Barre, VT. And there were cut downs scattered about Maine, running at places such as Beech Ridge, Oxford Plains, and Unity.

Apparently feeling its oats that winter, the Board made another call, one that worked passably for a while but would in the end contribute mightily to the end of the Arena. So very reminiscent of the decision to bring Wednesday night kart racing to West Peabody in 1960, the Norwood Directors agreed to make fuller usage of their real estate by building a drag strip. It would be a small one, they told the town. Just an eighth of a mile in length, focused on kids who wanted to exercise their street cars safely. Permits were drawn, and the strip eventually opened. It operated quietly for a few years. Then things became complicated.

As anyone would have predicted, the NASCAR Sportsman-Modified cars had a mixed start at Norwood. There was no base of equipment. Any local wanting to run had to build a car to a whole new set of rules. Some of the stalwarts took a wait-and-see attitude, while others such as Joe McNulty, Ray Janelle, Roland LaPierre, and Fats Caruso jumped right in. It was a rousing victory for the home team when Red Bolduc was first in the April 30 opener.

Right away, however, the whole scene had changed a great deal. The next week a newcomer, "Wild Bill" Slater of Danielson, CT took full measure of the field in a black coupe #V8. One of New England's beloved racing figures and a Hall-of-Famer, Slater was already at the top of his game. In 1959 he had driven the same Bombaci-Vitari car

(left) Joe McNulty came to Norwood from Gale's Ferry, CT. He drove Bob "Slim" Ross' #222 cars and he was renowned as a careful, money driver. When his work schedule changed, Ross gave the ride to a young Fred DeSarro. When DeSarro built his own #11, Ross sold the car to Dickie Williams. *(Cohen Collection)*

(right) Ron Narducci remembers Norwood: "I just had a little 292 Ford in my coupe when I was at Norwood. I was consistent, avoiding wrecks. To me it was kinda like running around the inside of a soup plate. But you could get your fill of soup in those 400 lappers. I'd hang onto the roll cage with my left arm to keep my head from falling off." *(Silvia Collection)*

to 15 wins at the New London Waterford Speedbowl. In 1960 he would become Norwood's first NASCAR Mod champ.

A mini-streak by Slater was halted by another Nutmeg-stater. Although Red Foote had raced Norwood during the early fifties, he was only an infrequent visitor during the hot rod era. Now he was back in Paul Smith's 312 Ford powered coupe, #J-2. Other honored names pulling in that year were Johnny Thompson, Ron Narducci, Jack Hart, Red Foote's brother, Russ, and Ernie Gahan aboard John and Sonny Koszela's #15 Woodchopper Special.

To fill out the show a new NASCAR Hobby division was organized, essentially an outgrowth of the previous non-Ford and Novice divisions. It featured coupes— flatheads and six cylinders at first—and by the mid-sixties was offering up great competition. Woody

Jack Glockner of Canton drove this novice machine for Eddie Gendreau, Jr. *(Gendreau Collection)*

There can be no question that Independent was hurting for cars when it went on the road. Their roster this night at Seekonk was a mixed bag: George Summers in a non-Ford #10; Freddie Schulz in a Flathead #14; and John Wholey in his #65 mini-sedan overhead. *(Summers Collection)*

Woodward, Bobby Pendergast, and Richard Parson were the top three point getters year one. A novice division was also in place.

Although the Directors put it to the cut downs by signing with NASCAR, they still intended to let the bugs run if Litwin and Gendreau could provide enough entries. This took time because the air was thick with bad feeling. Independent was booking shows at Westboro, Seekonk, and anywhere they could, but things were not going well. Finally, by the middle of June, it seemed there were sufficient cars willing to "cross the line" back to Norwood. On the 18th, nine entries, Fats Caruso, Leo Cleary, Fred Schulz, Bobby Sprague, and Fred Luchesi among them, ran a 25-lap feature. Al Stone reported that "the chopped hot rods were back as well as the popular names and enthusiasm was evident among the fans." However, just a month later, the cut downs were gone, unable to pull a viable field, never to return to Norwood.

A moment on June 18—a night that will never be forgotten—seemed to symbolize the demise of the little cars. On lap 24 of the main event, Red Bolduc raced off the second turn in a potent cut down owned by Bertha Small. For reasons no one has ever been able to fathom, the car suddenly shot hard right, plowing into the fence full tilt. Making a mockery of his Pop's words years before, Bolduc, a 36-year old member of the original Pawtucket posse, suffered a basilar skull fracture and severe brain laceration. He died at 11:00 AM the next morning.

News of the tragedy, of course, spread through the racing community like wild fire. Sadly, many sports journalists chose to make a nasty story of it, noting that on that same weekend Allentown, PA's Al Herman was killed at West Haven, CT in a midget. Ultra-popular Indy 500 winner Jimmy Bryan was hurled to his death at Langhorne, PA that Sunday afternoon.

The NASCAR performers were back in force for year two in 1961, but there was a decidedly different feel in the pit area. There was much communication, and memos and press releases were flying around everywhere. The explanation was simple: over the course of the winter Carl Merrill had accepted the new position of NASCAR Chief Steward and Director of Racing. The way NASCAR worked, the Board now needed to assume a greater role in the running of the show, and they decided that the hyper-organized Merrill was their man.

Given the whole cut down dynamic, Merrill's sudden NASCAR role at Norwood was a shock to some of the competitors. They felt that he had first dropped Litwin, Gendreau, and NARA by being Independent's business agent. Then he dropped Independent by going with NASCAR. Merrill's contention is that the hot rods were cooked, and he wanted everyone to be able to come back to the area's premier track.

The cut downs were able to struggle on for the better part of two years under Pioneer Auto Racing at Seekonk, Westboro, Thompson—anywhere they could book a show. The club was under the guidance of Dick Volante who now had Gavin Couper at the controls of his #33s rocketship.

Possibly the Norwood Directors' infatuation with their Daytona connection made them a little racier themselves. They scheduled two high-dollar national championship events for the Arena, bringing it wide publicity. First was the Yankee 500, a 500-lapper held on June 17 for the Grand National cars, now known as Nextel Cup. In the sixties before the proliferation of superspeedways, this division visited selected short tracks. Norwood's purse of over $10,000 was one of the largest ever paid in the Northeast. Emmanuel Zervakis took the top prize back to the Southlands in a 1960 Chevrolet, with an average

(left) Russ Foote stuck his toe into Norwood but not as deeply as his brother, Red, the Eastern Bandit. Russ retired following a dramatic flip out of the ballpark at New London in 1963. *(P. Conley photo, Cohen Collection)*

(right) Looking like the cat that ate the canary, Dick Volante is ready to go racin' at Hudson. When he ran Pioneer, however, he put Gavin Couper in his rocketship #33s. *(Volante Collection)*

(left) Quincy's honored wheelman, Larry Antonellis. *(P. Conley photo, Silvia Collection)*

(right) Few racers from the area surrounding The Pines ventured down to Norwood and NASCAR. Gloucester's Bob Pearson was the exception, and he remains a committed friend of racing today. *(Pearson Collection)*

speed of 53.827 mph, followed by Rex White, Ned Jarrett, and Buck Baker. The pace set a NASCAR Grand National record for a 1/4 mile oval, but grandstand attendance of 5000 on a day with perfect weather did not justify the costs of the event. It was not rerun in subsequent years.

The second national championship was the Minuteman 400, a Sportsman-Modified contest on Labor Day. It was won handily by Red Foote and, in one form or another, it continued for the next seven Septembers.

Familiar Norwood faces Hop Harrington, Red Hill, Fats Caruso, and Larry Antonellis made their way to victory lane in 1961. So did Connecticut invaders Johnny Thompson and Gene Bergin who drove an extremely innovative #15 modified owned by Ben Washburn of Bristol, CT. As great a talent as New England would ever produce, Bergin was respectful of the Arena from the start. He told Pete Zanardi that, "learning to handle Norwood was an intellectual experi-

Cy Parlin lands the Palmer Oil #97 after a sky ride. That's Red Foote in the #J-2 thinking about his left front while Wally Silva looks for room upstairs in the #107. *(P. Conley photo, Silvia Collection*

ence.... You don't want high RPMs because once you start spinning your wheels, it was all over. It was like being on skates and afraid to fall. You had to concentrate; you had to worry about the back end."

Curiously what likely gave Norwood the most notoriety in these years didn't even happen at Norwood. Of the 22 main events run in 1961, over half were won by a handful of renegades who were becoming known as the Eastern Bandits. During a narrow window of the sixties, the Bandits were on the loose, attacking racing in a way that is unthinkable today.

One of the effects of NASCAR's wiring a smattering of race tracks up and down the East Coast with a common sanction, common rules, and an annual point championship was that it was possible to race multiple times a week. If you were good enough, theoretically you could race for a living. But unlike the situation in the early fifties, the tracks were not within a couple of hours of each other somewhere in New England. In this deal, the circuit literally stretched thousands of miles from Louisiana through Florida and right up into Maine.

Ringleaders of the Eastern Bandits were Ed Flemke, Rene Charland, and Red Foote. A winter later, Denny Zimmerman and Ernie Gahan were riding with them. Others followed. They were racing everywhere and they were winning everywhere. There was a lot of "who were those guys!?" And, given that they were all New Englanders, the world usually considered Norwood Arena their home track.

Just thinking about the lifestyle of the Bandits will wear you to the bone. Schedules were in constant flux because of special shows, but a typical week might be Tuesday at Moyock, NC, Thursday at Fort Dix, NJ, Friday at Stafford or Richmond, VA. Saturdays at Norwood or Islip on Long Island or Manassas, VA. Sunday afternoon at Thompson followed by an evening in Utica, NY or, the afternoon in Marlboro, MD or South Boston, VA, and the evening in Old Bridge, NJ.

It was busy on this Saturday night. Travelers Herbie Tillman of Miami, FL, in the #16 coach and Rene Charland in his trademark #3 are chased around town by Fats Caruso and Jack Malone. Hop Harrington (#23) and Smokey Boutwell follow. *(P. Conley photo Silvia Collection)*

(left) Your basic Rene. *(Bob Hunter photo, Berggren Collection)*

(right) "Steady" Eddie Flemke in one of his many just-in-time manufactured racers. This one, first in primer as "The Grey Ghost," was later painted yellow. *(P. Conley photo, Silvia Collection)*

Put in perspective, all this was not happening in air-conditioned buses and haulers. It was pickup trucks towing open trailers at a time when the Federal Highway System was hardly in the shape it is today. Charland tells that the race driver often had some preference in sleeping arrangements. In his case, he would rest on the road, stretching out on the floor of the cab between the feet of his two mechanics.

Somehow the Bandits found the time and energy to build and maintain their cars in lightning-fast form. Particularly down South their win rate was extraordinary. The late Eddie Flemke, likely New England's most legendary stock car racer, told Mike Adaskaveg, "The Southern cars had better motors than us, but they were basic dirt chassis. Their cars weighed 3000 pounds. Mine was 2100. Rene came up to me one night after a show in Richmond and said 'Eddie, I just can't understand Grant.' 'Grant who?' I said. 'General Grant. It took him and all those men to defeat the Confederates back then. Now all it takes is you and me'."

Rich racing lore will follow forever the amazing exploits of the Bandits. Through the grinding trials of it all, a spirit of light-heartedness and good somehow thrived. Was there ever a trip when Joseph Maurice Rene Charland went through the Holland Tunnel headed South, way too fast, without seeding it with firecrackers?

In 1962 the Bandits were often out of town on business on Saturdays. A new and fan-grabbing dynamic excited Norwood. It was the incredibly strong season put together by Bill Slater and the chase given by Fats Caruso. Together the duo accounted for 16 wins in the 22-race season, and they were easily one-two in track Sportsman points. Johnny Thompson and Smokey Boutwell were one-two in Modified

points. Boutwell drove Ed Bowley's #F5 to three of the last five mains. The #F5 was the only modified to win.

Slater's accomplishments began with a record of the most consecutive wins, seven, at Norwood. The Connecticut driver just plain had the circular arena figured out. "Get a ball, put it on a string, and then start hurling it," he told Pete Zanardi. "It goes round and round. That's the way you drove Norwood Arena. You did not want to break that rhythm." Not to imply that Slater had always had things figured out. He smiles recounting the tale of his first race and a conversation as he waited, 138th in line, to enter the Lonsdale pit area in 1949. Hall-of-Famer Sammy Packard, the techman, approached Bill and asked him if he had a locked rear end. (Welding the spider gears so that both wheels turn equally would often make a car faster, but it was illegal.) Slater's response was to ask him to jack up the car. "I had no idea what that was. I wanted Sammy to tell me if I had one."

Slater was very active in the fifties, asphalt and some clay, but his career actually blossomed when Bob Vitari and Vic Bombaci chose him to steer their #V8, "the Connecticut Valley Rocket." By 1962 Wild Bill had become a definite stylist. He was aggressive and light-

(left) Ed Bowley brought a Daytona-style Studebaker to Norwood for Smokey Boutwell first, but this coupe was much faster. That's Red Labelle with the checkers. *(P. Conley photo, Silvia Collection)*

(right) Bill Slater (R) and his long-time confidante, Connecticut racing writer extraordinaire, Pete Zanardi. *(Berggren Photo)*

"Mr. Clean" reflects the flash yet again. That's Paul Conley with the camera. *(P. Conley photo, Silvia Collection)*

There was nothing pretentious about Fats Caruso. *(Silvia Collection)*

ning fast, but he paid heed to his "round and round" analogy. He was smooth as silk.

Many of Norwood's fans reacted to Slater enthusiastically because he also looked smooth. The black #V8 with yellow numbers and its white insides was impeccably maintained, always fresh and shiny. So, too, was Slater in his already retro uniform of black pants, a white shirt, white socks, and penny loafers.

In pursuit from the very first lap was an equally popular driver of totally contrarian identity. Mario "Fats" Caruso, the Shrewsbury Flash, had been one of the first to switch to NASCAR from the cut downs. He performed in a series of #69 cars for Worcester Sand and Gravel. Gaudily splashed with red paint and yellow numbers, these legendary rides were sometimes ragged but always quick. And Fats just made them quicker. He, too, was a stylist—mash the pedal, lean on the right rear, take no prisoners. He was not timid. He thrilled thousands as he powered off the fourth turn, wide open, slightly sideways, his right rear tire begging for mercy.

Irreverent and no-nonsense, Fats often seemed as brash off the track as on it. According to multiple reports, Fats would frequently venture down to the Norwood bar before the main event to scarf down a shot or two to "get ready." The grandest win of his career was in August of 1963 when he outgunned a stellar field in a 200-lap National Championship on the mile at Trenton. As the story goes, the #69 crew spent the entire purse money at the Frontier Club, a local C&W bar room, before borrowing a few bucks to struggle back up the highway to Worcester and Shrewsbury.

Slater and Caruso staged some incredible duels over the next couple of years on the Auto Mile. Ironically, just as the two gained fame together over the next decade in NASCAR, their NASCAR driving careers all but ended the same moment on June 30, 1968. Late that Sunday evening on Thompson's then thinly lit backstretch, Slater tangled with Jerry Dostie coming off turn two. With the front suspension

It is unlikely that three cars could be deeper into the pedal than Caruso, Slater, and Boutwell had them as they flashed by the line in 1962. *(P. Conley photo, Silvia Collection)*

damaged, the #V8 sat in the shadows in the middle of the track. The dirt embankments that protected the infield light poles blocked starter Jimmy Costello's view. As the lead pack raced off the turn, Caruso in Johnny Stygar's #$ Falcon slammed into the disabled #V8 at full speed. Caruso never even saw it coming. There was a horrifying mass of fire and wreckage as eleven cars came to rest near the entrance to turn three. Several drivers were treated for burns including Norwood regular Slim Jim Baker who helped rescue drivers from their burning cars. Slater and Caruso were in critical condition in Day-Kimble Hospital in Putnam, CT. Both faced long and painful recoveries.

Although Slater and Caruso continued their tear in 1963 with 19 wins between them, other old-time names were also getting things figured out—quickly. Hop Harrington had been driving a pretty #23 Ford coupe owned by a 50-year old grandmother from Pawtucket. Bertha Small was a true entrepreneur. An immigrant from Czechoslovakia, she counted repair garages and a laundry near Brown University among her holdings. She loved racing and was seen herself behind the wheel in the occasional Powder Puff. She simply refused to believe the sport dangerous, even after her beloved cut down shoe, Red Bolduc, had been killed. She was convinced he had had a heart attack before the crash. Harrington had bagged a show in both 1961 and 1962, but in 1963 he delivered Bertha's car to consecutive wins on June 15 and June 22. Then, on the autumnal equinox, September 21, he was back up front with a new and beautiful #74, a car he built with Red Hudson and Butch and Roland Fruzetti. The number and the names may have been from the fifties, but the technology was not. The pace-setting vehicle boasted torsion bars, Austin Healy disc brakes, and power steering.

The Lion was also stirring up the jungle. Cleary remembers being almost despondent when the NASCAR boys proved so fast in 1960. But his own psychology got a super charge when he picked up a ride

(left) The NASCAR #74 looked very different from the #74 the Harrington/Fruzetti team fielded with NEARA ten years before. *(P. Conley photo, Silvia Collection)*

(right) Norm Kies' drivers had New London, Plainville, and Riverside figured out with his #21 cars. He brought this #121 to Norwood and had the good sense to hire a Lion. *(P. Conley photo, Silvia Collection)*

in Norm Kies' famous #121 Red Ram. Leo won one late that fall. He then jumped into Henry Rufo's #53, left vacant by Red Hill. He won one in 1962, two in 1963. For 1964 he was back with his old buddy, Bernie Barrows. This was by no means a lavishly funded operation. The garage was so small, says Leo, that he and Joe Gerrior had to move the car over to the left to work on its right.

Nonetheless, Leo was ready, very much focused since his partying days were now over. He, Bernie, and brother Pat spent much time figuring out just what to weld up. Leo wanted something different, something new. It was driving him around the bend, "that guys like Charland and Gahan would start up front in their Sportsman cars, run side by side, and finish up front because no one could pass." The three backyard engineers developed an elegant set-up called the "Cleary rear." Essentially, it replicated the split-spring "Flemke front" in the back of the car. After a little sorting out, Bernie's #2 car proved awesome.

So was the manner in which the Leo chose to drive it. Simply put, the car handled well enough to accommodate the roar of the Lion.

Martin Bezema is still on the Auto Mile today, the successful owner of car dealerships. *(Grady photo)*

Cleary invented a new groove. He began going three deep all the way around Norwood. It was beyond frightening to watch. George Savary says, “Everyone was just plain afraid of him. Today he’d be considered a fruit loop, but, My God, was he fast.” Bernie’s car first took him to top money on July 11 of 1964. Making full use of his new designs over the next few years, Leo would end up second only to Bill Slater in all time Norwood Sportsman-Modified feature wins.

The autumn of 1964 also saw a couple of long time Norwood competitors from Needham come into the limelight. On Labor Day weekend and again the next week, Jack Malone put the blue #79 coupe up front. A successor to the #79 non-Ford driven by Fats, the car was co-owned by Dave Welch, a local excavator, and Greg Mills. Mills and Welch won with Freddie and Billy Shultz and Eddie Flemke as well, before Greg’s tragic death in a highway crash in 1974.

Jack Malone was by this time a successful real estate developer. One of his holdings, a store and garage strip near Needham Center, was fondly known as Gasoline Alley. It housed any number of racing teams over the years, including Bob Melnick, Ronnie Sayers, George Savary, Pete Hamilton, and Lou Austin. A frequent visitor was Needham’s Bob Bacchiochi. “Botch” hustled his #82 Sportsman to the fall championship on September 19, 1964.

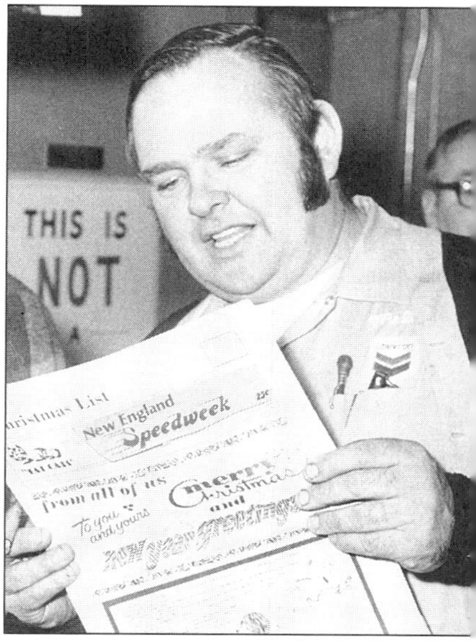

The racing community was stunned when everybody’s pal Greg Mills was killed on the highway. *(Ink, Inc. Collection)*

All the big boys were back in 1965. Not surprisingly the big names were the big winners; Johnny Thompson had his #122 Ford wound up tight to take six; Hop Harrington in the Ed Bean Dodge #1 had five; Cleary, Caruso, and Slater had two each. What was surprising, though, were four new Sportsman winners, each a young guy up from the Hobby Division.

Carl Merrill congratulates Johnny Thompson, July 28, 1968. That’s Assistant Starter Mike Favulli on the right. Like his Dad, Mike was a popular Norwood Official. He then became a fabulous NEMA driver before suffering career-ending injuries at Oxford Plains. *(Balser Photo)*

(left) Bob Melnick must have welded up hundreds of race cars in his shop at Jack Malone's Gasoline Alley. *(P. Conley photo, Silvia Collection)*

(right) Billy Schulz is trying hard. The Hobby division gave JC Crossley, Chuckie LeBlanc, and Bobby Saulnier a real workout with the track wrecker. *(P. Conley photo, Boyd Collection)*

From an undistinguished start in 1960, the division had grown well. Rules were gradually loosened, and by 1965 overheads were allowed as well as flatheads with multiple carburetion. It was no longer just the legacy of the six-cylinder non-Fords. As George Savary says, "It got to be real good competition. We'd watch the modified guys for sure, and they started watching us, too."

As is always the case, over a couple of years divisional stars began to shine. Glenn Legere, Jeff Reed, Bill Darling, Paul Susi, Ronnie Roberts, Bob Melnick, and Fran Voss showed flare.

Billy Shulz, Hobby champion in 1961 and 1962 in his #60 coupe, hopped in the #79 Mills-Welch Sportsman with a win on May 15, just the fourth night out. Then it was time for Bobby Santos, Hobby champ 1963-1964, setting records never to be broken. Known as the Frito Bandito, Hall-of-Famer Santos hustled his #87 Sportsman to victory on August 14.

The other two former hobbyists to win Sportsman mains in 1965 were emerging in a strangely parallel way to Paul Richardson and Jim Cheney that same year up at The Pines. Don MacTavish and Pete Hamilton were just about the same age, friendly rivals, and talented beyond definition. Both would quickly use their successes at Norwood to launch themselves onto the national NASCAR scene in a big way. Both became Hall-of-Famers. But, then, as happened with Cheney and Richardson, fate would split their futures forever.

Mac grew up in Dover, a natty, highbuck suburb of Boston. His circumstance was modest, however, since his dad left while Donnie and his sister Marcia were still infants. For someone bright, wired, and curious about fast cars, it was only a matter of time before he was off to nearby Norwood. By 15 he had his first car, a 1938 Plymouth four-door rampmobile. By age 17, in 1957, he was racing everywhere he could and winning.

Hal Cooper campaigned a #1 Hobby car. In 1963 a bad rollover in the first turn brought him debilitating injuries. *(Duncan Collection)*

Martha's Vineyard's Bart Kent was a gutsy Hobby shoe. Don Berrio, who is now a noted NEMA owner, partnered in this car. *(P. Conley photo, Silvia Collection)*

Glenn Legere took a ride up to Hudson one Sunday night in 1965 and won the show in his Hobby car. *(Duncan Collection)*

Paul Susi of the great Susi family of racing. *(P. Conley photo, Silvia Collection)*

Colorful Al Johnson, who often wore Bermuda shorts. *(P. Conley photo, Silvia Collection)*

Walter Scott won his share. *(P. Conley photo, Silvia Collection)*

MacTavish's travels in the fifties and early sixties were, truth be known, often pretty unsightly. He did show obvious signs of promise as a driver and certainly had a good sense for mechanics and engineering. He was a graduate of Franklin School of Technology. However, some of his early cars were substandard. One night he rolled

(left) Don MacTavish looks pretty darn pleased with his first trophy. And how about Miss Norwood Arena, 1958? *(P. Conley photo, Berggren Collection*

(right) Perfect formation. That's MacTavish in his #J, Jack Malone upstairs in the #L-1, and Doug McCarthy out front. *(P. Conley photo, Silvia Collection)*

hard at Westboro and his cage collapsed, costing him a chunk of his ear. He was at Norwood the next night, his ear bandaged. The roll bars were somewhat back in place, but not even butted up or spliced. They were simply pieced back in, laying on top of one another, and welded up.

The deeper Mac got into racing technology, the deeper he got into things that did his reputation no favors. He became the world's most innovative rule bender. He'd run multiple carbs, hidden beneath a sub-hood; he'd run an illegal Ford rear, wrapped with Marcia's sweater. "That's to keep the gear lube warm", he told Al Charbonneau, Norwood Tech Inspector.

When Mac moved up to the senior division, he preserved his edgy image by lettering his cars funkily, sometimes with overtly sexual connotations. Additionally, he supported his Sportsman operation by participating in Demo Derbies. He was just as good as they come, even winning the first ABC-televised World Championship demo in 1963. However, being seen as a demo driver was not thought proper for an upwardly mobile NASCAR racer.

When Mac wheeled his #J Sportsman into Victory Lane on August 28, 1965, a motley swarm of out-of-control guys called "the Clan" hooted and hollered with congratulation. Mac was no dummy, however. He knew at this point that he wanted big time, to go big time racing; he knew he would have to change his image.

Mac's buddy, Pete Hamilton, did not have this problem with public persona. Not that many people knew anything about him when he stunned the rail birds with a second place finish to Smokey Boutwell opening night in 1965. Folks sure knew him by season end, though, as he drove Ray Stonkus' #Flying 9 to four convincing wins over the summer and third place in the point standings. A commanding win in both legs of the Fall's World Series at Thompson capped off a fabulous year.

Hamilton, son of a professor and academic administrator from Newton, looked so freshly-scrubbed and squeaky-clean that it was hard to envision him in a race car. But, while working at Bob Bacchiochi's garage, he went to Norwood to watch Botch race. Swept away on the spot, he was there the next week in a Henry J Novice car. It must have been fun to watch. Pete laughs about "taking my helmet off and walking away, the car still upside down with the wheels spinning." (Hamilton's first night could have been an instant replay of another Hall-of-Famer, Don MacLaren. Big Mac's first lap ever was at Norwood in jalopy days. He, too, was in a Henry J. It, too, was upside down on the first lap.)

It would be one more week before Hamilton won in the novices, a scant four years till he won in the Sportsman. He attributes his success to focus and he is probably right. "After that novice car there was nothing else that I wanted to do with my life than be a race car driver. That was a gift. I am so grateful that I knew that so early. I don't think I had a lot of natural ability. That is what you see in a Bugsy or a Cale Yarborough. They don't need to know a shock from a spring. And Richard Petty—I think he didn't have enormous natural ability, but he sure had the drive. I did, too. That's what helped me, along with three or four great mentors."

Bob Melnick and Jack Malone tutored Peter during Hobby days in a #V8 coupe. By 1964 and 1965 in Ronnie Sayres' #720 Sportsman and the Stonkus' #Flying 9, the determined Hamilton was also now listening closely to the most learned Modified professor of them all, Ed Flemke. Hamilton's deep respect for Flemke, who died of a heart attack in 1984, is still obvious. He speaks almost emotionally about how Eddie was willing to share with him his "technique for racing." Not just driving or building a car, but a whole, integrated, attitudinal package. It worked.

That youngsters MacTavish and Hamilton were winning was incredible because it was high noon at Norwood. The great Nutmeg racer Dick Watson, who came to the Auto Mile from time to time those

(left) Before Ray Stonkus (holding flag) hooked up with Pete Hamilton, he campaigned his "Bay State Hustler" with veteran Wally Silva in the seat. Al Hurd drove it before Silva. *(P. Conley photo, Silvia Collection)*

(right) Bobby Santos in the #87 leads an unsightly Hobby scene. It's Ricky Riberio in the #Cloud 9, Pete Hamilton in the #V8, Jeff Reed in the #92, and Al Johnson dirt-tracking the #12%. *(P. Conley photo, Silvia Collection)*

Jerry Dolliver hustles Jr. Prescott's beautiful #24 ahead of Pete Hamilton, in his first Sportsman ride, and Hop Harrington on June 6, 1964. *(P. Conley photo Silvia Collection)*

years, recalls, "It was simply amazing. The competition was so tight, so intense. All the way around there would be constant bumps and bangs. Front, rear, the sides. It was nothing dirty. Just really good, fast racing."

A see-saw battle for the 1965 point championship thrilled the fans the entire year. On the last night, a hyper-motivated Leo Cleary was intent on taking the championship away from Bill Slater who had won the last three in a row. Only six points behind, Leo pulled out onto the track for the feature and stopped dead. Broken clutch linkage. Much to the Lion's surprise, he was motioned by relative newcomer, Fred DeSarro, to jump in his #11 Sportsman. Unfortunately for Leo, it was to no avail. Slater pulled it out, 1288 to 1244 points. "What a thing for Freddie to do," says Leo. "I didn't even know him at the time. In the end we were the greatest friends."

It could have seemed "déjà vu all over again" when "Wild Bill" Slater repeated the Norwood Championship yet again in 1966. But times were achangin'. Opening night he was caught in a nasty front stretch crash when Barney Mattie's #7 spun into the infield and slid back on the track into Slater. Slater's car hit the wall and flipped, wiping out the Rocket. In 2003 after a moderate stroke, Slater received a phone call from a man wanting to know if Slater "remembered the guy who put him in the wall at Norwood." It was Mattie checking in on an old friend. The recollections were much merrier than the event.

Some predicted that the 1966 crash would be the end of the Rocket, but two weeks later, a rain-out in between, the black and yellow coupe was right back in victory circle. All was not well, though, and by mid-season Bombaci and Vitari decided to call it quits, leaving Bill pretty much to his own devices. He did win the title, but the days of famed #V8 dominance were gone.

Bill Slater will always remember April 28, 1966. It was quite a crash. *(P. Conley photo, Silvia Collection)*

Jerry Dostie in Art Barry's #909, Seekonk star Dave Dias in his brother Manny's #3c, fun-loving Bobby Sprague in Harold and Preston Hathaway's #86, Doug McCarthy in the #4 Sportsman, and George Pendergast in the Pondue Bickie #53 were all first-time victors. In 1965 a trophy from Norwood was very big stuff. The merriment in the Pendergast pit after his 30-lap victory on June 16 was so spirited that he broke his arm.

One driver who had not run Norwood in previous years was first on July 9 and twice more, winning the Modified championship over a most frustrated Leo Cleary. Seekonk-schooled Bugsy Stevens came to Norwood with two main attributes—a boat load of natural ability and a bedraggled mechanic/owner named Lenny Boehler from Freetown. Everyone paid immediate attention. Pete Hamilton tells Bones Bourcier in the book *BUGSY!* that, "The Bug epitomized what a race driver should look like both on and off the track... He had an aura about him even then, close to cocky. I very much looked up to him."

Perhaps more important than what Bugsy did at Norwood was what he did for Norwood. Over the next three years, before the Modifieds left the Auto Mile, Bugsy and Lenny, Don MacTavish, George Colwell, Julian Garcia and Pete Hamilton, Dick Trabish and the two Rays (Stonkus and Spognardi) joined to form a kind of

(left) Dick Jackson, #27JR, Jerry Dostie, and Bob Bacchiochi battle it out. Dostie's #909 was owned by Art Barry, one of the Northeast's most accomplished owner-builders. *(P. Conley photo Silvia Collection)*

(right) Jack Malone leads Fran Voss in the #5A, Bobby Sprague in #86, and George Pendergast (if not Nutsy Fagan) in the #302. *((P. Conley photo, Silvia Collection)*

Jack Lundin's Explosive Career

Burlington's Jack Lundin is one of the select few to win at Westboro, The Pines, and Norwood. What makes the feat especially laudable is that his entire driving career lasted barely eight years.

Lundin was just plain predetermined to be a racer. His grandfather was an old-time motorcycle jockey back in flat track days. His dad was a drag racer, and, when he was growing up, they all went to the races.

As Lundin describes it, "I loved watching the MacLarens and Clearys of the world. They were my heros". So when he put together a little Chrysler non-Ford for West Peabody in 1959, it was natural that he would go to folks like Leo to find out what to do. Forty-five years later, he remembers the words of the Lion: "The better she rides, the faster she goes". With the advantages of having a dad in the pits and a grandfather's machine shop for support, he listened carefully. They made everything themselves—including the springs—all to Leo's specs, and they won the second night out.

In 1963 the Lundins ventured down to the Auto Mile. Their car was not well funded, but it sure did the trick. They took on the Hobby Division with a six cylinder GMC in a '37 Chevy frame under a massively lightened '49 Chevy body. The car had an internal porta-power, allowing Jack to adjust weight from the driver's seat. It also had adjustable motor mounts and drive-shafts of varying lengths to allow for major chassis adjustment. Right from lap one, railbirds considered this #1 car a contender. The Lundins reeled in a seventh place finish in points the first year, ninth the next. But in 1965, it was just plain hang on. Jack rocketed to the Hobby championship, winning an astounding, record-making 12 of the 25 features with 20 top fives.

With some time off to drive Forrest Dame's cut down at Hudson and The Pines, the Lundins' next adventure was a NASCAR modified. Despite their marginal financing, they were first the second night out at Norwood, nipping Hop Harrington on July 1, 1967.

Over the course of the next fall, Jack and his Dad built a glistening new mod that sat ready to go by December. That's when it happened.

The week before Christmas, during a heating system service call, a gas leak ignited, and the Lundins' home was blown up. Jack was at work, but his wife Catherine, their two children, and two cousins were inside. The force of the blast literally blew them into other rooms, and a bulldozer had to be brought in to open the house up, so twisted were the walls and doors. Amazingly, no one was killed, but the Lundins faced the full hardships of recovery from this kind of misfortune. Insurance was woefully inadequate, and Jack spent most of the next thirty years with two full time jobs, trying to catch up. That accomplished, he now builds racing engines in his Lundin Machine business in Burlington.

Jack in his tricked-out 1949 Chevy. *(P. Conley photo, Silvia Collection)*

Lundin goes inside to win in a Hobby coupe in 1964 *(P. Conley photo, Silvia Collection)*

Though he was never able to race again, the thrill of the game—and especially of Norwood—simply never left. "For us guys from Peabody and Pines, going to Norwood was like going to Indianapolis. Driving there was like driving Bristol. I still feel the itch. Catherine says that each year when the spring brings warmth, my blood turns just naturally to fuel."

(left) Bugsy Stevens and Lenny Boehler took a lot of hardware out of Norwood Arena. This time the presenter was Governor John A. Volpe. To his left, Miss Norwood Arena, Wes Plummer, and Herb Anderson. *(Merrill Collection)*

(right) Without George Colwell (L) and Lenny Boehler, there would have been no championships. No glory. *(Berggren photo)*

"Bandits Two." Off they went down the road, bringing further notoriety to Norwood. Picking up from Rene Charland in 1965, Mac put in a beyond-Herculean effort and earned the 1966 National Sportsman championship, running an amazing 122 shows. He was in the top five eighty times, first Sportsman 28 times, winner eleven times. All said and done, he accumulated 8968 national points. The much less-traveled Slater was second with 5768 and Charland was third with 5490.

Hamilton in Matteo Trotto's Worcester Sand and Gravel funded Sportsman and Stevens in Boehler's Ole Blue coupe waved to each other quite a bit over the next year, all over the East Coast. They brought home to Norwood both 1967 national titles, Sportsman and Modified. Bugsy and Lenny held a tight grip on the modified title in 1968 and 1969 as well. Bugsy writes in his biography, "Lenny and I weren't really aware that we were living this romantic gypsy lifestyle; we were probably numb…it was sleep and drive, drive and sleep. All those miles."

In 1967 the Lion in Norwood finally got his meat. A decade after winning the title in Longy's cutdown, Leo Cleary teamed with Massachusetts racing personality, Iron Mike Scrivani. The tough talking Scrivani, owner of a huge truck stop on Route 1, bought the equipment from an ailing Bernie Barrows. Leo finally had some bucks behind him. He was on the hammer. "In the last two laps, let the fenders fall where they may," became a favorite Leo-ism of the time. He won the track championships at both Norwood and Thompson. He shared the number of most wins, four, with a red-hot Freddie DeSarro in his #11 Sportsman. Gene Bergin was quick in Beebe

(left) Sam (Holland) the Bardahl Man greets Hobby sensation, Don Kibbe. *(P. Conley photo, Silvia Collection)*

(right) Moonlit mods of Don McCulloch #42, Frank Faria #34, popular Ronnie Roberts #33, and Bob Bacchiochi #4. *(P. Conley photo, Silvia Collection)*

Zalinski's #M-6, as was Freddie Shulz, replacing his brother Billy in the Mills-Welch #79. Bobby Melnick was a winner in his Gasoline Alley #45. Mike McClelland nipped Don Kibbe from another Hobby Championship. Fred Mancini, George Savary, and Jack Luciano followed. John Harcourt won the Junior Hobby contest over Butch Armstrong, Len Baker, Armando Viera, Jr., and Jerry Driscoll.

Leo made it two for two in the 1968 point chase over Jack Malone in talented Roy Devereaux's #L1 and Fred Shultz in the NuStyle #14. First time winners were the very popular Lou Austin in the Kevin Coan/Tuck Hoffman #73 Ford, East Providence's Frank Faria, and Hobby grad Jeff Reed, who beat Don McCulloch and Cleary on June 15. The season also saw a major change, mirroring a new look in Daytona. The Hobby division had been scrapped. The great old coupes and coaches were replaced with a late-model-bodied "Tiger" division. George Delmar pulled out an impressive ten of the twenty-two mains. Bill Singersen, Leo Nevins, Dennis Ryan, Mike Terrio, and Ken Phinney were also tough.

The people's choice, Lou Austin. From this picture you can tell what a good guy he is. He was also very fast in his #73 Ford, both at Norwood and Martinsville. *(Balser Photo)*

Pete Hamilton (L) and Don MacTavish looked a lot different from a lot of guys their age during the 1969 Vietnam era. *(Cohen Collection)*

Before it was even started, the 1969 season was knocked completely off its pins. Buddies Don MacTavish and Pete Hamilton were still sharing notes, still on the road, and still obsessionally focused on reaching racing's highest level. Newly fluffed and buffed, media-conscious Mac had put in some strong runs at Daytona's February Permatex races and he had recently been in upstate New York racing and building cars. Following his 1967 Sportsman title, Pete was already shopping for Grand National rides. He won Rookie of the Year in 1968 before losing his sponsor.

For the 1969 Permatex race on the 2 and 1/2 mile Daytona tri-oval, Mac had signed with New Jersey's Don House and had high hopes. Pete had run the car in the same event the year before and had looked good. Mac was also excited. He claimed he had a Grand National ride lined up for later in the year. As Pete watched from the Goodyear Tower and millions watched on ABC *Wide World of Sports*, the sleek #5 car crashed the wall with that horrid kind of violence after which everything goes silent. There was no chance of survival. One of New England's greatest hopes to reach the big time was dead. Hamilton admits that watching Donnie die was the hardest thing he has ever been through. He left the tower and walked to a quiet section in the back of the pits and wept. "The next thing I knew Richard Petty came along, grabbed me by the arm, and took me to his family area. He told me I didn't need press people watching me at that moment. He calmed me down. He was pretty darn thoughtful to a goofy rookie from Boston."

Hamilton seemed to have that God-given talent of making the most of anything. In an incredible sequence of twists and turns, his future proved to be as divergent from poor Mac's as Paul Richardson's was from Jimmy Cheney way back up in Massachusetts. The very next year, Pete Hamilton was right back at Daytona. Right in the Grand Nationals, the big boy division. And this time he was in a best-of-class

Pete Hamilton at work in the Petty Superbird. *(Berggren Photo)*

car—a #40 Superbird fielded by none other than Richard Petty and Petty Enterprises, with Dodge support to boot.

That Sunday the "goofy rookie" from Boston stunned the world by winning the Daytona 500 in a most magnificent manner, outdueling the Silver Fox of NASCAR, David Pearson. No one could have been prouder than the fans back up at Norwood. Their guy had just pulled off the most significant racing feat of any Massachusetts driver since Brockton-born Fred Frame won the Indianapolis 500 in 1932. And, just nine years before, they had watched with amusement as this kid slipped out of his overturned Henry J, the wheels still spinning.

Somehow it was almost as if the air would not clear in 1969, so devastated was everyone after Mac's crash. Even as Jack Malone wheeled the #L-1 to victory on the April 26 opener, the karma of the pits was bad. And, as is usually the case, money had its part in it. In contrast to the continuity of rules under NARA in the fifties, it seemed that NASCAR and Norwood management were changing things every two minutes. From 1960 through 1962, there had been the sportsman and modified divisions. For 1963 the mods were dropped, and "limited sportsman" cars were started ahead of the sportsmen in the features. In the fall of 1965 the modifieds were back with the sportsmen. Then, in 1969, it was modifieds only. New rule books almost always mean more expense for racers. Additionally, Norwood's payoffs were no longer as meaty as they were back in the fifties.

Before long a group of owners and drivers spearheaded by Dick Armstrong, owner of Fred Schulz' #14 coach, popped up. To Norwood's Board NEDOC (New England Drivers and Owners Club) it sure looked a lot like Independent, especially when the noise about

(left) Sometimes Bob Judkins brought his #2x to Norwood and he would win with Ed Flemke. Sometimes he went to Fonda where he won with Kenny Shoemaker. That's Angie Nardone kneeling. He was Mayor of the Infield. Dan Brundage holds the flags and Steady Eddie is in the office. *(P. Conley photo, Silvia Collection)*

(right) It was April 26, 1969. Joe Brady came with a late model modified Mustang with Ford big block power for Leo Cleary. Once they got it sorted out, they were really hooked up. *(Balser photo)*

the purses started. By the end of May there was a strike at Norwood, Thompson, and the recently-paved Stafford Springs.

In order to cover their fannies, the various track promoters did what Oscar Ridlon would have done. They brought in the midgets. In the case of Norwood, says Carl Merrill, "They played to about 100 people, max." By June negotiations were progressing, and the guys were back. In truth, however, it was not over. George Savary called it. "When we came back, management said 'no hard feelings', but I didn't believe it. I knew they had not wanted to give in." Merrill was once again in the middle. He claims he urged the Board "to play good ball, but they refused. They were just plain too hard-nosed." The Directors had already proven that, when ten years earlier they had dispatched the cut downs. Now they were seeing red about the replacement. Everyone knew that sooner or later a shoe was going to drop.

The season progressed quite unspectacularly. Johnny Thompson was like lightning in his checkerboard #122 Ford and got five wins. Nonetheless, all said and done, he was second in points behind fifties-style charger, Freddie Schulz. Brother Billy showed a lot of verve in hard-working Joe Buccilli's #3d with wins on July 5 and September 27. And old-timers packed the bar after Barnie Mattie brought the Red Devil #7 to the checkerboards for the first time since the fifties.

(bottom) The great Freddie DeSarro strikes a pensive pose. Rhode Island Fred was quieter, less high profile than a Bugsy. But, when he died at Thompson, there was a huge hole in everyone's heart. *(Lloyd Burnham photo, Berggren Collection)*

(left) Roland LaPierre Sr. guns his injected coupe past the final modified victory flag ever at Norwood. *(Balser photo)*

(right) Westboro grad Bobby Karvonen leads Booker T. Jones in the #27. Booker was one of the few minorities to try Norwood. Much loved, he became a Hall-of-Famer. *(P. Conley photo, Silvia Collection)*

On the final night, a cool October 4 evening, 54 year old Roland LaPierre, the former cut down star, thrilled the whole place with a winning drive in his under-funded #134 coupe. It was no cake walk. Running right off his bumper were Ed Flemke, Bugs Stevens, and Fred DeSarro.

On December 1 the real significance of Roland's romp sank in. It had been the last Modified race ever to be held on the Auto Mile. In a press release, Wes Plummer couched the ire of the Board towards the Modifieds by saying "the track management is of the opinion that a shift to the Late Model Sportsman division of NASCAR is the proper direction to move if newer fans are to be attracted to the track, if newer owners and drivers are encouraged to participate in stock car racing, and if a competitive field of race cars is to be maintained."

Trouble is, the Board—and NASCAR—were wearing rose colored glasses. It would be very difficult to come up with an example of A-frame cars ever having replaced Modified cars while not devastating the fan base. Norwood turned out to be no exception. Just as when the cut downs left The Pines, when the Modifieds towed out of Norwood, it was the beginning of the end. And, almost as if to provide a straight and fast route directly there, the Board offered up another misadventure. It was that drag strip.

Drag racing at Norwood cranked up tentatively in the early sixties, and, in fairness, pretty much in the way the Board had told the town it would happen. A modestly sized eighth-mile run was set up right near the oval. Local competitors brought in their street machines and tested them against the clock. Crowds were hardly huge, but the complexity was. No one was prepared for the countless recording of types of cars, classes, and the lines of kids revving their motors. It was a lot of work.

It must have been oh so easy for the Board to come to terms with the managers of the very successful New England Dragway in Epping, NH. These guys wanted to promote Norwood with a passion, and

NORWOOD

The Preservationists

Quite fortunately there has been a cadre of individuals committed to collecting and preserving all possible aspects of pioneering racing in Massachusetts.

For close to sixty years RA Silvia has been diligently compiling a wonderfully thorough library of regional racing materials in his home in Warwick, RI. RA's files cover all tracks in New England and virtually every division. He is widely recognized as the leading authority. Meanwhile, Tommy Caruso, whose interest is mostly in big cars and midgets, has collected a fascinating stable of cars, memorabilia, and literature —almost a museum—at his "old tyme" garage in Tyngsboro.

Two publishers, Val LeSieur and Dick Berggren have been consistently supportive of the heritage of the sport, both over a period of over twenty five years. Val's weekly paper, *Speedway Scene*, published in North Easton, has been the local racing bible. Phil Smith and Jay Hathaway have been particularly well-read contributors. Dick Berggren, through his work as a TV racing personality and his role as Editor of Salisbury's *Speedway Illustrated* magazine, has brought national attention to Massachusetts' rich racing past.

Many people, of course, have contributed to the hundreds of photographs in this volume, but none as fully as Norton's Bill Balser. Bill has been in the infields each weekend for literally fifty years, clicking away while dodging errant race cars. He is very much active today, supported enthusiastically by his eagle-eyed son, David.

Most especially over the last couple of years retroactive racing buffs have been running lots of laps on the Internet. Tom Ormsby's *www.vintage-modifieds.com* covers all of New England and it features Phil Smith's "Looking Back" columns. Don Thomas' site, *www.NorwoodArena.com*, has been really well received and Don is hosting annual Norwood reunions as well. Meanwhile, former racer Steve Newman maintains a great site, *www.ThePinesSpeedway.com*, while Lenny Maughn and North Shore race enthusiast Dwight Lowes have been running autumn get-togethers for Pines folks.

The new wave of enthusiasm for vintage racing has also given birth to two strong car clubs. Charlie and Mary Lima of New Bedford manage STAR, Senior Tour Auto Racers, that offer a field of restored or replica cars that actually compete on short tracks. New England Antique Racers (NEAR), run by Longmeadow's Al Fini and a very engaged Board, has also a full roster of historically significant cars. NEAR is better known, though, for its Hall-of-Fame that, to date, has bestowed upon over sixty of New England's greatest racers the honors so fully deserved.

Bill and Phyllis Balser *(Balser Collection)*

Val LeSieur—thirty years of weekly publishing of Speedway Scene. *(Balser photo)*

Dick Berggren—thirty-five years of writing and broadcasting. *(Berggren Collection)*

(left) (L-R) Butch Savary, Dan Brundage, and Carl Merrill congratulate George Savary for winning opening night of 1970, the first Late Model year. *(Balser photo)*

(right) George Delmar and his car owner, Monty Montecalvo. Delmar appeared to be on his way to bright late model stardom until he never returned from a race at Devil's Bowl in Fair Haven, VT. He was found in his crashed plane months later. *(Balser photo)*

they knew how. What apparently they did not know was how the Directors had characterized the drag strip to the town. The new operators went for it. The track was expanded to a quarter mile, and the muscled cars blasting down it were not from the driveway next door. Suddenly it was serious. A whole new deal.

A couple of injuries and a fatality were stern strikes against the strip. But what really put things over the top was a blow to the ear. When jet-powered dragsters were brought in for one of their dazzling nighttime fire and lightning shows, talented Norwood photographer, Paul Conley says he could hear them all the way from his home in Dedham Center. "It was deafening. Can you imagine what those folks were who lived just a few hundred yards away were thinking?" It's not hard to imagine. They were furious. Funny cars at 11:00 at night. No way. They wanted the place closed. The whole damn thing.

Norwood's operational team, Carl Merrill (Director of Racing), Russ Bears (concessionaire), and Neil Hawley (office manager), had ample things to worry about as spring of 1970 approached. The neighbors were up in arms, and no one knew if there would even be enough of these late model cars to put on a decent show. As would have been expected, a brief season was planned, just 21 nights. It was one cheap, stripped-down promotion. No race all year was more than 30 laps.

Bob (left) and Rick Healey in July 1971. *(Balser photo, NorwoodArena.com Collection)*

George Savary, saying that he really had nothing else to do, grudgingly put together a '57 Chevy. He won opening and closing nights, enough to earn him the Championship. His choice of weapon was on the money. '57 Chevies won 16 of the feature races. Dave Lind, Jack Peterson, and Len Baker got one each in a Ford, and Jerry Driscoll propelled his purple Plymouth to the podium on the fourth of July.

Bob Healey, son of Liz and brother of racer Rick, had the most wins with four. The most consecutive weeks in the top five was won by Dave Peterson, Jack's brother. Dave was carrying on the Peterson family's long and honored involvement in New England racing when he was killed in a modified at Thompson a couple of seasons later. Roy Chamberlin was the 1970 Street Division Champ. Paul Roche, Don Hunt, Bob Armstrong, and Joey and Steve Kourafas were also on the prowl.

Everyone was hoping for brighter days in 1971, but a message in the program said it all. It would be "...the year of challenge as we enter the era of ecology and play a part in a program of noise pollution." Carl Merrill was working intensely, mandating Thrush mufflers, monitoring the noise of the late models with equipment placed around the local neighborhoods. It was a touchy situation, and NASCAR was listening very closely. Aware that this thing could really blow up,

(left) Frank Hayes greets Dave Peterson with the checker. Some of the Tiger Division guys worried about the higher speeds carried at Thompson on Sundays. David paid the ultimate price. *(Balser photo)*

(right) Hold a race on the dirt at Lakeville or in the quarry in Barre, VT, and Jerry Driscoll would be there. Here he is at Norwood's warmup day, April 19, 1970. *(Balser photo)*

NASCAR really was aware of the noise problem. Bill France Jr. came up to check it out. That's Earl Grant to his right. *(Balser photo)*

Daytona insisted that the track not even mention the word "muffler" in any outreach whatsoever. In other words, muffle the whole thing.

Les Rose, Jerry Driscoll, George Savary, Armando Viera, Jr., and Ron Larkin were top dogs that year. Don Hunt, Frank Kuhlman, and Rick Healey were chief streets. Two divisions were created to try to fatten up the lonely pits. Chuck Whynot, smiling Jerry Capazzoli, and Slim Jim Baker had the fastest Volkswagens, while Russ Webber and Jim Cousin were best in the Limited Streets.

Dynamite Dave Dion *(Balser photo)*

One April day back in the sixties, three brothers towed a 1948 Ford down from New Hampshire to test out the Hobbies. Living just a stone's throw from Oscar Ridlon's Hudson Speedway, Dave, Paul, and Roger Dion were avid cut down fans, but they had other aspirations. "We had read in the papers about NASCAR. It sounded so professional. We wanted to join in and to run down South," says Dave. They decided to try Norwood and it sure was tough sledding. "I was absolutely scared to death driving down there. When we raced, I couldn't believe we could get into trouble going so slow, but we did. All three of us had the same level of knowledge. Nothing."

Eventually Vietnam forced an intermission, and when Dave was back, the Late Models were in. Everyone facing a new and unfamiliar rule book, the Dions fared much better and deep in the autumn of 1971 they finally won their first show. Busting with enthusiasm, off they went to Martinsville, VA's fall National Championship. Much to their pleasure, they qualified and ran well. The fuse was lit.

A sleek new Torino body and a snappy Trans-Am Ford motor from AJ Foyt's stable helped make them Norwood's Alpha car in 1972.

Jerry Capazzoli always had a grin. Sam Holland looks pretty amused, too. *(Balser photo)*

Dave says they were not appreciated by the locals. "Jack Malone, Bobby Melnick, Billy Hughes, and those guys had well-funded operations. They didn't take to us from Cow Hampshire. It got testy. One night I flipped the length of the backstretch."

When the dust finally settled, "Dynamite Dave" Dion had scooped the majority of the races, the September 2 Permatex (the final show), and the 1972 point Championship. It should have been very significant for Norwood that Dion that year went on the road, that endless vapor-trail he travels still today. He is New England's recognized master of Late Models. He has competed all over Canada, New England, in New York, Virginia, the South—anywhere the A-Frame cars are booked. The Brothers seemed to develop their own form of "technique", and their Fords have been upfront all over the East Coast. David says, "We just thrived on being outsiders. We were always better on the road than at home. There is something about going into someone else's stadium that turns me on."

Couldn't that have been spoken by Rene—or Pete Hamilton? It sure has the ring of another round of Eastern Banditry—someone yet again winning races, traveling all night, carrying laurels back to Norwood. The irony is that just as the Brothers Dion were opening up, Norwood Arena was closing down.

(left) Billy Singersen drove many divisions in the final years with great success. *(Balser photo)*

(right) Among the best of the seventies Streeters was Dick Inman, shown here In August, 1970. He died a month before his wedding in a highway crash. *(Balser photo)*

Veteran Jack Malone came back to spice up the Late Model field and he did just that in Joe Brady's #41. Brady, far right, is one of the most storied Modified owners of all times. *(Balser photo)*

You can bet that by 1972 the Board was pretty much fed up. The non-racers had been through 25 summers of racing, and now there was little to show for it. Shareholders had received no dividends. In fact, things were pretty darn squeaky financially and problems were growing like weeds. The town, mightily offended by the drag strip, was getting sticky about permits; the neighbors were relentlessly loud about the noise; the pit area never refilled after the exodus of the mods; crowds were terrible.

In times like these without committed leadership the Board Room can turn completely self-serving. That's just what happened at Norwood. According to Carl Merrill, faced with the Arena's unpaid note of $350,000 to a local bank, Wes Plummer went to lawyers and realtors to discuss selling the property. An auction was the way to go, and Plummer was assured the facility would bring $1,000,000. He instantly began making the rounds to shareholders, trying to buy up stock in advance of a sale. Hearing of the plan, Merrill, Russ Bears, and Harry Butters attempted a minority suit to block it. They failed.

On a gray morning that fall, a small group of suits assembled just outside the now tired-looking buildings and stands. Upon the auctioneer's opening, the bank was quick and businesslike to go to $350,000 to cover its exposure. Next a representative from the Faded Glory jeans company called out "$351,000." The auctioneer acknowledged and called for further interest. There was none. The words "sold for the sum of $351,000" were hardly out of his mouth when the Directors, completely aghast, looked at each other as if to say, "My God! We have just lost everything."

Faded glory, indeed.

(Carl Merrill Collection)

INDEX

AAA, 4, 88, 89, 93, 94, and throughout
Abbot, Ray, 111
Abbott, Art, 93
Abbott, Paul, 115
Ace Express Special, 123
Adaskaveg, Mike, 192
Alden, Mark, 60
Alexander, Bob, 174, 175, 184
Allard, Candy, 125
Allard, Lee, 65, 119, 121, 123, 125, 128, and throughout
Allard, Red, 13
Allen, Si, 60, 61
Allison, Bobby, 109
Alvarez, Pancho, 109
Ambrosio, Bill, 72
Ambrosio, Danny, 173
American Racing Association, 11
Anderson, Andy, 22, 155, 165, 168, 169, 170, and throughout
Anderson, Herb, 151, 171, 206
Anderson, Rufe, 8, 87, 91
Andretti, Mario, 180
Andrews, Bill, 11
Antonellis, Billy, 50, 51
Antonellis, Larry, 20, 27, 44, 173, 178, 190, and throughout
Aramian, Bill, 129
ARC, 45, 46, 55, 56
Archambault, Archie, 109, 116, 117, 119, 127
ARDC, 166
Arden, Carmi, 160
Arden, Emily, 160
Argentina, Rocca, 31, 78
Arlington Diner, 105
Armstrong, Bob, 215
Armstrong, Butch, 207
Armstrong, Dick, 209
Armstrong, Skip, 119
Army Corps of Engineers, 104
Arnold, Jeff, 128
Arrigo, Johnny, 44, 45, 46, 51
Arundel Speedway, 136
Ascot Speedway, 61
Astle, Deke, 37, 53, 62
Astle, Fred, 21, 56, 62, 177
Astle, Jon, 46, 62
Atherton, Barney, 109
Atlantic Auto Racing Association (AARA), 4, 11, 21, 24, 41, 42, and throughout
Auclair #L-1, 179
Austin, Lou, 139, 197, 207
Australia, 37

Bacchiochi, Bob "Botch", 26, 197, 201, 207
Bahre, Bob, 143
Bailey, Don, 11
Baker, Bob, 26
Baker, Buck, 190
Baker, Jim "Slim", 195, 216
Baker, Lenny, 47, 207, 215
Balch, Thomas, 86
Baldiga, Bill, 46
Baldwin, Choppy, 114, 116, 119
Balser, Bill, 27, 30, 173, 212, 213
Balser, Dave, 212
Balser, Phyllis, 213
Banville, Roland, 169
Barbeau, Henri "Red", 19, 21, 26, 169, 179
Bard, Bobby, 53
Bardahl Special #50, 109, 126
Barrows, Bernie, 176, 196, 197, 206
Barry, Art, 203
Barthell, Bill, 124, 125, 140
Barthell, Frank, 124, 125, 140
Barzda, Joe, 84
Batchelder, Dick, 143
Batmobile, 42
Bay State Midget Racing Association (BSMRA), 3, 4, 5, 89, 92, 93, and throughout
Bay State Railroad Company, 86
Bean, Ed, 171, 197
Bean Mountain, 178
Bear Ridge Speedway, 68
Bears, Russ, 214, 218
Beauregard, Dick, 23
Beauvais, Phil, 129
Becker, Al, 47, 49, 50
Beebe, Jack, 74
Beech Ridge Speedway, 136, 186
Beeso, Red, 42, 43, 47, 50
Belanger, Teddy, 106
Bell, Dave, 78
Belmont, Sparky, 93
Beneditto, Pete, 45
Bentley, Earl, 102
Bergeron, Paul, 117, 119
Berggren, Dick, 104, 170, 212, 213
Bergin, Gene, 190, 206
Bernardi, Johnny, 4, 5, 91, 153, 154
Bernstein, Bennie, 100
Berrio, Don, 199
Bertrand, Billy, 36, 40, 47
Bezanson, Buzz, 111, 115, 129
Bezema, Marty, 196
Bianchi, Bob, 181
Bigelow, Eliot, 51
Billington, Harry, 1, 2, 22
Bird, Amos, 76, 81
Bird, Steve, 76
Bishop, Rollie, 95
Bixby, Bob, 128, 133, 145
Black, Johnny, 3, 60, 90, 93, 155, 157, and throughout
Blaine, Eddie, 123
Blaine Special, 110
Blair, Bob, 3, 4, 86, 88, 90, 91, 96, and throughout
Blaisdel, "Colonel", 53
Blanchard, Dave, 73, 74
Blanchard, Don, 146
Blomberg, Adolph "Longy", 156, 159, 164, 174, 179, 181, and throughout
Blood, Milt, 26
Bloom, Herbie, 56
Blout, Cal, 181
Bodine, Geoff, 48, 6, 123
Boehler, Lenny, 53, 54, 74, 203, 206
Boise, Marty, 26, 36
Bolduc, Arthur "Red", 10, 13, 17, 160, 164, 165, and throughout
Bolduc, Moe, 116
Bolduc, Omer "Pop", 170, 171, 188
Bombaci, Vic, 193, 202
Bombaci-Vitari #V8, 186
Bombara, Steve, 47
Bonadies, Tony, 181
Bonin, Bob, 6
Bonnierick Special, 128, 139
Bonser, Bob, 137
Borden, Fred, 17, 17, 22, 23, 26, 28, and throughout
Borden, June, 44
Boston Garden, 84
Bouchard, Ken, 37, 49, 53, 75
Bouchard, Ronald, 37, 45, 49, 50, 53, 56, and throughout
Bouchard, Bob, 37, 49, 74
Bouchard, Bob (Salem), 135, 138
Bourcier, Mark "Bones", 203
Bourget, Tommy, 20, 49, 57
Boutwell, Judi, 118

Boutwell, Nathan "Smokey", 22, 111, 115, 117, 119, 124, and throughout
Bowley, Ed, 29, 114, 193
Boyd, Lew, 31, 35, 39, 42, 43, 81, and throughout
Brady, Joe, 60, 64, 210, 217
Brandy Brow, 128
Brawner, Clint, 180
Brazil, Larry, 109
Bristol Speedway, 205
Brokvist, Vic, 145
Brookline Speedway, 21, 26, 34, 37, 38, 49, and throughout
Brooks, Al, 47
Brooks, Bert, 16
Brooks, Dick, 64, 72, 117
Broulette, Ed, 36
Brown, Ed, 21
Brown, Howie, 127, 128, 129
Brown, Maxine, 127
Brown, Ray, 93
Brown University, 195
Brundage, Dan, 210, 214
Bryan, Jimmy, 188
Buccilli, Joe, 210
Buck Monies #516, 174
Bud Shirk Offy, 144
Bullock, Bob, 92, 93, 155
Bullock, Reggie, 165
Bunn, Hully, 11
Burke, Ray, 114
Burns, Dr Francis, 152
BUSCH Series, 75, 76, 141
Butters, Harry, 151, 218
Buzzell, Wally, 128, 147
Byron, Dick, 117
Byron, Leo "Tippy", 117

Cabral, Glen, 72
Cabral, Randy, 72
Cagle, Will, 61
Cail, Dick, 144, 145
Cameron, Bob, 9
Campbell, Wally, 11
Capazzoli, Jerry, 216
Carlson, Red, 45
Carmen, Dick, 180
Caron, Lenny, 131
Caron, Roy, 119
Carpenter, Frank, 56
Carrick, Hal, 102, 106, 108
Carroll, Johnny, 90, 158
Carter, Frankie, 114, 118
Carter, Jimmy, 127
Caruso, Ernie, 53
Caruso, Mario "Fats", 13, 16, 39, 59, 171, 184, and throughout
Caruso, Tommy, 212
Caruso, Funzie, 11, 45
Caruso Offy, 3
Casey, Don, 184
Cash, Jim, 53
Cast, Joe, 21, 46, 47
Casterline, Eddie, 87, 91, 93, 96, 97, 154, and throughout
Casterline, Pat, 155
Castor, Red, 11, 100, 107, 108
Chaille, Jerry, 142
Chamberlin, Roy, 215
Chapman, Wally, 109
Charbonneau, Al, 200
Charland, Rene, 191, 192, 196, 206, 217
Chase, Art, 171
Chatham Speedway, 67, 68
Chausse, Frank, 37
Checkered Flag Raceway, 130
Cheney, Jim, 135, 140, 141, 198, 208
Cherry Park Speedway, 8
Chesboro, Dick, 31
Cheshire County Fairgrounds, 1, 5, 22, 82
Chilly Willy #42, 111
Chitwood, Joie, 102
Circle Two, 174
Clark, Art, 161
Clark, Bobby, 57
Clark, Jerry, 15, 63
Clarke, Billy, 57
Cleary, Charlotte, 176
Cleary, Leo "the Lion", 17, 54, 60, 64, 65, 119 and throughout
Cleary, Pat, 176, 177, 181, 182, 186
Cleary Auto Body, 170, 175, 177
Cline, Dick, 145
Clothier, Ed, 40, 78
Cloutier, Bob, 109, 111, 121, 124, 133, 135, and throughout
Coan, Kevin, 207
Coastal Racing Association, 63, 66
Cody, Mun, 129
Coffin, Charlie, 127
Cohen, Bruce, 63, 81
Cole, Herb, 35
Collins, Don, 23
Colonial Garage Ford #130, 95
Colson, Frank, 74
Colturi, Gary, 52
Colwell, George, 203, 206
Comeau, Leo, 110, 182
Conant, Ralph, 43
Conley, Dave, 54
Conley, Paul, 193, 214
Connecticut Valley Rocket, 193
Conway, Frank, 128
Conway, Russ, 104, 114, 115, 120, 127, 131, and throughout
Cook, Bob, 26
Cook, Jerry, 64, 65
Coolidge, Cal, 46, 49
Cooper, Hal, 199
Corey, Pete, 10
Cortez, Tony, 37
Costello, Debbie, 23
Costello, Jimmy, 21, 23, 24, 28, 29, 30, and throughout
Cote, Andy, 52, 111, 116, 117, 174
Couper, Gavin, 10, 159, 160, 161, 162, 169, and throughout
Cousin, Jim, 216
Cox, Ashton, 155
Coy, Joey, 63
Coy, Johnny, 63
Crise, Captain "Red", 172
Crockett, Al, 120, 121
Crockett, Al Jr., 120
Crosley, 99, 100, 101, 170
Crossley, JC, 198
Crotty, Buddy, 124
Csiki, Joe, 14
Cummings, Harold "Red", 8, 9, 17, 157, 158, 159, and throughout
Curley, Ken, 53, 57
Curtis, Mark, 78
Custom Auto Body, MA, 10, 11, 12
Cyclone #5, 136, 140

Daab, Dave, 159
Dame, Forrest, 22, 124, 126, 127, 138, 145, and throughout
Darling, Bill, 198
Darling, Wayne, 57
Darlington Speedway, 12, 75
Davidson, Joe, 157, 169, 171
Day-Kimball Hospital, 195
Dayton, Ken, 164
Daytona Speedway, 165, 189, 208, 209, 216
DeAlmeda, Jack, 130, 131, 132
DeAlmeda, Tony, 130, 131, 132
Dean, Bobby, 115, 119, 145, 146, 148
Deboise, Teddy, 41
Deboise, Windy, 41
DeFusco, Don, 78
Delginio, Smokey Joe, 21
Delisle, Hermie, 3, 87, 88
Delisle, Ray, 22
Delmar, George, 207, 214
DeSarro, Fred, 53, 54, 187, 202, 206, 207, and throughout
Devaney, Bob "Barn Rat", 128, 135
Devereaux, Roy, 178, 207
Devil's Bowl Speedway, 214
Devoe, Ed, 66
Dias, Dave, 203
Dias, Manny, 203
DIEHARD 500, 75
Dion, Dave "Dynamite", 147, 148, 216, 217
Dion, Paul, 216
Dion, Roger, 216
Dionne, Bob, 178
Dionne, Don, 57
Doane, Charlie, 67, 68
Dodge, Hank, 100, 101
Dodge, Jackie, 99, 102, 106, 130

Dolliver, Brian, 119
Dolliver, Jerry, 102, 106, 108, 110, 119, 138, and throughout
Dolliver-Merrick #24, 108
Donati Hudson, 36
Dondero, John, 86, 87, 88
Donovan, Don, 122
Doody, Paul, 180, 181, 184
Dostie, Jerry, 194, 203
Doucette, Tom, 115
Dover Speedway, 136
Dracut Speedway, 83, 104, 105, 109, 117, 174 and throughout
Driscoll, Jerry, 207, 214, 216
Druand, Dick, 20
DuBois, Dick, 61, 70
Duchemin, Brownie, 129
Dudley, Wally, 20
Dudley Diner #59, 102
Duff, Al, 114
Duffries, Gary, 47
Duffries, Pop, 47
Duggan, Hank, 22, 124, 128
Duggan, Johnny, 124, 135
Dumas, Maury, 14, 117
Duncan, Ed, 33, 139
Dunlop, Bill, 37
Dunlop, Pam, 37
Dunn, Cliff, 171
Dunn, Mary, 62
Dunn, Ned, 185
Dunn, Tom, 62
DuPont, Tommy, 8, 161, 167, 169
Duquette, Norm, 178
Dusseault, Deuce, 138, 139
Dyer, Hank, Mr. and Mrs., 172
Dynamite Special, 9, 157

Earle, Dick, 37
East Lynn Garage, 95, 107, 108, 139
Eastern Bandits, 189, 191, 192, 217
Eaton, Johnny, 108
Edgerly, Dick, 121,129
Edwards, Bobby, 19, 111, 123, 138
Edwards, Eddie, 5, 7
Edwards Welding, 123
Egan, Dick, 93
Eggleston, Homer, 26, 37
Eldridge, Bill, 16, 117
Eldridge, Roy, 103, 128
Eli Whitney 50, 62
Eliot, Dick, 65
Elliott, Charlie, 136, 137, 140, 146, 148
Elsa's Lodge, 156
Elto #8, 85, 90, 92
Emmerick, Lee, 10
Empey, Anne, 31, 57
Eng, Ed, 88
Environmental Protection Agency, 69
Esty, Hobart, 148
Esty Lumber, 148
Ethier, Charlie, 5, 11, 13
Evans, Richie, 64
Everglade 300, 68
Evonsion, Steve, 53

Faded Glory, 218
Falconi, David, 38
Falconi, Jimmy, 38, 58
Falconi, Johnny, 15, 38, 58, 61
Falconi, Johnny III, 59
Falconi, Murph, 22, 23, 30, 31, 32, 38, and throughout
Falconi, Peter, 38, 44, 46, 57, 61, 66, and throughout
Falconi, Ricky, 33, 38, 39, 40, 44, 45, and throughout
Falconi Brothers Fuel Oils, 30, 31, 38, 59
Faria, Frank, 207
Farmer, Moe, 135, 138
Farnell, Mary, 106
Farnell, Ray, 99, 105, 106
Father Knickerbocker, 14,15
Faulkner, Dave, 31, 34
Faulkner, Wally, 6, 21, 24, 25, 20, 30, and throughout
Favulli, Mike, 162
Favulli, Mike Jr., 197
Fenton, Smokey, 78
Fiandaca, Pete "The Traveling Man", 36, 38, 74, 75, 76, 77, and throughout
Fini, Al, 8, 212
Finlayson, Paul, 102
Fisek, Joe, 121
Fish M-1, 164, 165
Flannery, Ralph, 13, 98
Flemke Sr., Eddie, 53, 59, 191, 192, 196, 201, and throughout
Flock Brothers, 11
Florian, Jimmy, 5, 6
Flying 5's, 29, 111
Flynn, Bill, 102
Flynn, Ed, 157
Fonda Speedway, 69
Foote, Lucien, 102
Foote, Melvin "Red, "Heavy", 10, 159, 164, 187, 189, 190, and throughout
Foote, Russ, 187, 189
Ford, Dick, 94, 106, 117
Ford Flatheads, 12, 19, 34, 41, 52, and throughout
Ford V8-60, 4, 5, 7
Fornoro, Nick, 172
Forrest, Art, 154
Foss, Bob, 93, 96
Fountain, Wayne, 47
Fox, Bob, 46
Fox Lounge, 43
Foyt, AJ, 216
Frame, Fred, 209
Framingham Motor Inn, 37
France, Bill Jr., 215
Franklin Fairgrounds, 2
Franklin Pierce College, 38
Franklin School of Technology, 199
Fraser, Al, 46
Fray, Lou, 148
Freeport Stadium, NY, 19
Frontier Club, 194
Fruzetti, Butch, 195
Fruzetti, Roland, 164, 195
Fruzetti #74, 164, 196
Ft. Dix Speedway, 75
Fuller, Bobby, 62
Fuller, Jeff, 43, 62
Fuller, Ricky, 67, 71, 72

Gadsby, Dick, 109
Gagne, Bob, 146
Gahan, Ernie, 21, 49, 115, 139, 181, 187, and throughout
Galka, Pete, 6, 7
Galluzzo, Jimmy, 48
Garcia, Julian, 203
Garfield, Curt, 57
Garganigo, Tommy, 32, 37
Gariepy, Paul, 72
Gasoline Alley, 97, 162, 197, 198
Gath, Happy, 98
Gattalia, Charlie, 11, 93
Gaumond, Dick, 10
Gauvin, Ed, 11, 94
Gazaway, Mark, 123
Gendreau, Ed, 167, 168, 188, 189
Gendreau, Eddie Jr., 187
Gendreau, Evelyn, 183
Gendron, Wayne, 51
Gerrior, Joe, 174, 196
Gessell, Ernie, 94
Gibbons, Chet, 5, 93
Gibbons, Mike, 174
Gifford, Tommy, 156
Gilbert, Ernie, 5, 94, 95, 116
Gillespie, Steve, 63
Giuliano, Lou, 93, 180
Glass, Bobby, 61
Glazier, Tom, 71
Glockner, Jack, 187
Goff, Hank, 56
Goldbug, 169, 170, 171
Golden Gate Speedway, 109
Goodyear, 208
Gorman, Julian, 72
Graham, Ralph, 47
Grant, Earl, 215
Grant, General, 192
Grant, John, 70
Grantz, Dave, 57, 139, 142, 146
Gravel, GeGe, 73
Grazio, Hector Jr., 132
Grazio, Hector Sr., 132
Greco, Billy, 53
Green, Don, 171
Green, Jimmy, 1

Grey Ghost, 191
Grez, W.J., 71
Griffin, Jack, 9, 17, 18
Gross, Freddie, 178
Gross, Mary, 178
Groveland Historical Society, 130
Gurney, Ralph "Iron Man", 9, 155, 161, 167

Hackle, Bob, 69
Halaquist, Ed, 22
Hale Hospital, 139
Hall, Don, 160
Halloran, John, 133
Hamel, Buster, 111
Hamel, Lenny, 100
Hamilton, Pete, 197, 198, 200, 201, 202, 203, and throughout
Handy, Brian, 33
Hansen, Harry, 115, 116
Hanson, Neil, 98
Harcourt, John, 207
Hardy Auto Body, 116
Harling, Ray, 171
Harmony, Ray, 132
Harper, Bob, 159, 168, 177, 181
Harriman, 112, 116, 95, 106, 112, 116
Harrington, Ralph "Hop", 10, 17, 160, 164, 167, 169, and throughout
Hart, Robbie, 32
Hart, Jack, 187
Hartman, Wally, 61
Harton, Lou, 139
Harty, Johnny, 13
Harty, Marty, 13, 16, 17, 22, 23, 27, and throughout
Harty Brothers, 26, 169
Harwood, Nancy, 30
Haskell, Brice, 114, 128, 129, 139, 146
Hathaway, Harold, 203
Hathaway, Jay, 212
Hathaway, Preston, 203
Havalotti, "Hard Luck" Joe, 47
Haverhill Court, MA, 132
Haverhill Gazette, 133
Hawk, Chief Sun, 84
Hawley, Neil, 214
Hayes, Frank, 57
Hayes, Sheila, 146
Haynes, Bucky, 155
Haynes #77, 92
Hazard, Russ, 21
Healey, Bob, 214, 215
Healey, Liz, 184
Healey, Rick, 214, 215
Heath, Don, 98, 99
Hebert, Ron, 135
Heidelburg, Methuen, MA, 133, 136
Heikkila, Walter, 49
Henderson, Doug, 128
Hendrickson, John, 114, 117
Hennebry, Joe, 3, 8, 9
Henry, Milt, 153
Henry J, 11,12, 99, 209
Herman, Al, 188
Hersey, Bob, 11, 177
Heywood, Jimmy, 36
Hialeah Speedway, 109
Hill, Ray, 1, 9, 10, 11, 18, 174 and throughout
Hill, Red, 13, 21, 173, 177, 181, 190, and throughout
Hiltz, Lee, 9, 92, 156
Hisso engine, 1, 2
Hitchcock, Bob, 28
Hoenig, John, 18
Hoffman, Tuck, 61, 207
Holbrook, Gary, 46, 57
Holinski Roadster, 140
Holland, Milt, 131
Holland, Sam, 158
Holman and Moody, 158
Holt, Jim, 169, 171
Hood, Billy, 57, 60
Horan, Jack, 10
Horne, Pete, 159
Horton, Lou, 59, 72
Hot Rod magazine, 170
Hough, Pappy, 11, 12
Houlihan, Dick, 71
House, Don, 208
Householder, Ronnie, 4
Howard, Chink, 11
Howard, Joe, 63
Howe, Ann, 17
Hoyle, Eddie, 53. 169, 180
Hoyt, Whitey, 126
Hudson, Ray, 98
Hudson, Red, 195
Hudson, Flo, 104, 136, 142
Hudson Speedway, 7, 8, 13, 39, 45, 74, and throughout
Hughes, Billy, 217
Hull, Harry, 153
Humphrey, Dave, 46, 51, 63, 148, 169, 173, and throughout
Hunt, Don, 216
Hurd, Al, 201
Hurd, Art, 106
Hurd, Lee, 106, 107
Hureau, Dick, 46
Hurn, Pete, 127
Hussex, Ricky, 71
Hutchins, Lloyd, 111

Illustrated Speedway News, 151, 152
Impala Special, 184
Independent Race Car Owners Association (IRCOA), 28, 185, 189
Indianapolis 500, 5, 84, 93, 96, 127, 188, and throughout
Ingalls, Slim, 164, 177
Inman, Dick, 217
International 250, 172
Interstate Speedway Park, 169
Interstate Stock Car Association, 160, 167

Jackman, Shirley, 31, 34, 45, 57
Jackrabbit #22, 157
Jackson, Dick "Jet", 21, 57, 203
Jacques, Al, 36
Jaffarian, Dick, 108
James Hanley Brewing Company, 161
Janelle, Emil, 165
Janelle, Ray, 8, 9, 72, 91, 161, 169, and throughout
Janisaitis, John, 45
Jarrett, Ned, 190
Jarzombek, Charlie, 65
Jellesma, Len, 62, 73
Jimmy Fund, 60
Johnson, Ace, 46, 49
Johnson, Al, 199, 201
Johnson, Bob, 74
Johnson, Warren, 146
Johnson, Wesley, 82
Jones, Booker T., 210
Judkins, Bob, 75
Judkins #2x, 48, 53, 210

Kane, David, 143
Kangas, Vic, 49, 50, 53, 75, 138, 142, and throughout
Karner, Josephine, 172
Karner, Rue, 172
Karvonen, Bob, 38, 211
Kauns, Chet, 109
Kay, Joey, 35
Kay, Johnny, 46
Keizer, Red, 157
Keller, Al, 91, 93
Kent, Bart, 198
Kiazim, Hank, 109, 110, 126
Kibbe, Don, 207
Kies, Norm, 196
Kimball, Red, 61
King, Kazzy, 100
Kingma, Rudy, 178
Kingston Fairgrounds, 160
Kinsman, Porky, 13, 44, 52, 111, 164
Kneeland, Froggy, 114, 129
Kneeland, Margaret, 20
Koopman, Ted, 37, 97, 154
Koopman, Tom, 37
Koopman Special, 91
Koszela, John, 187
Koszela, Sonny, 187
Kourafas, Joey, 215
Kourafas, Steve, 215
Krebs, Buddy, 52
Kuhlman, Frank, 70, 215
Kurtis Kraft chassis, 4, 7,19
Kutney, Ken, 41

Labelle, Red, 193
LaBonte Family, 107, 139
LaCuier, Hunk, 9
Lagasse Amusements, 100
LaJoie, Connie, 54, 55, 56
Lakeside Special #9, 117
Lakeville Speedway, 65, 69, 214
LaMachia, Blackie, 5
Lamereaux, Gil, 47
Lancey, Roger, 26, 27
Landry, Jim, 128
Lane, Howie, 147
Lang, Warren, 51, 58
Langhorne Speedway, 88, 188
LaPierre, Roland, 13, 19, 171, 186, 210
LaPierre, Jr., Roland, 15, 65
LaPointe, Ken, 139
Larkin, Ron, 216
LaRoche, Red, 108, 119, 122
LaRochelle, Joe "Fireball Joe", 57, 120, 147
LaRochelle, Leo, 117
LaRue, Ed, 43, 57
Lawler, Don, 100, 109
Lawrence-Eagle Tribune, 114
Lawrence General Hospital, 127, 148
Leach, Ray, 175
Leader Card Special, 3
Leaning #2, 21, 185
Leavins, Buzz, 36
Lebanon Valley Speedway, 44, 68, 69
LeBlanc, Chuckie, 198
LeCerte, Al, 119
Lee, Art, 170
Lee Speedway, 115, 126, 137, 139
Lees, Jim, 165
Legendre, Ralph, 164, 165, 177
Leger, Paul, 36
Legere, Glenn, 198, 199
Lemay, Joe, 70, 72
Lemuel Shattuck Hospital, 182
LeSieur, Val, 147, 212, 213
L'Etoile, Marcel, 68, 72
Levesque, Tiny, 45
Lewis, George "Wild Man", 8, 157, 158
Libbey, Jimmy, 50
Libbey, Byard, 50, 61
Lil Wonder, 123
Lima, Charlie, 212
Lima, Mary, 212
Lime Rock Raceway, 94
Lind, Dave, 70, 71, 72, 215
Litterio, Caesar, 19
Litterio, Sam, 19
Little, Bertha, 109
Little, Jimmy, 6
Little Beaver #3, 105, 109, 167
Little Princess, 140
Little, Gordon, 109
Littlefield, Helen, 160
Litwin, Frank, 157, 167, 168, 188, 189
LoGerte, Bill, 100
Longy's #515, 156, 159
Lonsdale Speedway, 7, 8, 16, 18, 20
Lotus, 17
Lovering, "Cowboy Jack", 102
Lovey's Garage, MA, 37, 45
Lowes, Dwight, 130, 146, 212
Lucia Brothers #0, 177
Luciano, Jack, 207
Lundin, Catherine, 204, 205
Lundin, Jack, 204, 205
Lundin Machine, 204
Luschesi, Fred, 10, 19, 21, 26, 78, 160, and throughout
Luz, Bob, 145
Lyko, Ray, 52
Lynch, Jimmy, 180
Lyons, Paul, 6

M&H Tire, 76, 179
MacDonald, Red, 116
MacLaren, Don "Big Daddy", 98, 103, 114, 117, 123, 124, and throughout
MacLeod, Fred, 91
MacLeod, Mac, 87, 92, 155
MacTavish, Don "Mac", 60, 198, 199, 200, 203, 208, and through-out
MacTavish, Marcia, 198
Magarvaro, Sam, 130
Maggiacomo, Jokko, 19
Magurn, Fran, 92
Maher, Audrey, 160, 161, 170
Mahoney, Joe, 31, 45, 55
Maki, Bruno, 10
Maki, Reino, 10
Mal Hallet Special, 109
Malone, Jack, 165, 179, 180, 191, 197, 198, and throughout
Manchester Motordome, 11, 24, 94, 95, 106, 107, and throughout
Mancini, Fred, 207
Mancuso Garage, 104, 105
Mann, Billy, 63
Mann, Dick, 124
Mann, Johnny, 63
Martel, Barbara, 110
Martel, Jim, 110, 116, 123, 127
Martin, Eddie, 35, 40, 51
Martin, Gordon, 11, 22, 161, 167
Martin, Joe, 51
Martin, Radical Rick, 62
Martinsville Speedway, 207, 216
Massachusetts General Hospital, 122
Mastriani, Dave, 47
Matthews, Paul, 145
Mattie, Barnie, 173, 184, 202, 210
Mattie, Hugh, 173
Maughan, Lenny, 130, 212
Maughan, Leo "Doc", 130
May, Steve, 58
McCallum, Jimmy, 36, 50, 53
McCann, Tom, 57
McCarthy, Bob, 146
McCarthy, Dick, 78
McCarthy, Doug, 200, 203
McCarthy, John, 46, 51
McClelland, Mike, 207
McClure, Al, 147
McCulloch, Don, 207
McDonald, Norm, 3
McDougall, Duncan, 71
McGee, Bob, 11
McGee, Jim, 17, 180, 181
McGinn, Mike, 71
McGovern, Hugh, 102
McGuire, Jim, 15, 184
McKay, Ernie, 127
McKennon, Al, 98
McKenzie, Doc, 13
McKinnon, Ralph, 111
McLeod, Mac, 13, 116
McNulty, Joe, 17, 186, 187
McNutt, Bill, 159
McNutt Offy, 3
Mechalides, Louie, 123
Medford Bowl, 11, 16, 94, 111, 174
Melinus, Shorty, 171
Mello, Chris, 163
Melnick, Bob, 162, 197, 198, 201, 217, and throughout
Menard, Basil "Jug", 7, 10, 156, 159, 161, 169, and throughout
Merrick, Bob, 102
Merrick, Buddy, 101, 102, 107, 117
Merrick, Kenny, 117
Merrick, Sonny, 116, 117
Merrill, Carl, 64, 164, 165, 177, 178, 184, and throughout
Merrimack Racing Association, 11, 99
Meservey, Dan, 66, 67, 68, 69, 71, 72, and throughout
Meservey, Danny, 72, 73
Meservey, Doug, 72, 73
Michaelson, Frank, 38, 39
Michaud, Jean, 57
Miller, Fran, 36
Mills, Greg, 184, 197, 207
Milton Marion Alfa Romeo, 84
Minuteman 400, 190
"Miss Newton", 164
Miss Norwood Arena, 121, 200
Mitcheson, Al, 92
Modestino, Lou, 68
Moffat, Jim, 22, 25
Mohawk Stadium, 13
Molaghan Family, 31, 54
Monadnock Speedway, 63, 74, 121, 142, 178, and throughout
Monaghan, Don, 121, 128, 129
Monahan, Dick, 57
Monast, Al, 117

Montecalvo, Monty, 214
Moody, Ralph, 8, 11, 17, 158, 159, 161, and throughout
Morin, Bob, 128
Moroso, Robbie, 59
Morris, Johnny Phillip, 173
Morton, Dave, 8, 22, 26, 30, 31, 42
Morton Welch Engineering, 110, 119, 182
Motor Wheel Enterprises, 24, 30, 41
Mundy, Frank "Rebel", 8, 9, 11
Murphy, "Irish" Jack, 29
Murphy, Billy, 123, 132
Murphy, Doug, 61
Murphy, Mike, 61, 123, 138, 142
Murphy, Paul, 61
Murphy, Stevie, 61
Murray, George, 32, 56
Murray, "Nasty" Neil, 63, 120
Murray, Richie, 70
Mystic Valley Racing Association, 99

NAPA Supermodified, 141
Nardone, Angie, 210
Narducci, Ron, 187
Narragansett Park, 170
NASCAR, 11, 12, 28, 35, 49, 56, and throughout
Nashoba Valley Rocket, 44
National Jalopy Association (NJA), 95, 98
National Marine Fisheries, 174
Nazareth Speedway, 73
NEAR Hall of Fame, 4, 7, 8, 19, 45, 49, 52, and throughout
Nelson, Buster, 13
Nevins, Leo, 207
New Bremen Speedway, 184
New Egypt Speedway, 75
New England Auto Racing Association (NEARA), 9, 167, 168
New England Big Car Assoc, 1, 21
New England Dragway, Epping, NH, 211
New England Drivers and Owners Club (NEDOC), 209
New England Midget Association (NEMA), 117, 146, 181, 197, 198
New England Mini Modified Association (NEMMA), 68, 69, 71
New England Speed Equipment, 19, 180
New England Speedways, Inc., 6
New England Stock Car Racing Association (NESCRA), 8, 94, 95, 121, 155, 156, and throughout
New England Super Modified Racing Association (NESMRA), 112, 137, 138,140, 142, 143, and throughout
New England Sweepstakes, 172
New London Speedbowl, 17, 18, 22, 23, 63, 187, and throughout
Newman, Steve, 131, 212
Nextel Cup, 189
Nicholson, Art, 102
Nielson, Joan, 160
Noel, Dick, 128, 131
Nordstrom, Walt, 181
Norfolk County, 152
North American Racing Association (NARA), 169, 173, 182, 184, 189, 209, and throughout
Norwood Arena Grand Prix, 167
Norwood Hospital, 159
Notte, John, 4
Noyes, Bo, 20, 28, 46, 57
Nutting, Russ, 47, 147

O'Brian, Bill, 128
Offenhauser engines, 47, 91, 94
Oilzum Trophy, 25, 131
O'Keefe, Curt, 63
Old Bridge Stadium, 18, 191
Ole Blue, 206
Olsen, Cigars, 119
Olson, Duncan, 47
O'Neil, Joe, 159
Onorato, Rocky, 44
Orcutt, Steve, 50
Ormsby, Tommy, 212
Oswego Speedway, 29, 131, 140
Otto, Ed, 172
Owens Motor Special, 168
Oxford Plains Speedway, 11, 37, 110, 186, 197

Packard, Sammy, 11, 156, 157, 193
Page, Jerry, 41
Page, Larry, 1
Palmer Oil #97, 190
Panarelli, Frank, 45
Panetta, Sully, 13, 19
Pappas, Mike, 116
Paquin, Hal, 6
Parkhurst, Bruce, 135, 138
Parkhurst, Parky, 111, 115, 117, 118, 124, 128, and throughout
Parkins, John, 144
Parlin, Cy, 109, 190
Parmenter, Gibby, 117
Parson, Richard, 187
Parsons, Johnny, 4, 5
Paul Clark Ford, 157
Pearson, Bob, 190
Pearson, Dave "Silver Fox", 209
Pederson, Robert, 121
Pendergast, Bobby, 188
Pendergast, George, 203
Perkins, Carl, 114, 115, 116
Perkins, Eddie, 123
Permatex race, 208
Perry, Don, 171
Perry #3a, 180
Peterson, Dave, 130, 214
Peterson, Freddie, 130
Peterson, Jack, 130, 215
Peterson, John, 151, 171
Petit, Paul, 11
Pettingill, Wes, 104, 131 134
Petty, Richard, 202, 208, 209
Petty Superbird, 209
Phinney, Ken, 207
Pickering, Red, 47
Pillion, Al, 22, 46
Pinecrest Speedway, 28, 174, 175
Pioneer Auto Racing, 189
Plainville Speedway, 196
Plamondon, Joe, 54, 56, 60, 62
Plant, Larry, 11
Plummer, Wes, 151, 206, 211, 218
Poe, Lenny, 57, 148, 155
Polish Hour, 157
Pond, Ronnie "Hawk", 47, 50
Pondue Bickie #53, 203
Pooler, Junior, 8, 19, 163, 166
Potvin, Ed, 31
Powers, Bobby, 142
Powers, Eddie, 85
Pratt, Dick, 65
Pratt, Frank, 32
Prescott, Junior, 119, 138, 202
Presley, Elvis, 17
Presutti, Frank, 138, 145
Procopio, Frank, 72
Progin, Bernie "Tinker", 26, 49, 138, 139, 142
Pulsifer, Bob, 26, 37
Purnell, Ralph, 88
Putnam, Lloyd, 21
Pyne, Jimmy, 50

Race Hill Farms, 75
Racing Corporation of America (RCA), 167
Randall, Bill, 4, 5, 91, 93, 94, 96, and throughout
Rattlesnake Speedway, 68
Readville Speedway, 4, 82, 83
Red and White Movers, 38
Red Devil, 139
Red Devil #7, 184, 210
Red Ram #21, 196
Reed, Jeff, 198, 201, 207
Reed, Jim, 172
Rettew, George, 47
Rexford, Bill, 11
Rhinebeck Speedway, 19
Riberio, Rick, 201
Rich, Win, 22
Richard, Leo, 13, 102
Richardson, Chet, 135, 140
Richardson, Ken, 135, 138, 140
Richardson, Maryann, 141